Among

all

these

Dreamers

SUNY Series in Dream Studies
Robert L. Van de Castle, editor

Among

all

these

Dreamers

**Essays on Dreaming
and
Modern Society**

edited by *Kelly Bulkeley*

State University of New York Press

Published by
State University of New York Press, Albany

For information, address State University of New York Press,
State University Plaza, Albany, N.Y., 12246

Production by Marilyn P. Semerad
Marketing by Dana E. Yanulavich

Library of Congress Cataloging-in-Publication Data

Among all these dreamers : essays on dreaming and modern society /
    edited by Kelly Bulkeley.
        p.   cm. — (SUNY series in dream studies)
    Includes bibliographical references and index.
    ISBN 0–7914–2929–6 (hc). — ISBN 0–7914–2930–X (pbk.)
    1. Dreams. 2. Dream interpretation. 3. Civilization,
Modern—20th century.   I. Bulkeley, Kelly, 1962–   . II. Series.
BF1078.A56 1996
154.6'3—dc20   95–46090
                                                            CIP

10 9 8 7 6 5 4 3 2 1

For Dylan and Maya

Contents

III. Dreams, Spirituality, and Modernity

IV. Dreams and Critical Reflections on "Our" Culture

Acknowledgments

The contributors to this book are a remarkably talented and creative group of people, and they have taught me a great deal about dreaming and modern society. It has been an honor to gather and edit their writings. My goal in *Among All These Dreamers* is to bring their work to a broader audience, sharing with others their ideas, insights, and perspectives. Jane, Marion, Kathy, Herb, Jayne, Tony, Carol, Jeremy, Mom, Wendy, Bette, and Johanna, I thank all of you for your help in making this book come to life.

This book, more than any of my other writings, has been heavily influenced by what I learned from my colleagues and students in the Soc. 2 program at the University of Chicago. The book's conclusion is, in one sense, my version of a Soc. 2 manifesto.

Carola Sautter and the editorial staff at SUNY Press have my deep appreciation for providing me and other dream researchers with the opportunity to publish our works through such a professional, high-quality press. SUNY Press' contribution to the development of the dream studies field cannot be overestimated.

As always, my family—Hilary, Dylan, and Maya, Tish, Ned, Michelle, Kevin, Jake, and Alex, Marie, Howard, Janys, Marie, Bob, and Henry—has been infinitely supportive during the long months of working on this book. I owe much thanks, and much love, to all of them.

Appearance is for me that which lives and is effective and goes so far in its self-mockery that it makes me feel that this is appearance and will-o'-the-wisp and a dance of spirits and nothing more—that among all these dreamers, I, too, who "know," am dancing my dance; that the knower is a means for prolonging the earthly dance and thus belongs to the masters of ceremony of existence; and that the sublime consistency and interrelatedness of all knowledge perhaps is and will be the highest means to *preserve* the universality of dreamers dreaming and the mutual comprehension of all and thus also *the continuation of the dream.*

—Friedrich Nietzsche

Introduction

Kelly Bulkeley

Dreams have proven to be valuable therapeutic aids in promoting the psychological healing and growth of individuals. Dreams have also helped scientific researchers learn new things about the structure and development of the human mind. But does the study of dreams have anything to contribute to a better understanding of *society*? As we approach the end of the twentieth century, modern Western society is suffering from a variety of troubles, conflicts, and crises. Can dreams be of any use in addressing social problems like violent crime, sexual abuse, ethnic and racial conflict, environmental degradation, and the worsening lives of underprivileged children? Can dreams provide any insights into the deeper causes of the ills that afflict our society, and offer any possible cures for those ills?

The most common answer to these questions is that studying dreams helps society by helping certain individuals learn more about themselves; the growth and maturation of these individuals then ripples through society, promoting the welfare of all. This answer is legitimate, but inadequate. It smacks too much of psychological Reaganomics, of trickle-down social reform. Is this really the best answer we can give?

No, it is not. The essays collected in *Among All These Dreamers* argue that there are a number of specific ways in which the study of dreams can be of direct, practical help in the process of creating and sustaining a more humane, more fully integrated society.

The first set of essays illustrates how dreams offer a valuable resource in practical efforts toward the resolution of particular social troubles. The second set suggests ways in which dreams can help us understand and relate better to "others," to people of different cultures, races, and genders. The third set looks at the potential of dreams to renew and revitalize the spiritual lives of people residing in a world torn by the forces of scientific rationality on one side and religious fundamentalism on the other. The last set of essays offers the study of dreams as a means of analyzing the complex interplay of social realities and individual dreams.

Together, the twelve essays remind us that we truly live "among all these dreamers"—that *all* people in our society, regardless of their class, their race, their wealth, their education, or their political power, are humans who dream. This book suggests that our dreams can be powerful agents not only in the healing of individuals, but in the transformation of communities as well.

I.

Dreams
and
Social
Reform

Chapter 1

Dreams and Social Responsibility

Teaching a Dream Course in the Inner-City

Jane White-Lewis

I feel very lucky. I have always loved my work as a psychotherapist and Jungian analyst. The intimacy of the analytic hour and the analytic relation is a very precious experience. It is a rare privilege to enter into the imaginal life—the dreams, fantasies and concerns—of another. In my work I am, it seems to me, a midwife—assisting, enabling new life to come into being. And as I bear witness to another's transformation, I am changed.

Quite content with my chosen profession, I was startled a few years ago when I was at a college reunion and the partner of a classmate challenged me on my work—the exclusiveness, the elitism of my work. We had been discussing therapy, short-term therapy and group therapy versus long-term individual psychotherapy or analysis. A cognitive therapist, my challenger believed wholeheartedly in the efficacy and value of short-term therapy. He asked me, "How can you do what you do—spend so much time with so few people, a privileged few—when there is so much to be done, so many people in need of therapy?" It was true. Given that I usually see my patients two or three times a week for years, I have worked, compared to this short-term therapist, with very few people. My response to his question was this: "Yes, I work on a small canvas, but my practice is composed mostly of therapists and educators, also a lawyer, an executive in a construction firm—and mothers and fathers, and potential mothers and fathers—that is, people who are in a position to impact others, to affect the lives of others. If I can work deeply and increase the consciousness of these people who are in contact with many others, then there will that much less toxicity in the world, and, through the ripple effect, my practice does not seem so small." That was my answer.

But this question—"How can you do what you do?"—stayed with me, troubled me, and began to take on a broader significance as I witnessed the appalling deterioration of life around me. Repeatedly, I would see the homeless struggling to survive as they huddled in cardboard boxes on the streets of New York or in the less public corridors of Grand Central Station. Repeatedly, I would read in *The New Haven Register* of drug-related crimes and the tragic deaths of young men of color in New Haven, the "City of Elms." Repeatedly, I would hear accounts from friends and patients of muggings, robberies, and street crimes. I ached with pain for the children, women, and men victimized by the social and economic conditions of their lives, and I raged at the previous president and administration who persisted in defending their privileged position, with no vision, no heart, no sense of social responsibility. But was I fooling myself? Perhaps I was no better, reassuring myself of the social impact of my practice as I worked as an analyst with mostly upper-middle-class, white patients in my comfortable office in the beautiful, serene New England town of Guilford, Connecticut. Wasn't this a luxury? But what could *I* do ? The problems were too immense. What could I do that would make a difference?

About the time I was wrestling with these questions, I decided to start graduate work at the Union Institute, which is a nontraditional, alternative, interdisciplinary graduate program. On applying to the program, my plans were clear. I had written on the psychology of nightmares and nightmares in literature. At Union I wanted to focus on the interface between psychology and literature and planned to study literary theory, theories of the imagination, and feminist criticism. One requirement of the program has to do with social responsibility. As stated in the catalogue, "The Union Institute does not support research in a vacuum, and it defines doctoral study as a force for social change." Each student must consider the social relevance of her/his work.

This aspect of the Union program—social responsibility—was given special emphasis in the particular opening colloquium I attended. To prepare for the colloquium our group was asked to read Jonathan Kozol's book *Savage Inequalities* (1991). In this powerful book, Kozol describes the appalling conditions he found in some of our city schools and compares these schools with public schools in affluent suburbs and towns. Kozol argues that in many ways our schools are now more segregated and less equal than before the Brown v. Board of Education decision in 1954; elite public schools have arisen within our public school system. By describing the conditions of inner-city schools and by relating his conversations with the school children, Kozol effectively conveys the real tragedy, alarming injustice and "savage inequalities" within our educational system. In my opinion, *Savage Inequalities* should be required reading on everyone's list. It is the kind of book that changes one's thinking, you learn something and can't unknow it, life just isn't the same after you read the book—at least that is how it was for me.

When I went to the colloquium I had been considering teaching a course on dreams in the local high school, in Guilford, to fulfill the internship requirement of the program. But after I read *Savage Inequalities* and after I heard one of my colleagues, a successful Afro-American executive, describe his plans to work with young men of color in the inner city to help them gain some sense of self-empowerment—it all fell into place for me. What is more empowering than knowing oneself, one's inner life, one's dreams, one's potential? I decided that I would not teach a course on dreams in Guilford, but rather in the inner city, in New Haven.

My next step was to visit the High School in the Community (HSC), an alternative public high school in New Haven. Founded in 1970 by a group of innovative, dedicated teachers in response to turmoil in the schools and in the city in the late sixties, HSC has attracted, over the years, students who are interested in more creative approaches to education and who are interested in interdisciplinary studies. The school is small (about 240), informal (everyone is on a first-name basis), and there is a lot of individual attention. Students apply to this magnet high school from all over the city. Because of too many applications, the students are chosen by lottery in each school district, and, as a result, the student body is diverse in both academic ability and ethnic/racial backgrounds. There are children of Yale faculty; there are students from the poorest, most stressed, most beleaguered neighborhoods in the city. From what I had heard about HSC, I thought that this school *might* be receptive to my proposal.

With some trepidation I called to set up an appointment with the principal. I was told that there is no principal at HSC; the school is run by the teachers. (A good sign!," I thought to myself.) The helpful voice on the phone suggested that I come to a teachers' meeting the following day to talk to the teachers about my idea.

Early the next morning I drove into New Haven and, without too much trouble, found the school—an old red sandstone building sitting on a tiny lot and looking like a child's tall and square drawing of a school. As I sat in my car for a few moments, I started to feel queasy and to hear voices saying, "A course on dreams? You must be crazy!" Taking some deep breaths and finding a wee bit of inner courage, I managed to get out of the car and locate an open door (the front door was locked). On entering, I found myself in a vast, dark hall. In a state of semi-paralysis I was contemplating my next step when a cheerful soul moved toward me and asked if she could be of help. I started to explain that I wanted to teach a course on dreams, but after only a few sentences, she stopped me. "What a great idea! But wait!," she said, "I want the others to hear too," and she called to a group of teachers to come and hear what I had to say. As the teachers listened with obvious interest, I told them why I wanted to teach a course on dreams and what I hoped to accomplish by teaching such a course.

I said that it seemed really strange that one hears almost nothing about dreams in school. We spend almost a third of our lives sleeping; dreaming is, as we all know, a wondrous aspect of being human. We are blessed with a dialogic imagination. Psyche loves stories—we love to listen to stories, we tell stories to others, we tell stories to ourselves in our dreams. But we don't talk about dreams in school. What a waste! There is so much we can learn from our dreams.

Studying dreams, I argued, has educational, creative, psychological, and social value:

1. By considering the images of their dreams as metaphors and imaginal expressions of their feelings and concerns, the students could move from concrete to more abstract, symbolic ways of thinking, thereby increasing their capacity to think symbolically.

2. By studying and reflecting on their dreams and by tapping into their imaginal worlds, the students could get a sense of their own cast of characters and inner literature, both as a source for their own creative expression and as a bridge to literature, to the imaginal worlds of others.

3. By considering dream figures as aspects of themselves and the dream as an expression of their inner conflicts, the students would begin to know themselves better. In dreams we find missing parts of ourselves that point the way to our psychological development; we also find the rejected parts, the inner enemies, the seeds of prejudice.

4. Increased self-awareness fosters self-empowerment, self-esteem, a fuller sense of agency and more responsible life choices—all of which have social implications.

To the extent that one is more psychologically conscious of inner conflicts, the less likely one is to project these conflicts, this toxicity onto the world and the less likely one is to act out in destructive ways.

The faculty response to my proposal was enthusiastic; they loved the idea. "Wonderful! It would help the kids with abstract thinking," said a math teacher (who teaches a course on math and art). "Connecting dreams with writing and literature—terrific!," said an English teacher. "I wish we could take the course," said several of the teachers. Within twenty minutes, I was signed up to teach an elective course entitled "Dreams and the Imaginal World" during the second quarter, November through January.

Before starting the course on dreams, I had had minimal teaching experience. Through an odd set of circumstances my first job had been teaching. Although my field in college had been economics (international finance), I found myself—after graduating from college in 1957—teaching seventh-, eighth-, and ninth-grade English at Hillsdale's School for Girls in Cincinnati, Ohio—not exactly preparation for teaching in a New Haven public high school in the 1990s.

Although I had certainly been thinking about the course for months, I had not done much actual preparation—no course design, no lesson plans. As this was new territory (to my knowledge, no one had ever taught a course like this), I felt that I had to get a sense of the territory before I could determine which direction I wanted to go. A few days before starting to teach, I did, however, begin to panic at my lack of preparation. Trying to comfort me, an experienced teacher friend reassured me by saying that I had been preparing all my life for teaching this course—which was true, I guess—but undoubtedly more teaching experience would have helped.

And so at the beginning of November I started teaching. About a fourth of the school had wanted to take the class; eighteen juniors and seniors were picked to be in the class. We met for an hour four days a week, Monday through Thursday for nine weeks. Then in January, I decided to teach a variation of the course the next quarter to a group of ninth- and tenth-graders. The comments that follow generally refer to both sessions.

On my first day of teaching I entered my assigned classroom and found a huge room, one of the four rooms on the first floor. Two walls were cut with enormous windows; large blackboards covered the reachable areas of the other walls. Radiators (which could not be turned off) clanked away; several windows were open in an effort to deal with the overheating and peculiarities of an antique heating system. I noticed odd iron doors on one wall, the remains of an even older heating system. Later I was told that this school was built in 1880 and is the oldest school in New Haven.

Several students were in the room eating lunch. The High School in the Community has no lunchroom—in fact, no gym, no library, no varsity sports, no lockers, too few computers, and no auditorium (PTA meetings and plays are held in the halls). But when the students, my students, entered the room, none of the dated, inadequate facilities mattered. Immediately the room became filled with energy and very contemporary as the students tumbled into the room with their bright colors and voices, laughter, flashy earrings, baseball caps, book bags—and curiosity. And so, with the aroma of lunchtime fried chicken still in the air and some sticky soda spillage on the floor, we began to get to know each other and to talk about dreams.

In one of the first classes, as an introduction to talking about images, the students made collages—picking out images that appealed to them from a pile of magazines. We talked about some of the images. For example, cars turned up in a lot of the collages. So we talked about cars—what is a car? How is it different from other modes of transportation? What might a car mean in a dream?

Because the students were most interested in understanding their own dreams, we spent a lot of time talking about dreams. At the beginning I tried a rather disciplined approach to group dreamwork with the students asking the dreamer for clarification of the images in the dream and for associations. What started as dream*work* usually shifted quickly into dream*play*," a free-for-all as everyone started associating to the dream, talking at once and addressing comments to a neighbor, if not the dreamer. At some point during this process, something would click for the dreamer, the "aha" phenomenon that dreamworkers speak of. I tried to get a word in now and then, generally making some effort to push for a more symbolic understanding of the images. It was primarily my task, I felt, to make sure that the experience was emotionally safe for the dreamer. As it turned out, there seemed to be something protective and self-protective operative in the room which kept the expression of feeling and dreamwork at a safe level. At the end of class, I would speak privately with the dreamer to make sure s/he was all right, to comment on the dream, and to suggest something to think or write about.

Other class activities included creating dream theater by enacting a dream, and drawing a response to her/his dream or to a dream told to the group. Sometimes the class would write about their dreams—dream the dream on (continue the story) or engage in an "active imagination," a dialogue with one of the dream figures. The students also wrote about their earliest memories, family stories, their own personal histories— that is, the imaginal context of their lives and their dreams. To understand projection and our tendency to color what we see, a couple of classes were devoted to projective tests—the Rorschach and the TAT. We talked about the literary use of dreams in novels and short stories and dreams in movies. A published poet friend of mine came, read some of her work and spoke of her own process of transforming her dreams into poetry.

The major project for each course was to keep a dream journal, to make daily entries. If the student could not remember a dream, there were many other possibilities—for instance, childhood dreams, in fact any dreams from the past, dreams of friends or family members, any dreams encountered in novels, short stories, poems and on television. The journals were mostly kept at home; I would, however, review them and comment on them several times throughout the quarter.

Although I had had an intuitive sense that a dream course could be valuable, it was only in the classroom that I fully recognized the powerful potential and endless possibilities inherent in teaching a course on dreams at the high school level. Let me give you a few examples of what can happen.

There was Rick's dream, for instance. As I listened to Rick telling his dream, I was startled by the remarkable similarity to the beginning of Dante's *Divine Comedy*. The next day I brought in a translation of the *Divine Comedy*. No one in the class had heard of Dante (although one girl said she had a friend named Dante, who, in fact, turned up in the second course). It was a marvelous moment (especially for Rick) when I read his dream and then the beginning of Dante's poem, and the class recognized the connection between the two, the connection between our dreams and great literature. They *got* it—the fact that creative possibilities that lie within each of us, in our dreams.

And then there were those students who claimed that they could not write well or hated to write, but who discovered a "voice" when they wrote out of their personal experiences and feelings. Often associations to remembered dreams led to painful events and current concerns—the death of a father from AIDS, the sudden death of a beloved teacher, a devastating house fire, the break-up of a family because of divorce, the terror of living in New Haven and the fear of being shot. When these students wrote about their dreams and the associations to their dreams, they began to discover not only their potential for writing powerful and eloquent prose, but also the relief that comes from giving expression to the pain and tension within.

There is, I discovered, a real societal value in talking with high school students about their dreams. Dreams proved to offer an amazing opportunity to talk about issues in a nonjudgmental way. For instance, many of the students reported dreams of police. A fairly typical dream involved the student being engaged in some drug-related activity and hiding from, arguing with, or running from the police. I asked the class, "If the dream is a reflection on an inner state or conflict, who is the cop?" Their own inner authority figure, their conscience? If the student can consider the cop as an inner figure and the image of the dream reflecting an inner conflict, then there is the possibility of taking some responsibility for the choices being made and not unconsciously acting out, projecting the disapproval onto the outer cop/parent/authority figure.

Another example: Many of the young women dreamed of having a baby, and usually jumped immediately to a concrete interpretation—the baby in the dream represented the baby they wanted to have with their boyfriend. Teenage pregnancy is a real problem for many of these girls. One of my sixteen-year-old students was a teenage mother. What if the baby in the dream is understood as some young part of the dreamer, some potential that need to be mothered? A literal pregnancy is not the solution for a young woman who wants to fill her inner emptiness with a baby, to feel more important by becoming a mother. The last thing in the world these young women, these children, need is to be trapped into a lifestyle that will interfere with any attempt to get an education. If the child in the dream can be considered as an inner child, inner potential, that needs to be mothered, cared for, educated— there is a possibility of choices and a chance of escaping the hopelessness and despair of being poor and uneducated with few options.

As you can imagine, the teaching was not always easy. Some days were difficult and discouraging. And I made mistakes as I struggled to learn what worked and what did not. Whenever I got into my lecturing mode—talking about Freud versus Jung, or archetypes or whatever—I could see their eyes glazing over (the fact that the class was right after lunch and the last period of the day didn't help). When I let go of having to *teach* them and stayed with their imaginal material, anything I wanted to teach emerged; that is, the theory would naturally come out of the practice. For example, one of the students, Tina, dreamed of a girl she hated, an excellent example of what Jung calls the "shadow." Her image was engaging and memorable and offered an opportunity to talk about this useful Jungian concept without my launching into a boring presentation.

In the first group I made a major mistake in trying to teach *Wuthering Heights* which I had adored when I had read it at about age twelve. Brontë's literary use of a dream in this novel is brilliant. In the third chapter, a nightmare appears which shapes and resonates throughout the novel. But most of the class hated the book; the language was so difficult that it was like reading a foreign text. They refused to read it. I even tried showing a film version of the novel; most of the class dozed off during the viewing. In the second group, instead of watching *Wuthering Heights*, we watched an episode of the popular soap opera "All My Children" and ended up having a lively discussion of themes and archetypes.

All in all, teaching the dream courses at the High School in the Community has become an important part of my life. This experience has had an enormous impact on me; I suspect the same is true for many of my students. And, of course, the effect of introducing dream studies into the curriculum had been felt beyond my particular classes. Often my students introduce me to their "dream characters," their friends who appear in their dreams, who then proceed to tell me one of their dreams. Teachers in the school are curious about the course, frequently ask me about their dreams, and bemoan not being able to take the class. On occasion I am invited to a literature class to speak about a dream in a text (e.g., *Macbeth*). In addition, students who are not in my class stop me in the hall and ask, "You're the Dream Lady, aren't you? Well, I had this dream last night and . . ." or "What does it mean when you dream that. . . .?"

I realize that I have been especially fortunate to have found such fertile ground; perhaps not all schools would be so supportive and receptive to including dream studies in the school curriculum. And yet, perhaps my experience is not so unusual after all. Dreaming is, after all, a universal phenomenon. Let us not underestimate the innately human fascination with dreams and the desire to find some meaning in a dream. Maybe it would *not* be so difficult to introduce dream studies into school curricula.

It seems to me that there is a danger in the field of dream studies of a certain smugness and self-satisfaction. We know how important dreams are to us and we talk to each other about them. I do not, in any way, want to diminish the importance of this exchange, which can be enormously valuable both personally and professionally. But can't we do more in terms of the world around us? Are we doing the best that we can do? When are we going to put social responsibility as a priority? We have enormous unrealized potential and each one of us has the capacity to "make a difference."

My choice has been to work in an inner-city school. Listening to the dreams of inner-city kids and taking the students and their imaginal lives seriously, has made me acutely aware of the power of dreams in an educational context. Schools are an obvious place to start, as there are many opportunities at all levels no matter what one's interest. Each one of you—writers, psychologists, psychiatrists, anthropologists, teachers, artists, dancers, dreamers all—could find a way to contribute in a school setting. But there are, of course, many other forums in the community besides the schools where we can contribute. Isn't it time that we *do* contribute and share, more consciously and conscientiously, our riches with others?

Chapter 2

The 55-Year Secret

Using Nightmares to Facilitate Psychotherapy in a Case of Childhood Sexual Abuse

Marion A. Cuddy and Kathryn E. Belicki

This is one woman's story of a lifelong struggle to cope with the negative effects of childhood sexual abuse. Her story is, in fact, three stories. We begin this essay by telling her stories, although they did not unfold as neatly as we have described them here. Her disclosure of life events was propelled, partly by her dreams and partly by other therapeutic factors. One purpose of this essay is to illustrate how dreams illuminate experience and move us forward in development. A second purpose is to draw attention to the issue of childhood sexual abuse and the mistreatment of survivors of sexual abuse to highlight broader societal flaws. Embedded within this latter issue is a mental health structure that failed this woman over fifteen years of depression and suicide attempts and a culture that neglects older women. As we shall see, one of the ways she was failed was by a lack of willingness to hear her story; a failure that societally we are at risk to perpetuate, given the recent tendency to disbelieve reports of abuse.

Victoria's Stories: The Public Stories

Victoria was the fifth of six children born to her parents. Her father was a widower, with three sons when he married Victoria's mother.

13

When Victoria was two years old, her youngest sister was born. Their father, on his way to get the physician, was struck by a train and killed. Victoria's memories of her father were vague, but she had pleasant memories of throwing herself in his arms when he returned from work. She had some pleasant childhood memories of her mom cuddling her, but for the most part felt anger toward her mom, who returned to working outside the home to support the family. Victoria also had unpleasant memories of her brothers teasing her, making her their scapegoat. Growing up in the depression meant poverty, although her step-brothers contributed to the family income.

Victoria married at the age of 19. Records from previous hospitalizations indicated that Victoria had a "happy marriage." Her husband died in 1972 of a brain tumor, after a brief illness. The birth of their first child required high-forceps delivery resulting in hydrocephalus, and after approximately a year of intensive caretaking she died. Subsequently Victoria gave birth to another daughter (Lisa) and four years later a son (David). For most of her married life, her husband's parents resided with them. Victoria worked as a bookkeeper/clerk from the time of her second daughter's birth until her son was born and resumed working again when he began school.

Victoria had two previous admissions in 1981 to the hospital where one of us works (MAC) as well as numerous admissions to various other hospitals in her home city because of depression and suicide attempts either by cutting her wrists or overdosing on prescription medication. Victoria was a sixty-seven-year-old widow when she was transferred from a psychiatric hospital to the inpatient program of the first author in April 1991. Victoria had been hospitalized since October 1990 because of suicidal ideation. Two separate series of electro-convulsive treatment, in the fall of 1990 and January 1991, had provided very temporary relief of the depression and suicidal thoughts before she, again, felt a "black cloud" descending over her. Victoria experienced her transfer to this hospital as rejection and abandonment by the psychiatrist and staff who had been treating her, and she had resisted the transfer. As a result, she was transported by ambulance and admitted as an involuntary patient on the grounds that she was a danger to herself. Initially, she was placed on one-to-one observation. Victoria's anger at being "dumped" was evident from the outset by her sarcasm and demands for comfort. On her third day in hospital, she purposefully and secretly burned herself with an iron while a staff member was present, unaware of what Victoria was doing. I (MAC) met Victoria for the first time within minutes of this incident.

On the one hand, Victoria's history provides sufficient grounds for depression and suicidal feelings and attempts. It could be argued that the depression resulted from unresolved grief following the death of her husband and perhaps was related to the other losses, also unresolved, of her first-born daughter and her father.

On the other hand, the first several months of hospitalization and therapy can only be described as stormy. Victoria's presentation did not fit consistently with her history. She was angry with the caregivers for holding her a prisoner, made incessant demands on them by her numerous physical problems for which she wanted medication, and began burning herself with cigarettes. Further, Victoria was slow in developing trust, initially feeling that although talking was helpful she had to guard against saying too much in case she got herself into trouble. She despised herself for any show of weakness or vulnerability, including tears. During her fourth month of hospitalization, Victoria made a suicide attempt. Curiously, she expected that she would be abandoned by her therapist (MAC) as a form of punishment. She told me she thought I might return to continue the therapy after she had "toughened up." She also anticipated some form of punishment from staff for the suicide attempt.

Victoria also began voicing anger: toward her brothers for chores she was required to do for them as a child, including serving meals and ironing their clothes; toward her mother for returning to paid employment to help support the family; and toward the fathers of her friends as a teenager, who she said had something wrong with them. Over the weeks, Victoria became aware of the depth of her anger, but also afraid of her anger.

Early in the therapy process, I had enquired about a history of sexual and physical abuse. Victoria denied sexual abuse, but said her mother had hit her several times. She also reported verbal and emotional abuse by her brothers.

The Untold Story: The 55-Year Secret

Victoria had never forgotten being sexually abused by one of her full brothers (Mark). She had, however, done her best to push it aside and pretend it never happened. Much to her surprise, she disclosed the abuse as she entered the sixth month of therapy. The details emerged more slowly than her feelings of responsibility, shame, guilt, fear, betrayal, and anger. The abuse occurred over three years, several times a month in Victoria's bedroom. At times, Mark came to her room early in the morning after her mother had left for work. (In part, Victoria's anger at her mother for deserting her and returning to work was thus explained.) At other times, the abuse occurred at night. Her brother admonished her not to tell and brought her gifts to buy her silence. Victoria rejected the presents, but kept the secret because of her own feelings that what was happening was bad and wrong. There was another reason for keeping the secret. Victoria revealed that prior to the abuse by Mark, one of her step-brothers had openly approached her for sex. She had told her mother who then ordered her half-brother out of the house. Given that Victoria had both positive and negative feelings for Mark, her fear of what her mother would do to him helped prevent her from telling anyone.

Victoria also had the experience of several of her friends' fathers fondling and grabbing her, as a teenager. She had a further experience of a friend's uncle trying to grab her, and other girls, when they went swimming.

Two weeks before the marriage her husband-to-be raped her, resulting in her first pregnancy. Victoria always felt that her husband's rape had somehow caused her daughter's physical problems. Despite the public tale of this being a happy relationship, the marriage was, in fact, largely unsatisfactory, as her husband worked long hours during the day and made extra money working evenings. At first, she had been upset with her husband working long hours, but over time became relieved that he did. Victoria reported that the best years were those she was most busy working, helping with her church and school organizations, and raising her children.

After five months of therapy, the source of Victoria's anger toward herself, men, and her mother had meaning. Still to be explained, however, was that her suicidal ideation predated, by several years, the sexual abuse by her brother. I wondered aloud to Victoria if something else had happened. Victoria was willing to consider the idea but had no memory of what had led up to her suicidal ideation, only that it had seemed to always be present.

The Secret Story

There was a final story that Victoria did not tell even herself until she found sufficient safety and personal strength. She was raped at age five by a neighbor. The rape occurred on a sunny afternoon in the woodshed attached to her home. Prior to the rape, Victoria had been a "happy-go-lucky child." Immediately following the rape she was dazed, then defensively forgot it. However, when Victoria was approximately eight years of age, a neighborhood boy drowned. Victoria thought dying by drowning was "a quick way to go and headed for the river." She was stopped by an adult and did not make any further behavioral gestures to kill herself until she was in her late forties. Nevertheless, she continued to be besieged with thoughts of killing herself.

In therapy, Victoria had made several references to disliking the woodshed, along with a strong feeling of fear, before the following nightmare occurred shortly after she had disclosed the sexual abuse by her brother. "I was between 10 and 14 and was naked. My sister was there and a big bulky man in farm clothes. It was in the kitchen of the old house. It seemed as if my sister was pushing me out to the woodshed. The man was in the doorway between the kitchen and the woodshed. Dark, lots of hair, moustache. I was too terrified to talk or scream."

Over the next several months more details of the neighbor, the woodshed, and her reaction emerged until she was able to give a complete description of the rape. She remembered the neighbor who raped her pushing her backwards, with the rape occurring while she was lying on her back. Victoria described the sun streaming in through a window with the woodshed being a contrast of brightness and dark shadows. After the rape, she lay there for a long time "in a daze." She said to her mom "he hurt me." but when her mom asked "who" Victoria said she did not know. She refused to go back into the woodshed, terrified he would rape her again. Victoria did not experience the rape as a sexual act. At five years of age, she had no understanding or words to explain to her mother what happened other than "he hurt me." Victoria had kept this story from herself as well as from the world. Once she allowed herself to talk about the sexual abuse by her brother without dire consequences, she became more open to allowing herself to reexperience the earlier trauma and did so initially with oblique references to the wood-shed, later followed by the nightmare.

Discussion

How did the secrets emerge? The first author approached Victoria with the working assumption that there were ample reasons for all her symptomatology: that extraordinary symptoms meant extraordinary life-experiences. Victoria's words and actions were listened to in a way she had never experienced before. She never planned to tell anyone about the sexual abuse. (However, as part of every assessment and therapeutic contact, we routinely ask if the person has experienced sexual and physical abuse.) Victoria's initial denial of sexual abuse is not uncommon; most survivors find it very difficult to disclose. The act of asking makes it clear that the therapist is willing to hear this material and informs the client that it is significant. Such an invitation paves the way for future disclosure.

Recently, there has been increased concern about the creation of "false memories" of childhood abuse by manipulative therapists. This concern has gained tremendous media attention since the founding of the False Memory Foundation in 1992 by Pamela and Peter Freyd, fol-lowing their daughter's private accusation to them of incestual abuse by her father. The foundation has skillfully mounted a media campaign against therapists and self-help book authors who work with or support individuals recovering memories of abuse. The Freyd's daughter, Dr. Jennifer Freyd, never intended to make her accusations public. However, recently, in response to the increased attention to the False Memory Foundation, she has spoken publically about the foundation, arguing that her parents invented it as a weapon against her (Freyd 1993).

It is beyond the scope of this chapter to fully summarize the data pertinent to this controversy. In our own research we have found, con-sistent with Herman and Schatzow (1987), that delayed recall of trauma is common among survivors (Belicki, Correy, Cuddy, Dunlop, and Boucock 1993). Furthermore, we have found that individuals with corroboration for their abuse are as likely to report disrupted memory as are those without corroboration (Belicki et al. 1993). This finding is consistent with the documentation of others that individuals with verified histories of abuse or trauma quite commonly show some to considerable "forgetting" of the events (Herman and Schatzow 1987; Terr 1991; Williams 1992). It seems clear, therefore, that motivated forgetting of trauma and abuse is a valid phenomenon, and needs to be considered in effective therapy.

The course of therapy was intense, long and arduous. Victoria was plagued with suicidal ideation. The struggle to live or die occupied her waking thoughts and hence large sections of the therapy. Victoria had been making suicide attempts for more than fifteen years and could not simply stop this activity. Taking a risk by engaging in an unknown therapeutic process that *might* show her a way to feel better, was an enormous task for her. Moreover, she was sixty-seven years old at the time and, like many older women, felt that nothing but despair lay ahead of her. However, prior to disclosing any of the sexual abuse, Victoria had access to her dreams and nightmares, and she was able to use them in meaningful ways.

After disclosing the sexual abuse by her brother, she struggled with still wanting to deny *it* ever happened. Like many survivors, she also experienced terror that she would not be believed. There is a realistic core to this concern because of our general cultural tendency to downplay the prevalence of sexual abuse and other trauma (Herman 1992). However, an added weight for Victoria was that we furthermore tend not to think of older women as having been sexually abused. Our culture is heavily sexualized but also obsessed with youth and beauty. Thus, older women are not considered sexual beings, and therefore, the possibility of them having been raped as children or young women eludes us. As a result, Victoria felt defeated in ever being able to come to terms with her abuse.

Dreams as Vehicles of Insight and Change

Victoria did not disclose the sexual abuse until the sixth month of therapy, and within a week had the woodshed nightmare. She continued to record dreams but it was four months before the next sexual abuse dream occurred, although not recognized by her as such. During these four months, she was still struggling with whether or not to deal with the effects of the sexual abuse, one of the effects being suicidal ideation. Before and after disclosing the sexual abuse, her dreams contained themes of food/hunger, betrayal, anger, frustration, and disdain toward men. A dream which contained many contradictory elements and ended with her being empowered was followed two nights later by a dream in which she was sexually abused by a female nurse. It could be that she had made the decision to work rather than to die which allowed her to have another dream of sexual abuse. Two months later she dreamt on consecutive nights of "a vicious circle, in a group, a torrent of sound and abuse."

It is not possible, in this space, to unfold the therapy and dreams/nightmares as they occurred. Rather, we have tried to illustrate the various issues Victoria confronted by providing a sample of her dreams and also to elucidate the power of dreams and some ways to work with them. The dreams and nightmares Victoria described over this two-year period of therapy illustrate much of what we can learn from dreams both about ourselves as individuals and as members of social groups. At times, we use the same dream to explain several points because dreams can communicate a multitude of messages and feelings. We begin with an examination of what we call the emotional reality of the dream, that is, the dream reflects how the client is feeling and has felt for some time.

Dreams as Depictions of Emotional Reality

Dreams reflect the emotional reality of the dreamer and therein offer a specific opportunity to learn about ourselves and each other. Dreams can be a special assessment tool for therapists. It is as if, when we dream, we stage a play in which we enact through situations the theme of "what it feels like to be me." For example, a very common theme for Victoria was hunger. Frequently in her dreams, she searched for food and despite her best efforts was left frustrated and hungry. Sometimes she would feed others, but when she would turn to satisfy her own hunger she would encounter obstacles such as no bowls available for her cereal. And in this way she poignantly played out in her dreams her profound neediness, the inability to meet her own needs, the absence of caring others to help her meet her needs, the demands of others upon her to meet their needs, and the feeling that life simply threw obstacle after obstacle at her.

Emotional realities occur in contexts, and dreams give us clues to the real life contexts that shaped this individual's experience; however, we must exercise care in differentiating what points directly to real life and what points to a metaphor. Although dreams depict emotional realities, we can make the mistake of overlooking the fact that these personal realities have emerged from a context. King (1992) has argued that therapists need to be far more sensitive to the traumatic origins of nightmare content. She points out it is easy and comforting to interpret the common nightmare of being chased by a monster as being a dream about projected anger, and to not recognize in this dream the real individual, experienced as a monster, who led the dreamer to disown anger in the first place. Similarly, the first clue to Victoria's third, most hidden life came from the nightmare of the woodshed. It would have been a clear mistake to treat this dream as purely metaphor.

However, another mistake is also possible: to treat a dream metaphor as literal fact. During one period of hospitalization, Victoria dreamed of being sexually abused by a nurse. As far as we can determine this dream had no literal basis in reality, but it was a profound statement as to how she felt about hospitalization and nursing care. Most commonly a dream will depict the emotional reality while pointing to the external source of that reality. For example, in the first dream she recorded in therapy, Victoria found herself naked and unable to move or do anything but weep. People passed by and stared at her and then moved on, uncaring and unhelping. Finally, an ambulance arrived and from it emerged six attendants whom she described as "keepers." They conveyed her to the hospital stretched out naked across their knees. This is clearly a dream about feeling exposed, helpless, and receiving assistance only at the expense of being a prisoner. It was a very apt description of her feelings at the time about herself and her hospitalization. However, the dream also points to her real life-experiences of being stripped, and of being treated as a prisoner by a succession of men often under the guise of being cared for.

Dream Interpretation Should Come from the Client

The above example points out the need to "tread gently" with individuals' dreams. Dream "interpretation" should come from the client and while this "rule" is always important with dreams, it is particularly important with trauma survivors. Therefore, while we can learn much from listening to dreams, whether our own or others', we must proceed carefully in interpreting these experiences. We feel strongly that therapists should resist offering interpretations or even assuming they know what another's dream means. Insofar as we have common experiences with another, we may upon hearing a dream have some, or even considerable, insight into its meaning and/or origins. However, any interpretation we offer is at best a statement of what that dream would mean if we had dreamt it. And in pronouncing such an interpretation, however correct it might be, we take from the dreamer their authorship of this exquisitely personal creation. This is particularly problematic with abuse survivors who have already had so much of their personal power stolen.

Helping individuals arrive at their own understanding of the dream they have created can be one of several effective ways of empowering clients. There is no need for advanced training in dream interpretation techniques. Simply listening carefully, reflecting back the readily apparent themes, and asking the dreamer about the dream (what they think it means, their associations to the objects and people, the dreams) can aid the dreamer in deriving what they need to hear from their dream. We can offer an illustration of this process, following Victoria's in-hospital suicide attempt she had the following dream. "I dreamed of living in a cottage and coming to a store everyday or almost everyday that was run by [pastoral counsellor] and you" (MAC). Victoria had no ideas as to what the dream meant. She was asked why people go to a store—"To buy, to look, to compare." She was then asked what the ultimate purpose was—"To buy." When asked, "To buy what?," Victoria responded, "To buy what you want." When confirmed that going to a store was to get what you want and what you need, Victoria responded that she understood what the dream could mean, specifically, that there were people who could help her.

Dreams Help Articulate the Background of One's Experience

Dreams help articulate what Gestaltists call the ground (vs. figure) of our existence. This background is ordinarily very difficult to notice, let alone label and articulate. We do not notice the air that we breathe unless it suddenly changes and becomes a focal part of our experience.

However, if that background air is polluted, it can do much damage long after we have stopped noticing it. Similarly, a person whose life has been steeped in violence will not notice or comment upon the violence, but it will be in their dreams as part of the background. Victoria's first dream in therapy poignantly described the general feeling tone of her life in ways that she was unable to convey in direct conversation. She dreamt that she was in hospital and that all the patients went out on a picnic. However, she missed the bus and was all alone and so set out on her own, walking. "I couldn't find anyone and every place seemed strange. I was hungry . . . so I stopped for food, ate a hot dog and a piece of pie. . . ." However, the food did not satisfy her. Lost and hungry, she starts to cry. Children point at her and make fun of her. She wanders into a strange house and "the next thing I knew, I was naked. In the house, people kept coming in and they would stop and stare at me but I couldn't talk or move, I was like a board. All I could do was cry."

Dreams as an Efficient Way of Communicating

Why bother with dreams in therapy? Can we not accomplish all the above without dreams? It could be argued that the information obtained from dreams could be obtained by simply talking to the person. While this may be true, the characteristics of dreams make them a particularly fruitful source of insight. Because dreams involve imagery they permit us to think about and communicate many issues simultaneously. For example, Victoria's dream of being sexually abused by a nurse was replete with multiple meanings. In the dream she is in hospital but has recovered from a major illness and is beginning school. However, she finds she does not have appropriate clothes: all she has is a ski jacket and a short, thick gown which falls off every time she opens the jacket. As a result she is frequently naked and keeps trying to get clothed. She also searches out a bathroom as she feels very "dirty" and wants to get washed. However, all the sinks in the hospital bathrooms are inadequate. Some have no water while others have water, but no soap. She finally goes to school and finds that she is attending a course entitled "political science" but it turns out to be a course for mentally abused adults. Just as she starts talking in class, a nurse comes in and starts stroking her sexually. Victoria objects strenuously and leaves the class to get away from the nurse, although this means not completing what she had begun in class. The nurse pursues her and her sexual caresses become violent. Victoria fights back but the nurse just smiles. The dream ends with Victoria being carried to isolation. There are many issues in this dream: the fact that Victoria has been sexually abused, her simultaneous optimism and fears about therapy, her current vulnerability due to inadequate resources (as shown by her lack of clothes), her profound feelings of being soiled which are so common in sexual abuse survivors, her indictment of the inadequacy of the medical system in assisting her (the inadequate washrooms), the stirring of political activism as a response to her dilemmas (and a movement from defining her problems as being medical to being political in origin), and her feeling that nursing care is abusive, and blocking her growth. Could she possibly have conveyed as much in the same number of words through ordinary conversation?

Dreams May Highlight What Is Consciously Overlooked

In dreams we can attend to the feelings and perceptions that we have neglected during the day. In other words, the very things that escape our conversation are sometimes addressed in dreams. For example, Victoria's dream of going to a store staffed by two of her therapists (described above) occurred at a time when she was feeling hopeless and helpless) and had attempted suicide. In contrast to these conscious feelings, the dream conveyed a sense of hope (that her current two therapists might meet her needs). In addition, in this dream Victoria adopted the active role of the consumer who comes to a store not only to buy, but in her own words "to look, to compare."

Dreams Are a Relatively Safe Way to Approach and Communicate Emotion

Initially, Victoria had great difficulty expressing anything but anger, feeling that any other emotion made her too vulnerable. Even when she occasionally expressed her feelings of loss and sadness and became tearful, she maintained it was not permissible to be sad because she wondered how her therapist would take advantage of her in this vulnerable state. She was also afraid that she would become like some of the other patients in hospital, that is, psychotic, helpless, and vulnerable. Victoria's fears are an extension of the fears referred to in Ellenson's (1985) description of forty women with a history of incest who denied various psychological symptoms of distress because of a fear they would be labelled as "crazy." Her therapist provided her with encouragement to keep talking and working while also expressing her doubts that she would become psychotic.

In general, people who would never describe personal feelings are often quite comfortable describing a dream and this was true of Victoria. Thus, Victoria was not only able to experience profound grief in her dreams but felt comfortable sharing these dreams with her therapist. In addition, material that is too painful too recall during waking often first emerges in dreams, and this was certainly Victoria's experience. An advantage of dreams in this respect is that they can be dismissed as "just a dream" if the dreamer is not ready to accept the reality of the experience.

In the context of therapy, a client's dream can be a means of communicating feelings about therapy that they might not feel comfortable saying directly to the therapist. Returning to Victoria's dream of going to the store staffed by two of her therapists, which occurred after her suicide attempt, Victoria noted that one of the reasons she goes to stores is to comparison shop. At this early stage in therapy she was not comfortable about discussing her need to test the quality of her therapists, so she instead created a dream and shared that. Thus, dreams inform the dreamer, and those who participate in her development, about how therapy is unfolding.

Dreams about the Therapy Process

King and Sheehan (1996) in their work with trauma survivors have identified several stages that characterize phases of therapy. They have entitled these stages of dreams Resistance, Discovery, Effects, Growth and Understanding, and Renegotiation. In Resistance dreams the client is actively avoiding knowledge about what has happened to her. Early in therapy Victoria had several dreams in which she approached houses or rooms, only to find the doors locked. In discussing these with her there was a sense that there was something behind those doors she needed, but was not willing or able to yet access.

In Discovery, the dream dwells on images, thoughts, and feelings directly associated with the abuse. We have already described Victoria's woodshed dream. The following would also be best described as a Discovery dream. Victoria dreamt that a female hospital staff member unjustly accused her of causing another woman staff member to lose her job. Victoria argued with her about it to no avail. A male staff member "Jim" then came and the two took Victoria to a small, country home where they left her. Jim returns. Victoria seeing him "went up some crooked old stairs to the second floor and managed to crawl to the top, but there was a stick I had put across the top and tried to crawl under. During this time I could hear Jim come in and start up the stairs looking for me. I couldn't move, I was paralyzed, lying on the floor. I paniced in my dream and realized this was the end. He was going to rape and kill me and that was final." She awoke screaming.

Effects dreams depict the impact abuse or trauma has had on the dreamer's life. The following poignant dream is an excellent example. Victoria dreams that she goes to visit a couple with whom another friend of her's, "Mary," is staying. "I went to the second floor and the couple said to come back later. I tried to wake 'Mary' up a few times but was unable to, so I went back outside. I had a very precious book and was afraid of losing it. I went outside and started to walk. A couple of children came along and started to taunt and tease and kick and hit me. They tore my outer clothes off of me and stole the precious book from me. They started to run and I ran after them. They turned between some houses and disappeared. I kept running but found myself only in underpants, bra—no shoes either. I was frantic, covered with mud and completely lost between houses (with pavement all around) in an area I actually know (from where I used to live). It had started out as a pleasant dream but ended up as a terrible nightmare. I was distraught, crying, and completely disoriented. There was a row of churches (which is not true). I was tired and full of mud." The book that was stolen was a book for survivors of sexual abuse that had been provided by her therapist. Victoria found this book helpful in dealing with the effects of the sexual abuse.

In Growth and Understanding dreams, clients begin to move beyond their typical way of responding to or thinking about the abuse. In the following dream Victoria moves from her usual passive stance in dreams toward adopting a more active and effective role. "Betty had a car and I was with her. We went through some streets. People were jeering, in crowds, especially men, old and young, who clung to the car and somehow managed to get inside. They ran and shouted and Betty seemed drugged or drunk but she would not move and let me drive so I drove and turned the wheel from the side. Finally, somehow, I was in the driver's seat and the clinging and shouting got worse. The men in the back kept leaning over and feeling me and I lost my temper. We were lost in the streets and I would turn down one and see what looked like a main street but it turned out to be another side street. We finally made it to a church and I got out and went inside and the men seemed to melt away."

Renegotiation dreams are so named because King and Sheehan argue we should not use the language of resolution or completed healing in describing the end stage of therapy. Trauma cannot be excised from the life of an individual like a cancerous tumor, survivors cannot be healed from abuse in the way that they recover from a virus, putting the disease behind them as if it never existed. They can however come to terms with their experience and find new ways of thinking and acting. This is very evident in the following dream. As described throughout this chapter, common themes in Victoria's early dreams included being clothed inadequately, being hungry and unable to get sufficient food, being passive in the company of powerful men, and being victimized without redress. Contrast these themes with the following dream. "I was out walking, tall, well dressed with a special blouse on. I met up with a man, Joe, who was very drunk but I knew him well. He was more confused than drunk. I took him into a seemingly respectable restaurant but the staff seemed to be rough and rude. I ordered coffee and buns. Pastries also came. The food was very good and plentiful. Joe was disordered and I did my best to button his shirt and fix his tie. Somehow the waitresses caught my blouse. Tore buttons off at the cuffs and neck. There was a special decoration which was also torn off. I said firmly that I would take action about my clothes. There were four police officers there partying and I approached them about it. I took the restaurant owners to court and won. Later I met Joe and his parents and sister on a train and they congratulated me on it."

These stages do not typically unfold in a simple sequential fashion. A dreamer may be having reconciliation dreams around one abusive event while having resistance dreams in association with another circumstance that they are not ready to face. In Victoria's case, Resistance, Discovery, and Effects dreams occurred almost interchangeably for quite some time in the early and middle periods of therapy. However, this typology of dreams does offer us a guideline for tracking a client's progress with a specific issue.

Dreams as an Active Component of the Therapeutic Relationship

To this point we have discussed many ways in which dreams can give us insight into ourselves and others. They can also play a valuable role in actively moving the person forward in their development.

When we pay attention to dreams, certain reliable changes occur (Ellenberger 1970). Dreams become more vivid, easily understandable, and creative. It is as if mere attention to the dream makes it more likely that the dreamer will start to use the dream as a vehicle for actively thinking about their concerns. One of the benefits of this sharpening of the dream process is that dreams naturally provide a safe arena for trying out new behaviors and attitudes. For example, Victoria had a delightful evolution of one dream theme over a period of several months. As noted above, early in the therapy she had a dream about being carried into an ambulance and conveyed to the hospital. There were other dreams in which she was carried into a vehicle. Later, she progressed to actively entering a vehicle albeit in the capacity of passenger. Then, she had a dream in which she found herself driving the car but from the passenger's side; finally, she graduated to being the driver of a car and quickly following this was a series of dreams in which she adopted extremely active roles. Her progress in dreams predated any signs of such empowerment in her real life. We have similarly observed, with many others, that often changes first appear in dreams and then later emerge in waking behavior. The dream permits the person to do a trial run of the behavior or attitude and examine its consequences.

Finally, the therapist can very actively work with the client to make use of the dream environment to facilitate the client's development. These strategies were not employed with Victoria; however, with other clients we have used a variety of techniques. These methods are described in the dream literature and include such strategies as having the client elaborate and more fully explore the dream by such means as drawing the principle scenes or role-playing the dream from the perspectives of different characters or even objects within the dream; With nightmares, clients can imagine how the dream could end in a more satisfying way and rewrite the dream (or draw it, or role-play it) with the new ending. Finally, some people can be taught to work with the dream while dreaming.

Nightmares and Trauma

Nightmares, per se, did not have to be directly addressed with Victoria. However, many survivors of childhood trauma and abuse are profoundly troubled by their dreams. It is beyond the scope of this essay to discuss the many techniques that can be helpful. There are many discussions of this issue in the literature, including Barrett's book (1996) *Trauma and Dreams.*

Societal Issues Demonstrated by Victoria's Life and Dreams

Victoria's life-story poignantly illustrates several pressing societal issues, two of which we have addressed in this paper. In closing, we want to make some general comments about the prevalence of sexual abuse and the inadequate and damaging responses society makes toward abuse survivors.

Victoria is only one of a multitude who have been forgotten by the systems which purport to treat emotional distress. She is of a gender that is not taken seriously and of a generation that has only recently, yet still sporadically, been offered psychotherapy. She is of an age group that receives the most medication, both prescription and over-the-counter. Being in hospital does not make her better: Victoria cycled in and out of hospitals and emergency departments for more than fifteen years. Her dreams speak eloquently of the revictimization process that occurs within our hospitals.

Victoria is of a generation that taught children to be seen and not heard and women to be subservient to the needs of husbands, children, and extended families. She learned her lessons so well that she sought to silence herself permanently to end the emotional distress. Even then apparently, no one was able, or perhaps no one tried, to give her the opportunity to see herself as a valuable person.

The exact prevalence of sexual abuse is debated and will be for some time until we get resolution about such issues as to how to define sexual abuse and how to actually assess its prevalence. However, a review of the studies which have attempted to estimate prevalence, shows that despite differing methodologies and samples, sexual abuse is widespread. Certainly, we have found no difficulty in obtaining samples of sexually abused individuals for our studies (Cuddy and Belicki 1992; Belicki et al. 1993). A recent community study found that 27% of women and 16% of men reported childhood sexual abuse (Finkelhor, Hotaling, Lewis, and Smith, 1990). Clinical studies, that is of persons asking for professional help, find higher rates of childhood sexual abuse. For example, Briere & Runtz (1987) reported a rate of 44 percent of women seeking counselling at a crisis intervention center. Whatever the exact prevalence of sexual abuse may be, it is clear that it is not rare.

There have been many discussions of the societal factors that contribute to such a dismaying prevalence of sexual abuse. North American society is extraordinarily violent. It is also a very sexualized society as evident in our popular entertainment and literature. Naomi Wolf (1991) presents an excellent discussion of the dehumanizing course of sexuality over the past thirty years. She argues that the mass production of the sexual images of women "may have produced a generation that honestly believes that sex is violent and violence is sexual, so long as the violence is directed against women" (p. 163). Further, she notes that young girls are rated on their beauty, with their bodies being sexualized before they have the opportunity to discover their own sexual feelings. However, men do not have to earn their sexuality with their appearance. Men's sexuality "does not lie dormant waiting to spring into being only in response to a woman's will" (p. 156). Thus, women learn early how to look sexual, but not how to feel sexual.

Damaging as actual abuse is, our response to it often deepens the wound. First of all, there is a widespread tendency to overlook and underestimate the existence of abuse. Studies of both therapists and survivors, using a variety of methodologies have clearly demonstrated that abuse tends to go unreported in therapy. In recent years there has been a quickening of awareness by therapists but fast on the heels of this development came resistance in the form of disbelief of people's (primarily women's) accounts of sexual abuse. As noted above, the media has recently given attention to the suggestion that many accounts of abuse, particularly those recovered in therapy, as Victoria's third story was, are confabulated. It is clear that false reports of sexual abuse do exist, but given that most statistics on sexual abuse have been collected on individuals responding in an anonymous format during an era when the vast majority would not have discussed their experiences with a therapist, it is equally clear that the majority of reports of sexual abuse cannot be dismissed in this way. Given that sexual abuse thrives by intimidating victims into silence, when professionals suggest that many reports may be confabulations not based in reality, they collude with abusers in maintaining an atmosphere conducive to sexual abuse.

We are very concerned about the intimidation of survivors and therapists that is happening because of the False Memory movement. To clarify our position, we do not advocate pressuring a client to retrieve memories even when a therapist feels certain they exist. The therapist may be wrong, but most importantly such pressure tactics are disempowering of the client, which is simply incompetent therapy. However, we feel therapists need to ask about abuse and sensitively raise its possibility (making clear it is just a possibility) when a client presents suggestive data, such as a dream. We hope Victoria's story will be encouraging in this respect.

There is nothing intrinsically difficult about detecting a sexual abuse history even when the client does not share it initially due to reticence or repression. We have demonstrated that even untrained university students provided with only a single nightmare can identify individuals with a history of sexual abuse at a rate far exceeding chance (Dedonato, Belicki, and Cuddy 1993). Why then have we been so slow to identify this epidemic of abuse and why is there such resistance to it (e.g., the popularity of the False Memory movement)?

Judith Herman (1992) has an eloquently simple explanation. She points out that victims demand more of us than offenders. When we become aware of atrocity, we experience pain and are pressed to action. It is easy to send money to worthy causes such as Amnesty International because this course of action does not require us to change ourselves. In the same way, it is easier to deny or ignore the existence of sexual abuse than to do something about it. If we questioned the sexual imagery in a beer advertisement, we might feel pressure to change. In other words, if or when we feel pressure to change, the equilibrium of our life is disturbed. On the other hand, offenders require very little of us. If we will only ignore them and continue on with our lives unchanged, they can flourish.

We revictimize survivors in a multitude of ways. For example, individuals who have spent their childhood surviving sexual violence may not have had the time or resources to develop the social skills and graces that mark mature adults. This can then result in their being rejected socially or delayed in developing a vocation. If they resort to a life on the street (consider the many prostitutes sexually abused as children), we will marginalize and dismiss them as being less than human and not deserving of the rights accorded mainstream individuals.

If the victimized children are sufficiently disturbed, they will likely be stigmatized with psychiatric labels and immersed in a system that describes them as diseased. These people are not seen as the heroic survivors of intolerable childhood conditions but as somehow inadequately "built" or more blatantly at fault for their problems. Victoria's dreams were replete with both her acceptance of the medical metaphor of trauma (with many dreams depicting her circumstances as involving disease and hospitalization) and also her damning indictment of the failure of the medical system to help her. We need new metaphors both for understanding trauma and for describing the therapeutic process by which halted or distorted development is generated and renewed. The medical metaphor not only mistakenly directs attention to the diseased individual but paints an unrealistic, and limiting picture of therapy as "healing."

Epilogue

Victoria made tremendous progress with the use of therapy and the help of her dreams over three and one-half years. Throughout the course of therapy, Victoria lived in the community off and on, for up to a year at a time. She has been out of hospital for the better part of a year, living in a supportive environment, and out of therapy for several months, as of early 1995. Therapy for younger adults dealing with sexual abuse is estimated by Graber (1991) to require three to five years.

There are no such estimates for people in Victoria's age group. One could anticipate that the many decades she and others have spent trying to push back the negative thoughts and feelings would prolong the therapeutic rebuilding process, but to date, we have no answers about this. However, we do know that holding onto the secret of sexual abuse escalates the degree of trauma. The therapeutic process could, perhaps, be compared to renovating a building that is valuable, and worth saving and restoring. The work is difficult: it takes patience; it takes precision; it takes time; it takes many resources; it takes many skilled workers.

Victoria's dreams charted a course from feeling lost, abandoned, and forgotten to feeling strong, empowered, and in control, and back again. Dreams hinted at secrets through locked doors and houses, or houses without keys. Her dreams, over time, moved from passivity to action. In essence, her dreams tell a story, with a dream or several dreams, representing a chapter in the story. We cannot predict how the therapy would have unfolded or differed if Victoria had not had access to both her dreams and her nightmares. In this case, it is clear that dreams and nightmares made a valuable contribution to the therapeutic process. We have attempted to point out the issues many survivors of sexual abuse confront both in their waking and dreaming lives, and further, to explore how they can be used in the therapeutic process.

References

Barrett, D. 1996. *Trauma and Dreams*. Boston: Harvard University Press.

Belicki, K., B. Correy, M. Cuddy, A. Dunlop, and A. Boucock. 1993. Examining the authenticity of reports of sexual abuse. Paper presented at the Annual Convention of the Canadian Psychological Association. Montreal, Canada, 27–29 May.

Briere, J., and M. Runtz. 1987. Post sexual abuse trauma: Data and implications. *Journal of Interpersonal Violence* 2: 367–79.

Cuddy, M. A., and K. Belicki. 1992. Nightmare frequency and related sleep disturbance as indicators of a history of sexual abuse. *Dreaming*, 2(1): 15–22.

Dedonato, A., K. Belicki, and M. Cuddy. 1993. The effect of instructions and rater characteristics on raters' abilities to detect abuse histories from nightmare content. Paper presented at the Annual Convention of the Association for the Study of Dreams. Santa Fe, NM, 1–5 June.

Ellenberger, H. 1970. *The Discovery of the Unconscious.* New York: Basic Books.

Ellenson, G. S. 1985. Detecting a history of incest: A predictive syndrome. *Social Casework 66*: 525–32.

Finkelhor, D., G. Hotaling, I. Lewis, and C. Smith. 1990. Sexual abuse and its relationship to later sexual satisfaction, marital status, religion and attitudes. *Journal of Interpersonal Violence 4*: 379–99.

Graber, K. 1991. *Ghosts in the Bedroom: A Guide for Incest Survivors.* Deerfield Beach, FL Health Communications.

Herman, J. L. 1992. *Trauma and Recovery.* New York: Basic Books.

Herman, J. L., and E. Schatzow. 1987. Recovery and verification of memories of childhood sexual trauma. *Psychoanalytic Psychology* 4: 1–14.

King, J. 1992. Theories about dreaming: Let's regain our balance before we fall into the pool. Paper presented at the Annual Convention of the Association for the Study of Dreams. Santa Cruz, CA, 23–27 June.

King, J. and J. Sheehan. 1996. The use of dreams with incest survivors. In D. Barrett (ed.), *Trauma and Dreams.* Cambridge, MA: Harvard University Press.

Terr, L. 1991. Childhood trauma: An outline and overview. *American Journal of Psychiatry, 148*: 10–20.

Williams, L. M. 1992. Adult memories of childhood abuse: Preliminary findings from a longitudinal study. *The Advisor 5*: 19–21.

Wolf, N. 1991. *The Beauty Myth.* New York: William Morrow and Company.

Seeking the Balance

Do Dreams Have a Role in Natural Resource Management?

Herbert W. Schroeder

Managing the natural resources of our nation has become a complex and difficult challenge. As our population increases, so do demands for economic prosperity, material good, and consumer products. Great pressure is being placed on natural environments to provide wood, minerals, and other raw materials to satisfy these demands. At the same time, more and more people are turning to natural environments as settings for recreation, beauty, inspiration, and relief from a stressful, urbanized world. Fears of global atmospheric change and mass extinction of species have lead to call for protection and preservation of biological diversity in ecosystems. In the midst of conflicting demands, values, desires, and fears, government agencies that manage public lands and resources often find themselves beleaguered by controversy, politics, and lawsuits.

Resource management agencies have traditionally viewed natural environments in a pragmatic way, as a source of goods and services to satisfy the needs and desires of human beings. Professionals within these agencies ideally seek to base their decisions on scientific knowledge and a rational analysis of alternatives. As a social scientist working in a public land management agency, I have often been urged to focus on objective data and scientific information relevant to "real world" decisions. Many of my colleagues in the Forest Service and at universities believe that anything that is not measured objectively and quantitatively will have no impact on the decision-making process. In this atmosphere of rational planning and scientific research, it seems almost absurd to ask whether there could be a role for dreams in natural resource management. Dream studies, with their focus on the "inner world" and subjective personal concerns, seem very remote from the practical, day-to-day concerns of natural resource managers.

Perhaps, on occasion, a dream plays an important role for an individual in their work or career; but this is seldom if ever acknowledged or discussed openly. For example, one individual who works in the field of natural resources reported that a dream played a pivotal role in the choice of a career:

> A number of years ago, when I was working/living in a field unrelated to the environment, forests, natural resources, etc., I had a dream. This dream opened a new door—leading me to new work and thought, to an area that *fits* my life in a way no other has. . . . This is what I remember of it:
>
> I was facing east, deep in a forest of large, old trees. The foliage was dense, perhaps there were vines or moss in the trees, adding to the depth and shades of green. Sunlight was making its way through the green—from the east (maybe an hour after sunrise). Mostly the sun made the leaves glow, some shafts pierced through. There was a communication between the trees and I—not verbal yet not ephemeral either. There was a rightness, a sureness I felt in being there, as well as an excitement, a charge.
>
> I woke with a line in my head: 'That's what I do with my life— It's with the big green stuff.' (The 'big green stuff' is trees.)
>
> Since that time I have pursued an advanced degree, changed jobs and have "come down where I ought to be" (in the words of the Shaker hymn).

The person who had this dream gave me permission to include it in this chapter, on the condition that it be kept completely anonymous. The reason for this condition was a fear that admitting to being so influenced by a dream would lead to a loss of credibility as a natural resource professional.

It's not hard to see how this might happen. The very nature of dreams makes it unlikely that they would be viewed as relevant to a natural resource management profession. Jung (1964) observed that dreams manifest the subliminal "fringe of consciousness" in which clarity of definition and logical relationships are lacking. Dreams often seem to "evade definite information or omit the decisive point" (Jung 1964, 52). They appear contradictory and ridiculous compared to the "rational" thoughts of waking life. The irrational and unpredictable qualities of dreams seem totally contrary to the kind of precision, logic, and objectivity that is required by science.

Furthermore, dream interpretation in our culture almost always focuses on the significance of the dream for the individual dreamer. Resource managers in public agencies, on the other hand, are most concerned with the impact of their decisions on larger groups of people—communities, populations, and society as a whole. The individual and personal nature of most dream studies is not easy to relate to this larger scale of collective decision-making.

A closer look, however, shows that the gap between dreams and scientific natural resource management may not be as wide as it first appears. "Irrational" processes such as intuition and imagination have always played an essential role in the creation of new scientific theories, and dreams sometimes provide the impetus for important scientific discoveries. The most famous example of this is the chemist Kekulé's dream, which led him to his theory of the ring structure of the benzene molecule (Strunz 1993). While the end results of a scientific investigation are judged according to standards of rigor and rationality, the process by which the end result is reached may (and probably must) draw on intuition, hunches, feelings, and other irrational mental processes.

The importance of intuition in the initial stages of scientific creativity is well recognized. It is perhaps less well known that intuition and unconscious associations can play a role in people's understanding of scientific ideas even after these ideas have been formulated in logically rigorous terms. Jung noted that even the most matter-of-fact ideas and terms are colored by subliminal meanings and emotional undertones:

"[W]hen an exact definition or a careful explanation is needed, one can occasionally discover the most amazing variations, not only in the purely intellectual understanding of the term, but particularly in its emotional tone and its application." (Jung 1964, 28)

Thus even a precisely defined scientific concept may have emotional and symbolic significances that go beyond its immediate, logical definition. Scientists, however, tend to focus exclusively on the precise, logical definitions of terms, and to disregard (or seek to eliminate) the vaguer, intuitive significance that these terms have.

This can be seen in a recent debate that has arisen over the concept of the "balance of nature." Environmentalists often speak of the balance of nature as an ideal condition that needs to be preserved and protected. From a scientific and mathematical viewpoint, balance can be defined in terms of whether or not a stable equilibrium exists in a biological system. Recent developments in ecological research and chaos theory suggest that natural ecosystems in general may lack such equilibria. For this reason, some ecologists now claim that environmentalists are mistaken in evoking the balance of nature as a reason for protecting ecosystems— because such a balance never really existed in the first place (Kaufman 1993).

This argument seeks to dismiss the balance of nature by reducing it to a precise mathematical definition and then showing that this definition fails to apply to real ecosystems. But the balance of nature has a much broader significance than what is conveyed in this mathematical definition. Balance is a metaphor that we apply in many areas of our personal and public lives. It connotes a complex range of emotional, social, practical, ethical, and spiritual meanings. We speak of eating a balanced diet, of living a balanced life, and of having balanced relationships. We seek to maintain a balance of power between nations and within our own government. When we are uncertain about future events, we say that the outcome hangs in the balance. Balance is central to our concept of justice, symbolized by the scales on which evidence is impartially weighed.

The idea of balance is fundamental to many spiritual belief systems. Chinese philosophy sees the universe in term of two complementary principles: the passive yin and the active yang.

The yin-yang symbol, the *Ta ki*, depicts the perfect balance of the two great forces in the universe . . . held together in tension, but not in antagonism, as mutually interdependent partners; one in essence but two in manifestation. (Cooper 1978, 196)

The idea of balance and reciprocity between humans and the natural world is fundamental to Native American traditions and rituals.

[T]he world exists as an intricate balance of parts, and it was important that humans recognized this balance and strove to maintain and stay within this balance. . . . Thus, offerings were not so much sacrifices, . . . but rather a fair exchange for what had been taken, to maintain the balance. (Booth and Jacobs 1990, 38)

Celtic myth also depict the theme of exchange and balance. In one story there is a description of a valley in which two meadows are divided by a river.

Black sheep graze in one, white sheep in the other. Whenever one of the white sheep bleats a black sheep crosses the river and joins the white flock, turning white itself in the process. When one of the black sheep bleats, the opposite occurs. (Rutherford 1990, p.107)

This transformation between black and white symbolizes a dynamic interchange that maintains balance between the ordinary mortal world and the magical Other World.

These examples show that the idea of balance is a root metaphor (Bulkeley 1991c), used by many cultures to express their fundamental understanding of the universe and the proper role of humans within it. This understanding of balance is not simply about mechanistic physical and biological processes; it includes the pychological, social, and moral spheres a well. Thus, even if scientists can prove that stable equilibria do not exist anywhere in biological systems, the metaphor of balance will still have practical and ethical implications for our relationship with nature. In fact, the attempt to reduce the balance of nature to purely empirical, scientific term may itself be viewed as a symptom of imbalance in our way of looking at the world.

According to the Chinese tradition of the Tao, maintaining balance in the natural world requires that there also be balance within the human pyche (Miyuki 1985). Vice-President Gore expresses essentially the same view in his book, *Earth in the Balance*. Gore views the global environmental crisis as "an outer manifestation of an inner crisis that is, for lack of a better word, spiritual' (Gore 1992, 12). He sees the human psyche as consisting of two impulses—one that seeks to conserve and protect the world, and another that seeks to manipulate and physically transform the world. In our culture these impulses have fallen out of balance, with the manipulative impulse dominating in our attitude toward natural environments.

In the resource management professions, the deeper feelings and values that connect people emotionally to environments are often viewed as "subjective," and therefore less important than "objective" scientific facts. Thus, in resource management our thinking and decision-making about natural environments tends to become detached from our feelings for these same places. The solution to the environmental crisis, in Gore's view, is to restore balance in our attitude toward nature, by reconnecting thinking with feeling and facts with values. Consistent with this, there are now increasing calls to broaden the training of natural resource professionals by including nonscientific studies such as art, ethics, and philosophy (e.g., Bowers 1992; Crowfoot 1990; Sturgeon 1991).

If the solution to the environmental crisis is to restore balance in ourselves and in our relationship to the natural world, then dreams may have an especially appropriate role to play. Jungian psychologists see dreams as performing a compensatory (i.e., balancing) role in the psyche. That is, dreams help restore and maintain psychological balance by complimenting and compensating for distortions in the egos waking view of reality. They offer "a counterpoint (often a more inclusive viewpoint) to the attitude of the dominant ego-identity" (Hall 1983, 37).

This compensatory role of dreams is usually viewed with respect to the psychological development of the individual, but dreams might also help to compensate for distortions and imbalances in our collective, cultural views of the world. Bulkeley (1991a) points out that Western culture is unique in restricting dreams to a strictly personal context. Indigenous cultures almost universally look to dreams for guidance in the affairs of the larger community. Bulkeley (1991a, 1991b) has argued that dreams can help bring about a change in the basic attitudes and values of our society with respect to nature. Dreams point beyond the dualistic categories and structures of our daily lives to show us that "we are all members of a web of being that extends to the whole of the Cosmos" (Bulkeley 1991b, 161).

Bulkeley (1991b) suggests that dream studies should be included as one component of environmental educational programs. This could help to bring about a transformation of consciousness, which many environmentalists believe is necessary if the human species is to survive the environmental crisis. To this I would add a complementary suggestion: methods for working with dreams in therapy and other "personal growth" contexts could benefit by drawing upon the scientific study of nature, to provide amplifications of dream images and to connect dreams with the larger world of nature and society.

This possibility became a matter of personal experience for me as a result of having the following dream:

> I am with a small group of people. After traveling for a while, we arrive at a place that is like a zoo or aquarium. There are wolves living in a tank of water here. . . . They are intense and full of life. They are wild, but also very intelligent, loyal, and friendly. Once a person and a wolf get to know each other, a very strong bond forms between them. On a previous visit, one man in our group became close friends with a very large and strong male wolf. Now he sees this wolf again and approaches it. . . . The man and the wolf sit or lie very close together, looking directly into each other's eyes. The wolf's face seems almost like a reflection of the man's (and vice versa). There is a very intense, almost fierce, feeling of trust and affection between the man and the wolf. I know that most people would regard these wolves as very dangerous, but it is clear from their behavior that they won't hurt us, as long as we are friendly towards them.

The dream made a strong impression on me, and I wrote it down, as well as I could remember it, after waking up. A few days later, I was driving along an interstate highway and stopped at a rest area. There on a bulletin board I saw a poster, and on the poster was the face of a wolf that closely resembled the wolf in my dream. The poster announced "Wisconsin Wolf Awareness Week," a program to educate the public about wolves in northern Wisconsin. The coincidence of seeing this poster so soon after my dream about wolves prompted me to follow up.

On returning home I called the phone number on the poster and requested information about the Wisconsin wolf packs. From the brochures and booklets that were sent to me, I learned that wolves had recently begun to reestablish themselves in northern Wisconsin, now that bounty hunting had ceased and the animals were protected by law.

A few weeks later, I was handed an announcement for a lecture about the wolves of Wisconsin, to be held at a nature center close to my office. Again, prompted by the coincidence with my dream, I attended the lecture. There I began to learn about the social structure of wolf packs, their relationships with other species (including humans), and conservationists' efforts to promote the coexistence of humans and wolves in Wisconsin. At the lecture, I signed up for a weekend workshop on the scientific study of wolves, which was to be held at the University of Wisconsin's Treehaven environmental education center near Rhinelander, WI.

As I drove towards Treehaven on a cold February afternoon, I had a peculiar feeling. I felt like I was approaching a frontier—a place where I might make contact with creatures coming from outside of our civilized, human world. I knew that I would not have been coming to this workshop if I had not had the dream about wolves. I was letting a dream influence events and choices in my waking life.

The workshop was led by members of the Timber Wolf Information Network (TWIN), a Wisconsin group working to increase public knowledge about wolves. The workshop included lectures in which we learned scientific facts about wolves—their ecology, social behavior, predator-prey relations, and conflicts with humans. We were given presentations and demonstrations of methods for studying wolves—including tracking, trapping, and radio monitoring.

The program also included a survey of myths and cultural beliefs about wolves. In particular, two Native American stories about wolves provided interesting associations to my dream. The Haida Indians of British Columbia have a story about two wolves who swam out into the ocean to kill whales. A great storm and fog came, so that the wolves could not get back to the shore. They had to stay out in the water, and so became sea wolves (Lopez 1978, 92). My dream of wolves living in a tank of water at an aquarium seemed like a curious, modern echo of this older legend. Another story, the creation myth of the Ojibwe people, tells of how the Creator gave the first man a wolf to be his friend. The man and the wolf traveled the world together and became very close, like brothers. Later, the Creator told them that they had to part, and from then on would follow different paths (Benton-Banai 1988). Again, my dream seemed to be echoing this story of close friendship between a man and a wolf.

In addition to teaching facts about wolves and methods for studying them, the workshop included an "experiential" component. Several times, we went out to an area where wolves live, to look and listen for signs of their presence. On the first night of the workshop we went to the territory of the Averill Creek Pack—the southernmost wolf pack in North America. Our instructors imitated the howling of the wolves, hoping to produce a response from the animals. But it was a windy night, and we were unable to hear any reply.

The following afternoon we returned to the same area to look for tracks and other physical signs of the wolves. Eventually we came across the tracks of five to seven wolves where they had crossed a road. On the bank of snow by the side of the road was a urine scent-mark, apparently made by the alpha female. We followed the trail back into the woods, to see where the wolves had been coming from. The wolves had walked along the icy surface of a frozen river. We found some of their scats, and a little farther on, our guide noticed some wolf fur lying on the ice. We passed the fur from hand to hand. The strong canine smell of the fur was unmistakable. Later, we found the mostly eaten carcass of a fawn that the wolves had killed. This somewhat grisly sight underscored what we had learned about the role of wolves as "master" predators in their ecosystem.

That night we came back to the pack territory once again, for a last attempt at howling to the wolves. The weather had changed—the night was absolutely still and the stars were out. A crescent moon hung close to the horizon as we drove from place to place within the wolf pack's territory. Standing by the side of the road, I could hear the sound of trees in the woods, cracking and popping in the intense cold. My toes were freezing, my legs were shivering, and I was very tired from a weekend of almost nonstop activity.

The Northern Lights hung in the sky, looking like pale, luminous clouds. Later in the night they became like pillars of white light, reaching high into the darkness and converging on a single point at the zenith. We had still heard no trace of the wolves. Dick Thiel, our guide, walked down the road, to stand alone as he howled. Over his head I could see the constellation of Canis Major, the Great Dog. Dick kept calling to the wolves as the rest of us stood, straining to listen while our feet went numb from the cold. Then for a brief moment, I heard a distant sound—like a faint siren—first one, then several in harmony. The wolves had answered.

That one moment of communication between humans and wolves seemed to be the experience my dream had been leading me toward. As brief and as distant as the wolves sounded, I still felt privileged to have heard them. In that moment, the wolves of my dream had become real animals, out there in the night. The experience of the dream and the weekend of the workshop had come together into a more significant experience than either the dream or the workshop alone would have been. The workshop, especially the tracking and the howling, gave substance to the dream; and the dream lent emotional and imaginative depth to the workshop.

This experience has led me to believe that there could be great value in bringing together dreams and the scientific study of nature. As I said at the beginning of this chapter, I think that many professional resource managers are unlikely to see much value in paying attention to dreams and other kinds of intuitive experiences. But I think it is equally true that many people who are deeply interested in dream work and imagination may not appreciate the importance of paying attention to the objective, "outer" world.

Indigenous cultures such as the Native Americans are increasingly looked to as a source of spiritual wisdom by people who are dissatisfied with the rationalistic and mechanistic character of our modern Western worldview. One aspect of these cultures that is attractive in this regard is their emphasis on imaginative forms of experience such as story-telling, dreams, vision quests, and shamanic journeys. There is a plethora of books, tapes, and workshops that promote these aspects of native cultures for the benefit of nonnative people. But we must remember that the imagination of native cultures was grounded in a very practical and detailed first-hand knowledge of the objective world in which they lived. When a native American dreamed or saw a vision of an animal, a plant, or a landform, that element of nature was most likely already a familiar part of their experience. They had a great deal of practical knowledge to draw upon in understanding these dreams. Our urban lifestyle, by contrast, deprives us of this kind of grounding in nature, and our dreams about nature may thereby become detached from the objective natural world.

My experience with the dream about wolves and the events that followed has convinced me that the study of wildlife can provide one avenue for bringing the dream world and the objective world back together. In tribal cultures, hunting provided a context in which people spent time closely observing and learning the details of how wild animals behave. Most of us do not hunt for a living anymore, but scientific observation and study of wildlife may provide an alternative way. Careful study of animals requires one to enter the animal's world and to exercise great concentration and discipline in following and observing the animal—much like hunting. I suspect that many wildlife biologists develop a genuine sense of kinship with the animals they study, although they may be reluctant to talk about such a subjective, nonscientific aspect of their work.

Obviously, we cannot all become professional wildlife biologists, but amateur study and appreciation of nature is available to everyone. As one example, Pepi (1985) describes an approach to nature appreciation based on the journals of Henry David Thoreau. Pepi's approach "consists of deliberately integrating thinking, feeling, and acting in order to obtain the richest experiences possible from natural objects and events" (p. ix). He emphasizes the importance of making connections between feelings on the one hand and objective elements of nature on the other. The most satisfying experiences occur when feelings about a natural phenomenon come together with knowledge about the phenomenon to create "felt-significance." (Although Pepi does not mention it, I would add that imagination was also a part of Thoreau's method. A good example of this is found in the well-known essay "Walking." Thoreau's [1981, 408–10] description of an imaginary "shining family" that lives in Spaulding's woods has a decidedly dreamlike quality.)

An approach similar to Pepi's could be used in working with dreams about natural phenomena. When you encounter an animal in a dream (or in active imagination, or any other imaginative practice), follow up by learning something about the animal. Read a book or attend a lecture. If possible, go to where the animal actually lives and observe the animal first-hand (being careful not to disturb the animal or it habitat in the process). Then look back at your dream in light of your new experiences and knowledge. Weaving together experiences of the dream world and the objective waking world in this way may lead to an experience of the "felt-significance" of this animal for you.

Going even farther, you might think about doing something to take your dream out of your personal sphere and into the larger world, where it can make a difference. For example, you could get involved in conservation efforts or recovery programs for the animal you dreamed of. This will probably require you to do even more homework. To work effectively on resource management and conservation issues requires not only motivation and imagination, but also a good scientific understanding of the issues.

Combining dream work and scientific study of natural environments in this way can help to restore balance in our attitude towards nature, because it bridges the gap between objective, scientific concepts and the deeper, vague, but powerful feelings and meanings that we hold for natural environment and organisms. This kind of work can also help to bring our inner psychological or spiritual quests back into the context of community (where it always has been for indigenous people). Modern American culture is highly diverse and individualistic, and lacks a strong, commonly-held tradition by which to understand our relationships with each other and with the natural world that surrounds us. Nevertheless, small groups of volunteers are now forming for the purpose of restoring endangered ecosystems and species, and within these groups there is emerging a new sense of community that includes both people and the natural world.

My dream of the wolves showed the possibility of a reunion of human and nonhuman communities. It lead me to northern Wisconsin, where a reunion of sorts is now taking place between people and wolves. My dream depicted a balanced relationship in the symmetrical image of a man and a wolf, face to face in a bond of affection and loyalty. That same kind of affection and loyalty can be seen in the way that the members of the Timber Wolf Information Network have devoted their time, their energy, and in some cases their whole careers to helping wolves make their home again in Wisconsin.

The value of this dream did not lie in any personal interpretation or insight it gave me into the workings of my own mind. The value was in the experience to which it led me, of actually going to where the wolves lived and seeing the physical signs of their presence; of hearing people call out to the wolves and hearing the wolves answer. I understand this dream about wolves much better after learning something about these animals and how they live, and after spending a weekend with a community of people who love them. Experiences like this are one means by which we can continue seeking balance in our relationship with the natural world.

References

Benton-Banai, Edward. 1988. *The Mishomis Book: The Voice of the Ojibway.* St. Paul, MN: Red School House.

Booth, A. L. and H. M. Jacobs. 1990. Ties that bind: Native American beliefs as a foundation for environmental consciousnes. *Environmental Ethics* 12(1):27–43.

Bowers, C. A. 1992. The conservative misinterpretation of the educational ecological crisis. *Environmental Ethics* 14(2):101–27.

Bulkeley, K. 1991a. Dreaming to heal the earth. *Dream Network Journal,* (Spring/Summer): 8, 10, 55.

———. 1991b. The quest for transformational experience. *Environmental Ethics* 13(2):151–63.

———. 1991c. Dreams, spirituality, and root metaphors. Presentation at the Eighth Conference of the Association for the Study of Dreams. Charlottesville, VA, 26 June 1991.

Cooper, J. C. 1978. *An Illustrated Encyclopaedia of Traditional Symbols.* London: Thames and Hudson.

Crowfoot, James E. 1990. Academia's future in the conservation movement. *Renewable Resources Journal,* 8(4):5–9.

Gore, A. 1992. *Earth in the Balance: Ecology and the Human Spirit.* New York: Houghton Mifflin.

Hall, J. A. 1983. *Jungian Dream Interpretation: A Handbook of Theory and Practice.* Toronto: Inner City Books.

Jung, C. G. 1964. Approaching the unconscious. In C. G. Jung (ed.), *Man and his Symbols* (pp. 1–94). New York: Dell.

Kaufman, W. 1993. How nature *really* works. *American Forests* 99(3,4):17–19, 59–61.

Lopez, B. H. 1978. *Of Wolves and Men*. New York: Charles Scribner's Sons.

Miyuki, M. 1985. The arts of Mr. Hun Tun. In R. Hinshaw (ed.), *A Testament to the Wilderness* (pp. 19–36). Zurich and Santa Monica: Daimon Verlag and the Lapis Press.

Pepi, David. 1985. *Thoreau's Method: A Handbook for Nature Study*. Englewood Cliffs, NJ: Prentice-Hall.

Rutherford, W. 1990. *Celtic Mythology*. New York: Sterling.

Strunz, 1993. Preconscious mental activity and scientific problem-solving: A critique of the Kekule dream controversy. *Dreaming* 3(4):281–94.

Sturgeon, K. B. 1991. The classroom as a model of the world: Is there a place for ethics in an environmental science class? *Environmental Ethics* 13(2):165–73.

Thoreau, H. D. 1981. Walking. In L. Owens (ed.), *Works of Henry David Thoreau*. New York: Avenel.

II.

Dreams
and
Dialogues
with
"Others"

Reflections on Dreamwork with Central Alberta Cree

An Essay on an Unlikely Social Action Vehicle

Jayne Gackenbach

For almost fifteen years I worked primarily at Midwestern universities, in their departments of psychology. When I was put up for full professor, the colleague who was nominating me said that although I deserved to become a full professor he "wished I hadn't done the research I had done." That is, dream research. Would that this was an unfamiliar theme in my professional life, but exempting my colleagues, who also thought this was a scientifically valid if not important subject to investigate, most of those I came into contact with both professionally and personally thought dreams were "interesting" but not to be taken seriously. Thus when I moved with my family to Canada it was with eager anticipation that I took a job teaching two psychology classes at a nearby Native American college. I knew little about Natives* but I had heard about the deep reverence with which they held dreams.

---

*The term "Natives" refers to members of the aboriginal cultures of what is now Canada. Although the terms "Indians" and "Native Americans" are also frequently used to refer to these people, this chapter will use "Natives." Likewise, the chapter will use "reserves" as a synonym for "reservations" and "bands" for "tribes."

In the ensuing years I have become increasingly involved with Canadian Aboriginal people. Dreams play a central role in all of my relationships with these people.

Over the last three years I have taught primarily Cree, but also Ojibway and Blackfoot, at two all Native Colleges, Yellowhead Tribal Council and Blue Quills Native College, and in mixed Native/white classes at two community-college settings some distance north of where I live in Edmonton, Alberta. To teach Natives you have to go to them as few travel to the major universities for eduction.

There are two other ways in which I have become involved with Natives in Alberta, as a dreamworker and personally. As a dream-worker, I conduct workshops on dreams with a Cree woman for both whites and Natives. I have also conducted some research with my students on the relationship of dreams to waking autobiographical incidents and am currently working on a book about the death of a Cree woman.

Personally, I have become deeply involved with the extended family of the Cree woman with whom I do workshops. This involvement is primarily as a sort of surrogate grandmother to two of her great-nephews but also as a close personal friend to her niece (their mother). Finally, on a deeply personal level my own dreams have shown a marked increase in animal, Native, and elder imagery. Although I was right in general in my assumption about Native attitudes toward dreams, it has been a long haul to this validation. Simply put, being *around* Natives is not being *with* Natives.

The one million Aboriginal people in Canada make up almost one-twentieth of the population, a much larger percentage than in the United States. A Native woman from the United States visiting Alberta commented to me how good it felt to see on a daily basis references to Native issues in the media. The Canadian Native has been compared to the blacks in the United States in terms of their higher incidence in prisons, on social assistance, and using medical services. Yet the rights of Aboriginal peoples are at least twenty years behind those achieved by their counterparts in the United States. Furthermore, it has been argued that the attitude of the Canadian government is more restrictive toward Natives than is the case in the United States.

In many ways the Native community in Canada is like that of other poor peoples but there are differences. Due to the vastness of the land mass, many Canadian Natives are physically isolated, so their access to mainstream resources is difficult. This is exacerbaced by strong family and community ties as well as widespread dysfunctional-family-of-origin problems resulting in even less likelihood of changing their situation.

This was driven home to me when I realized how quickly I had come to almost "expect" personal horror stories from my Native students. For instance, during a workshop I was facilitating on dreams in a nearby community, there was only one Native woman in the group. After each nonnative participant had processed a dream using Ullman's group technique (Ullman and Zimmerman 1979), the Native woman who had largely been quiet told us her dream and her story. It was filled with violence, incest, alcohol, and the other ingredients of Native childhood I had come to "expect." I did not realize what my mind set had become until I looked at the faces of the other women in the group (all mental health workers) which showed their horror at this Native woman's story. Only then did I realize how deeply immersed I had become in the stories of pain among my Native students and friends. Although I try to not become insensitive to these tales, I realize also that to react too strongly to such a tale is to cut off the teller. A certain nonjudgmental acceptance of the brutality is expected if self-disclosure is to proceed.

Although attempts are being made to move more services to the reserves (e.g., most have schools to grade 9), they are as yet inadequate (e.g., Natives often quit school rather than leave the reserve). Another problem is in the nature of the two cultures. For instance, communication styles differ. Natives use nonlinear styles which allow and indeed expect uncertainty and are accompanied by nonverbal cues, like avoidance of eye contact with an authority figure, which make it confusing when they move into the dominant culture.

In sum, the situation of Natives in Canada today is similar to that of blacks in the United States in the 1950s, with repression and prejudice very alive. It is based in part on the belief that they are creating their own problems as evidenced by their failure to succeed at most white enterprises (e.g., huge failure rates in college programs). In the period since I started working with Natives I have realized that the naive idealism of spiritual seekers toward Natives is as one-sided and prejudiced as the "dirty drunk" stereotypes which are quite alive in Canada. Thus it is

important to strive for a middle ground integrating their peaks and
pains. Another aspect of this middle ground is to demystify whites as
either great or evil in Natives' eyes.

In this chapter I will discuss the possibility of using dreams as a
vehicle for generating and nurturing cross-cultural dialogue. This
dream-based dialogue can be expressed in various forms: from Native to
whites, from whites to Natives, between whites and Natives, within
whites and within Natives.

Dream Dialogues: From Natives to Whites

I have been facilitating dream workshops for natives and nonnatives with Ravenwoman, a Cree woman in her fifties. Born in a band
north of Edmonton, Ravenwoman's father is Cree and her mother is
Mohawk. Her maternal grandmother was a medicine woman who was
very proficient with dreams, using them as spiritual guidance.
Ravenwoman's great-grandfather was the founder of the band, while
her grandfather was the chief for thirty-three years. He was the most
important influence on her during Ravenwoman's formative years. She
would take dreams to him and he would teach her the way of the dream
including the ceremony that was used in greeting the dream. When she
was about three years old, she told her grandfather about a dream of a
white wolf. This told him that Ravenwoman was dreaming for the people and he began her training in earnest.

Ravenwoman has been my primary teacher/friend in my relationship with Natives and dreams. Speaking in some detail about her dream
life gives the nonNative some sense of its importance and place in
Aboriginal cultures (Gackenbach 1992).

"For a lot of people dreams are teachings. My grandfather believed
that if you listen to your dreams you could learn things my ancestors
knew now to do," Ravenwoman recalls. When she was quite young she
took on the responsibility of the younger children, which is a common
practice among Native families. Ravenwoman relates how her teaching
dreams of that period used to help her take care of the younger children.
For instance, her mom and dad had gone grocery shopping, which usually involved an overnight trip. She was left with her siblings and a
babysitter with not much food in the house. Ravenwoman dreamt of

someone "showing me how to pick some herbs and some onions." When Ravenwoman awoke she told her brother that she "dreamt where we can find some things we can make a soup out of." They went and picked the things and the sitter helped them cook it. "It was good!"

Ravenwoman recalls another incident which happened during her preschool years when her brother lost money their mother had given him for milk. He came home and knew he was in trouble. He told Ravenwoman to find it in a dream. As he expected her to be able to do this, it is likely she had been doing it before. She says she recalls that incident because they would be in trouble if it were not found. In her dream she asked a lady to find it. They retraced his steps and found it in the dream between the slates of a wooden sidewalk. Then she awoke and they went and got it.

Her mother had eleven children in sixteen years, so there were several at home when she was sent to residential school at six and a half years. Her older brothers also went. She says, "I made the mistake of telling the nun about my dreams and I was told it was the devil. . . . I learned then not to talk to other people about it . . . [and to] pretend I wasn't different."

After she left the convent school, she would dream often of the devil, although she never knew what he looked like. He was always trying to get her and she would wake up crying and screaming. Ravenwoman's fear of the devil was there because of her mother's strict Catholicism. However, these dreams were as fearful as what she learned about the devil at school. In a typical dream of this period, she would be in a one-room house with her brother and sister who were smaller than she was. The devil was trying to get in first by the door, which she blocked, then by the windows, which she also blocked. Then he came down the pipe of the pot-bellied stove and tried to get the lid off. Ravenwoman struggled with him over the lid and screaming she would wake. Unfortunately, yet also "statistically normal," Ravenwoman's childhood was marked by her own illness, rape, violence, and alcohol abuse.

During the time she was having the devil dreams, she noticed that the learning/teaching, freedom, and future dreams all shut down. But as she moved into adulthood these precious dreams returned. She now dreams for the family, for instance. She was told in one such dream some years ago to call all her brothers and sisters together and warn them that one of their children was in deep trouble. They needed to be especially alert and protective for two weeks. Only one sibling, her sister Delcy, did not come to the meeting. Two weeks later, Delcy's daughter committed suicide. Even Ravenwoman's oldest brother, who says he does not "believe" in dreams, will come and perform a ceremony if Ravenwoman says he should because of a dream she's had.

Raven woman spoke of an experience which she had twice as an illustration of the difference a lifetime makes. The experience first came at the age of eight or nine, and reappeared a second time after menopause. Ravenwoman saw a big ball of light, pulsating energy with a voice which filled the room. She writes:

> This was a spiritual dream of God appearing to me. In this dream I began by being afraid of something unknown to me and I wanted to hide, then I decided to pray, for in my dream I knew he would help me. Then this big ball of pulsating light appeared and I could hear the words this ball of energy was saying as an echo in the room. It said, "I am the goodness that you must follow and if you believe in me and trust me I will always be there to help you. If you wake up now you will see me." I woke up and saw this light beside my bed and I was no longer afraid. I ran to tell my parents and they said it was only a dream, it had not really happened.

The most recent one occurred after she had been up awhile praying and using her pipe. It appeared in the midst of this ritual. It explained about God and that God could help her and her people. "When we pray to God we are looking to the goodness within ourselves." While with that ball of energy she said, "I had no room to be anything else but me—the real me." She said, "What I felt was a total trust. . . . I felt humble." "If you can feel kindness and love coming from energy, that's what it was." When I asked her what was happening in her life as an adult about the time of the experience, it turned out to be a period of considerable stress. At the school she was working for as a play therapist, six of the children were suicidal, her son had just broken his back, and they had just unexpectedly adopted another son who had fetal alcohol syndrome.

She explained that the same experience separated by almost fifty years took on a different quality. "It's like when you go to a movie when you [are] a child. You see this movie and you think how fantastic and so on. Then you go again and see it as an adult but as an adult you pick up the real characters; you pick up the depth; you pick up what's really happening." These experiences, she explained, when they occur around menopause have meaning, richness, and depth. The message to her is: "This is what I've been trying to tell you all your life."

As can be seen by this brief biography, throughout her life dreams have played a central role for Ravenwoman. Also relevant to our work is her other training. She completed a Bachelor's of General Studies in Arts and Sciences degree program with an emphasis in psychology and Native history. Ravenwoman is currently a school counselor at her band's school. She also has received intensive training in a wide variety of mental health issues.

Out of our histories and trainings we have dialogued at length about all aspects of our cultures but especially about dreams. What has been refreshing is the similarities between her understanding of the dream in her culture and the scientific understanding I bring to our dialogue. For instance, she always speaks of dreams as teachings about what we need to know in order to proceed clearly into our own futures. Certainly, a perspective consistent with the information processing perspective of REM sleep dreams, which are easiest to recall (Belicki 1987). If we all paid attention to the cutting edge of our own mental capacities, REM-sleep dreams, would we not be better prepared for our own future choices? The view of dreams as teachings seems to me to also echo the classic psychoanalytic perspective of dreams reflecting deep psychic issues. Although Ravenwoman would agree with this, she looks to the dream for specific and concrete direction regarding the issue at hand. Again, her view parallels approaches in contemporary dreamwork which value the problem-solving capacity of these night experiences (but perhaps not as concretely as Ravenwoman).

But there are also differences in our styles of working with a dream. Ravenwoman tends to be more sensitive to specific items of content as having meaning, while I tend to focus more on the process of the dream. To illustrate, I recently had a dream of two white tigers lying on a stage. I walked up to them and was unharmed despite my hesitation. Ravenwoman said in her "read" of my dream that white animals represent the spiritual and are a positive signal, while I read it as what am I afraid to approach. One is an object emphasis based on cultural teachings, while the other is process-oriented focusing more on relationship between dream items.

Dream Dialogues: Within Whites

Initially Ravenwoman's object-based interpretations made me uncomfortable as they tend to be at once specific and vague. But then my dreams began to evidence more and more animals and Natives and most recently elders. Clearly my work with Natives was bleeding into my deep unconscious, so it made increasing sense for me to use cultural interpretations.

One very strong dream identified my "totem" animal* and was best understood using a Native cultural perspective. I dreamt:

> I was at an event of some kind largely outside. There was a hole in the ground that was an entrance to a big underground cavern. It was partially blocked by a concrete square but I saw in it a saber that I knew children who were coming to the event would try to get and possibly would fall in. I thought of going down to get it as I sat on the edge of the opening but saw that it was very gravelly and that I'd slip into the deep cavern. Then a big turtle came into the cavern from below and I asked her to get the sword. She did and came out of the cavern and gave it to me.

When I woke I assumed the turtle was of the Teenage Mutant Ninja Turtle variety as my eight-year-old son used to play with. This may have been mixed with a turtle character in a book I had read him the night before, an association consistent with the helping children theme of the dream. But it lacked a depth that I also felt came from the dream. Then I found the cultural interpretation that turtle is the "oldest symbol for planet Earth and is the personification of goddess energy, and the eternal Mother from which our lives evolve" (Sams and Carson 1988). This interpretation spoke strongly to me in that the turtle in my dreams was clearly female and came from deep within the earth to help me in my work. It wasn't until a month later that it was suggested to me that the turtle might be my totem. These interpretations do not work at odds to each other, rather they complement each other. One takes the waking precursors and associated them with my current concerns, while the other moves the dream experience to relevant cultural contexts.

---

*A totem animal is a spirit helper which often comes to a person in a dream (Harner 1980).

Dream Dialogues: Within Natives

Although I have learned from Natives and Ravenwoman about dreams and especially my own, it is also clear to me that within Natives there is a wide range of attitudes toward dreams. These range from confusion and ambivalence to an almost sacred acceptance.

Although I started with a largely professional relationship with my Native students and coworkers, it has evolved in some cases into deeply personal relationships. Although these personal relationships have gradually grown, several events coincided about a year ago which significantly deepened my relationship with Ravenwoman's family. By chance, during Ravenwoman's sister's (Crowwoman) last weeks my sixteen-year marriage broke up partly due to my deep involvement with Crowwoman's family. Thus I found myself with my children only half the week (as we had agreed to literal joint custody) and felt a void. Crowwoman had been raising her daughters' sons and although her daughter took over their care during Crowwoman's last months she was/is ill-prepared for the task. Thus I became a sort of surrogate mother/grandmother to them.

I suppose this all sounds very commendable on the surface and certainly the liberal "do-gooder" in me was attracted to this new role. But the reality of being deeply involved with Native children who come from a multigenerational highly dysfunctional family has only hit home more recently. I have struggled with transference issues with both Crowwoman's daughter and her grandson. We are all clearer that I am not Crowwoman, I am their friend. These are the primary relationships I have with this family as well as continuing a close personal friendship with Ravenwoman. I am also quite close to another cousin and am in a relationship with a Cree man from another reserve. With many of the rest of this family I have a positive relationship but we are not as close.

One of the critical experiences of my acceptance into this family was when Ravenwoman's youngest sister called me one day with a dream about Crowwoman. Gena said that Ravenwoman wasn't at home when she'd called to ask her about the dream so she thought she would call me.

So how do dreams figure into this complex web of family relationships? As in other Native families with whom I have come into contact, dreams also play an important role in this one. From the dreams/visions of Crowwoman during her illness to dreams of her by the various family members since her death to dreams about other aspects of their lives.

From the beginning of Crowwoman's illness she generally turned her life over to an eighty-two-year-old shaman, the Old Man. She refused the radiation, chemotherapy, and surgery the Western doctors had suggested, saying that she didn't want to poison, burn, or cut her body. She wanted to heal or die the traditional way.

Her healing regime with the Old Man included a flour, pepper, and mustard poultice. It was put over the cancer area, left on overnight, and taken off in the morning. There would be sweat underneath which was thought to be a cleansing force. The Old Man and Crowwoman had a dream experience with the poultice which seems to signify her confusion about the role of dreams in her own culture.

She was staying with the Old Man and his family for about six weeks. He'd given her this poultice to put above her groin area on her right leg over the cancer. She had been using the poultice fairly regularly. One night she had a dream that the poultice was pulling out a yellow bile from her. A few days later, the Old Man stopped by her room in the morning and commented to her that he had had a dream about her poultice and that it was doing the same thing, pulling out yellow bile. Immediately after these concurrent dreams, Crowwoman stopped using the poultice. She told her sister, Ravenwoman that it was uncomfortable as it was always tugging.

When she told me the dream and the following week came back and told me the Old Man's dream and that she'd stopped using the poultice, my obvious question was, "Crowwoman, are you sabotaging your treatment? Do you need to die? Do you want to die? Is that maybe what's going on here?" She was not offended by my blunt questions, rather she clearly responded, "Yeah, I've thought of that and I don't know." She wasn't sure, but it was something that she had thought of. I told her that I felt that the concurrence of both dreams so close in time was an indication that it might work. At the least it would be helpful. She agreed but did not continue with the poultice.

When I asked the Old Man about the poultice dreams after her death, I explained the mutuality of them but not the dreams themselves as he said they should not be told. They both spoke to the fact that Crowwoman could be helped if she did something which she had been avoiding doing. The Old Man chuckled when I told him this and commented good naturedly, "Well, I should quit smoking but I don't quit smoking. I guess there's a need yet for me continue to smoke." We don't always do what we need to do.

Since Crowwoman's death many family members and friends have had dreams of Crowwoman. Geoff, the Old Man's son and a shaman in his own right, kept having dreams of Crowwoman and called for a Ghost Dance to contact her. Ravenwoman dreamt shortly after her death that she saw Crowwoman dancing in radiant joy with pearl anklets. Her grandson, Ret, dreamt that she was in a body bag in his mom's closet, and that there was a way for her to come alive. I too have had a powerful dream of her since her death where she encouraged me to dance and not work so much. The dreams and visions vary but what all seem to hold conotant (white and Native) is the "reality" of these dreams as visitations by Crowwoman with specific messages.

I am also part of the day-to-day dialogue in the family involving dreams. So, for instance, a family member to whom I am close dreamt of being with a very attractive man. We talked about her concerns about physical beauty in processing the dream. What has become clear to me is that dreams are as much a part of daily conversation in all aspects of the family system as is cooking dinner. Although I knew intellectually how deeply dreams were regarded and had some feel for it with my students, the pervasiveness of this has been driven home by my personal involvement with this family.

Dream Dialogues: Between Whites and Natives

In addition to the dialogues Ravenwoman and I have conducted about dreams, I have been doing research on the relationship between dreams and waking autobiographical incidents in Cree versus whites in the Central Alberta area. This research further delineates the impressions of cultural differences regarding the dream which I have been getting as a teacher, writer, and friend. The dreams which were collected as part of an in-class activity were factor-analyzed separately for Native and nonnative students from two classes on developmental psychology (Gackenbach and Prince 1992).

Natives in this sample conceived of dreams along several distinct and meaningful dimensions (i.e., transpersonal or spiritual as separate from personal conflicts), whereas nonnatives were more likely to cluster these concepts of dreams into a single dimension. These findings reflect the Native idea that dreams are messages from other worlds and the opposite belief in nonnatives that all dream elements are parts of the individual psyche.

Supporting this empirical work is my experience of dreamwork with Natives; I have tried to promote the idea that even dreams of spirits were personal. I met resistence. Over time I have come to more fully appreciate the different dream forms of which they speak. To illustrate, the following dream-experience is clearly transpersonal and seen as concrete in that the dreamer was certain this was a visit/message from her dead mother. Yet as the story unfolded, it became clear there were powerful emotions involved. These manifested in a very real transpersonal connection. DS told me of a recurrent dream she had as a child a few days before the class did a dream incubation technique. She wrote:

> The dream I had that always made me wonder is a circle of trees and a little opening where a road comes in and my mother walking on that road toward me inside that circle with a rock in the center, a bag I put my sweet grass in after I had picked it and braided it. The part I can't understand is she disappears just before she reaches me to hold my hand and I wake up. Some day I would like to touch her hand in my dream to see what happens.

DS's mother died three hours after birthing her. DS was raised by her grandparents and physically abused by her grandmother, who blamed DS for the death of her mother. DS hated her grandmother and was glad when she died, yet the interference of the grandmother into the connection between DS and her mother continued in DS's eyes even after her death. She told me of a time after the death of her grandmother when she tried to contact her mother in a sweat lodge ceremony designed specifically for that purpose. DS explained that her grandmother came in spirit to the sweat and blocked DS yet again from connecting with her mother.

DS told me after class that when she told her grandfather about her dream as a child, he said that if her mother touched her she'd die. The dream in his view represented her mother watching over DS. So because of her death and the grandmother's influence DS was never able to truly connect with or "touch" her own mother.

A few days later we did a dream incubation technique for solving problems. DS wrote:

> Last night I had been thinking and worrying about my daughter who is in an abusive situation and her boyfriend took her to Saskatoon. He is abusing her out there.
>
> I fell asleep and I dreamt about my daughter sitting in that circle I use to sit in my own dream and I was the mother who was reaching for her hand. And when I touched her hand and she smiled, my phone woke me up and it was my daughter and she was at a police station and said she ran away from [him] and the police were going to take her to a WIN house and bring her home to me in the morning.

From my white cultural perspective it seems that the recurrent dream of childhood certainly echoed her distance from her mother, due primarily to the mother's death and the rejection of her grandmother. The second dream with her own daughter showed what she had achieved in her own family that which was denied to her in her family of origin, connection with her daughter. In DS's mind the dream-experiences had their own reality, their own firmness that plainly said it all. And the "proof" of the spiritual/transpersonal nature of the experiences was that she touched her daughter's hand at the moment the phone rang. There was certainly no doubt in DS's mind about the transpersonal nature of these dreams prior to the last one with her own daughter. It was more for my benefit that she told the last dream to me. DS knew the surrounding psychological aspects of the dreams but did *not* interpret the dreams in that way. She stayed very firm in her belief in the other worldliness of the source and meaning of the dreams.

Dream Dialogue: From Whites to Natives

The primary way which I have worked with dreams with Natives has been as a teacher. In every class I have taught to Natives, I have included a discussion of dreams in at least one of three ways: lecture, self-disclosure, and/or assignments. Inclusion in lecture ranges from asides which might highlight the course material (i.e., telling about the relationship of men to women in the dreams of women as a function of

time of menstrual cycle during a lecture in social psychology on interpersonal attraction) to formal inclusion in the course syllabus.
Regarding the latter I have included dreams in Introductory Psychology classes as a separate topic, in Developmental Psychology as an
aspect of the development of thinking and feelings, in Personality as
part of certain classic theorists, and in a special topics class on Altered
and Higher States of Consciousness. I have found that not only are they
appreciative of any information on dreams but frequently ask me for
more information, including asking me about a specific dream they
have had.

I should point out that my approach to teaching these same psychology courses to nonnatives is basically the same, with less of an
emphasis on dreams. I find that although they are also quite interested,
it is not with the intensity and focus of the Natives. This cultural attitude is also evident when nonnatives approach me with a specific
dream. They follow the white cultures "etiquette" of asking about a
dream, minimizing it by laughing at the very idea that such things
could be taken seriously. This sort of apologetic laughter is almost, but
not entirely, unheard of with natives who approach me about dreams.

The most fruitful way that I have worked with dreams with Natives
in the classroom is via written assignments. In conjunction with a section on dreams I might ask the class members to write out a dream and
hand it in to me. They are always given the opportunity to not have me
read it. But usually they are eager for me to read the dream and comment on it. They are extremely unlikely to share a dream in an open
classroom setting, whereas high self-disclosure was forthcoming within
the privacy of the homework assignment.

I have found that Natives are equally willing to share dream and/or
autobiographical information with me and at times both are at a fairly
deep level of self-disclosure. At this point I have probably read about
500 dreams/autobiographical assignments, with about half to two-
thirds relating to dreams. For instance, from a victim of sexual abuse:

> The lecture on sexual abuse as well as John Bradshaw's film were both very
> disturbing for me because as a child I was sexually abused for a period of
> nine years from the time I was eight until I was seventeen years old. I am
> currently in counseling and I just found the film very "enlightening"
> because it showed me or made me think about all the other people who
> have been abused and I didn't feel quite so alone.

Such tales of horror and fear also come out in their dreams. A Native woman writes of a memorable dream:

> I got separated from my two girls and my husband. The people were gathered in a domelike room and everybody was scared and I kept thinking about my girls and my husband. There was no electricity and no one was allowed to go outside of the dome. There were many people injured and many that were dead. Many of the people were burnt up and looked horrible. I didn't get the chance to find my girls because I would wake up.

Interestingly, Natives are not nearly as interested in my feedback on their autobiographical stories as they are in my feedback about their dreams. In fact, my impression is that it seems to be an infringement on their privacy to say much about their life stories but a betrayal of trust to *not* say anything about their dreams.

When I am teaching a longer section on dreams, I try dreamwork techniques both in and out of class. I would say in general that they are either lost about how to do the technique or at best resistant. For instance, in one guided imagery technique where they worked individually after the first few steps, the level of classroom buzz elevated making it apparent that this was not something with which they were comfortable. I closed the technique early and when reading the dreams and what they had written about them I found that they quite understood how to do the technique but that the sensitive personal issues were much closer to the surface than I had ever experienced before with this technique.

In another class I was able to get further with the same technique. The dream of LM illustrates the potential effectiveness of this technique for helping the dreamer bridge cultural beliefs to an interpretation of the problem. LM writes of her dream and immediate reaction to it:

> A couple of months ago I had a dream that the mushums [Cree for grandfathers] were telling me that they were going to take my son, Conrad, away from me. I asked them why, but they would not answer and the dream ended. I keep praying to them to tell me why they were going to or let me know what they mean. But nothing has happened. Now I worry constantly about my sons.

As part of the technique she rewrote the dream from the point of view of the grandfathers:

I am a grandfather, in the spirit world. I watch over people that need guidance. I am worried about Conrad, because he's really feeling left out or neglected and I have to let his mother know. I shall warn her in her dream. If I say I am taking away her son, she then might pay attention to his feelings of neglect. It will help guide her through this phase of his life.

It turned out that she had recently had a second son and was concerned that her first son, who was sixteen when the baby was born, was feeling neglected. She wrote to me about this in a later assignment:

> Then in class when I wrote about it. [I] had another dream that night. This time telling me that I've done everything to make my son happy. I have not neglected him and I think in a way, that since having a new family and a baby, he felt left out.

It is important to note that she had found the solution in the dreamwork technique, however, it seemed to me that her acceptance of the solution was contingent on getting a verifying message from the grandfathers in a subsequent dream.

In general when Natives give me a dream to "read," they want an interpretation of the message it is conveying. Thus they defer to my authority on dreams as they would to an elder or another dream "reader." They also ask many people what they think of the dream and do not reject each interpretation, rather they seem to take them all in and mull them over. Never really coming to a firm conclusion about any one dream. In contrast, the newest thinking on dreams in our culture is that the dreamer is the owner and final authority on his or her own dreams (Ullman and Zimmerman 1979).

I try to bridge these two belief systems by offering some interpretation in the form of questions which seem generated from the dream imagery. In this way, the answers remain with the dreamer and I have served as a gentle guide who nudges them to consider it from another perspective. This on occasion leads to a dialogue especially when the dream has had a very powerful impact on the dreamer. In any interpretations/discussion I never shy away from transpersonal interpretations. So if I am told a dream of a deceased relative, which almost universally is seen as a visit, I honor it and go to what message the relative has for the student.

It quickly became apparent to me that some belief systems, views of "reality," are best left in place. I in no way accept that my ontological position is the "truth" and am quite adamant with my students about the arbitrariness of white cultures' view of reality as bounded, separate, and linear. In fact, my own private ontology is very consonant with Natives, so the shift to a view that dreams of the dead are always visits with messages rather than unprocessed deep unconscious material bounded in the individual psychic was quite easy for me to make.

I do not want to characterize my dreamwork as not without the influence of my own culture. I do emphasize that it's the message that is most important and don't engage in arguments of ultimate reality of its source.

Conclusion

I have sketched in this chapter the pattern of relationships I have developed with Aboriginal people in central Alberta. These relationships range from personal to professional. Through them all I have tried to support who they are in their full range, as complex, fully functioning members of Canadian society as well as the inheritors of a rich spiritual tradition in which dreams are central. It is from this connecting in dreams that a multifaceted cross-cultural dialogue has emerged.

I am aware that I am in a position to reenergize the value of the dream and indeed the value of many of the traditional spiritual teachings for the Natives I come into contact with. In my role as teacher, with a doctorate in psychology, they listen to me about the science of dreams and states of consciousness which I integrate with standard psychological concepts. In some ways my teaching serves as a stamp of approval from white society, encouraging them to appreciate some of the truly beautiful traditional teachings. I do not presume to tell them anything about the specifics of their traditions, rather I speak simply of the science and clinical work with these states of being and emphasize my belief that my culture was and is simply wrong in dismissing or minimizing them.

This role was especially brought home recently when I was asked by students at Yellowhead Tribal Council to teach a class on these extraordinary states of consciousness including dreams. We had daily in-class activities to personalize the material. These ranged from dreamwork to testing their ESP using Rhine's Zener cards. Although this was my first attempt to directly bridge the Western scientific understanding of these states of being with people of a culture which deeply regards them, I am hopeful that I will be able to offer it again at Native colleges.

There were many moments of confirmation for the value of the class from the students but perhaps one of the strongest was from a Cree man in his mid-thirties with tattoos all over his arms. I knew his father was a medicine man and he had repeatedly made mysterious asides to me about the spirit world, including warning me that I should be afraid of it. His gruff exterior could be daunting. At one point he told me a dream and was quite eager to hear what I would say about it. In our conversation about the dream he clearly experienced the "aha" which manifested as a startle response in him. I had approached the dream in a *Native* manner looking for the direct guidance it offered and he was shocked that I would suggest a direction for guidance that he had not thought of or that no one else to that point had suggested to him. I knew at that moment that I had gotten through to him in a way that all the lecturing in the world had not. He had told me in the past of his own ambivalence about going into the "family business" (medicine man). I believe that my Western scientific support of the states of consciousness dealt with in his father's work had an influence on him. This is but one example of what I believe is the potential impact of the proper introduction of this material to peoples who fundamentally believe in these states of being but in whom white cultural influence has sown serious doubts. I accomplished in this course, with more depth than ever before, my goal of supporting Natives who look back to their own culture for spiritual guidance.

A second social action agenda I strive for in my work comes out of a curious phenomenon Ravenwoman and I have repeatedly experienced in workshops, classes, and our daily lives. It is the naiveté that *both* cultures have with respect to each other. That is, the almost reverent awe that each culture can hold for the other's "authority." This is not only in terms of dreams but many areas of the transpersonal/personal domains. Let me illustrate.

I had Ravenwoman come to a dream class I was holding through the extension faculty at the University of Alberta. The students sat in a circle around her in a hushed silence, quite literally hanging on her every word as she spoke simply about her experiences with dreams and the spirit. Afterward, as we walked through the parking garage to our cars, Ravenwoman turned to me and asked, "What's wrong with those people?" We both shared a good giggle over her puzzlement and agreed that the classes' attitude toward her was silly. But what we found equally silly was virtually the same reverence paid to me when speaking on psychology and even on dreams to Natives. The white "doctor" is seen with a deep respect that seems as overdone in its apparent depth as was the respect that was paid Ravenwoman.

The flip side of the reverence attitude is the anger of the Native and the nonnative toward each other. This is nicely evoked by a student's poem which came to her while falling asleep. She was taking a Native Studies class where she was learning about the atrocities which occurred to her people around the time of colonization. Not normally a poet, the first two lines of the following poem came to her in this sleep transition state. She got up and spontaneously wrote out the entire poem.

Purging

At last I have found a voice from which to speak
To the Queen of England, from her subject so meek.
How can you sleep at night, mind peaceful, body limp
You enjoy life to the fullest with nary a hint
Of how your old money came into your hands. . . .
On the backs of others in a faraway land.

Your monarchy grew by leaps and by bounds
Not once did you question how your fortune was found.
Do you let your mind wander to the days of old
How your ancestors reached out and went for the gold.

In their greed they staked claim for a flag and some rules
Saying, "nobody's here, just savage fools."
You said you discovered the land, therefore, you own
All riches and resources the Indians call "home."
We thought you spoke truth with your treaties so grand
We lost our lifestyle and you took the land.

Some tears, some bitterness and plenty of hurt
A people worn down by your laws and your dirt.
Exploitation, assimilation, words . . . not easy to say
From a people who survived and won't go away.

Like the Phoenix we're rising, from bended knee
From alcohol, poverty and racism, we'll soon be free.
We'll learn your language, your laws and your game
While we nurture our own and be rid of the shame
Of being an Indian, scorned by the whites.
We'll keep our pride and get on with the fight.

Should your sleep be disturbed with dreams of fright
Reach to the Creator for visions of light.
Undo the wrongs done to people of old
With harmony restored the truth will unfold.

—Linda Anderson
Spring 1993

It seems that there is little middle ground in the relations between our cultures in Canada. Thus this is a second agenda I have in all of my work with Natives and about Natives. Too many of my "New Age" contemporaries refuse to see that Nintendo is as popular with Native children as it is with our own; that although violence and abuse is frequent, it exists alongside an incredible sensitivity to what we have come to call the transpersonal or the spiritual as well as an emotional openness; that hockey is the way "out" for Native teens just as basketball is for inner-city blacks in the United States, and that young adult Natives feel the same pressures to go into the "family business" as whites do—in other words to honor the families' heritage/teachings.

I have been attempting to achieve this middle ground or place for cross-cultural dialogue through dream-based work at many different levels. This vehicle for understanding each other seems to facilitate living *with* and not just *around* Natives.

References

A version of this chapter was presented at the 10th annual meeting of the Association for the Study of Dreams in Santa Fe, New Mexico, June 1993.

Belicki, K. 1987. Recalling dreams: An examination of daily variation and individual differences. In J. I Gackenbach (ed.), *Sleep and Dreams: A Sourcebook* (pp. 187–206). New York: Garland.

Gackenbach, J. I. and W. Prince. 1992. *Dreams and autobiographical experiences from Alberta natives and nonnatives.* Paper presented at the annual meeting of the Association for the Study of Dreams, University of California, Santa Cruz, June 1992.

Gackenbach, J. I. 1992. Adaptiveness of childhood transpersonal experiences in two Cree women: A study. *Lucidity* 11: 107–22.

Harner, M. 1980. *The Way of the Shaman.* New York: Bantam.

Sams, J. and D. Carson. 1988. *Medicine Cards: The Discovery of Power through the Ways of Animals.* Santa Fe: Bear & Co.

Ullman, M. and N. Zimmerman. 1979. *Working with Dreams.* Los Angeles: Jeremy P. Tarcher.

Black Dreamers in
the United States

Anthony Shafton

I

Since midcentury the different currents of interest in dreams in the
United States have been giving impetus to one another. The discovery
of REM in 1953 started a second, post-Freudian revolution in the science of dreams. Jung's psychology finally took hold. And a grassroots
"dream movement" began with the spread of Perls' Gestalt therapy
techniques (1969) and with popular books by Ann Faraday (1972) and
Patricia Garfield (1974). The dream movement arose as a "hybrid product of the self-help, alternative health therapy, consciousness-raising,
and human potential movements" (Maguire 1989, 22). It emphasizes
practical applications of dreamwork, creativity, spirituality in both religious and nonreligious senses, psychic events, and lucidity—not to
exclude insight and healing as in conventional therapy. Above all, it
encourages dream sharing among peers and other forms of de-profes-
sionalized dreamwork: dreams belong to dreamers in their everyday
lives and do not, in most circumstances, require to be interpreted by
professionals in clinical settings (Hillman 1988). Meanwhile, clinicians, experimenters, and theoreticians have contributed to, and in turn
been influenced by these developments.

Taken all in all, interest in dreams is at an unprecedented level in the United States, and growing. We who value dreams regard this as an encouraging sign for our culture.

But one disappointment has been the lack of much racial diversity in the dream professions and at dreamwork venues. We in the dream movement need to come to grips with this reality, if we mean to promote dreamwork as a credible instrument of social healing. The underrepresentation of African-Americans is especially unfortunate, in view of their numbers and importance in the nation. This racial imbalance struck me when I attended my first conference of the Association for the Study of Dreams (ASD) in Chicago in 1990. The ASD is a broad organization for all dream-minded people. It sincerely welcomes academicians, clinicians, and community dreamworkers of all stripes, and also solicits participation by interested laypersons. But as I was leaving the hall after the president's opening address and looking the membership over, I noticed that there were no black faces. This confirmed the impression of racial uniformity I had already formed in the course of reading the dream literature, many of the authors of which I was now surveying. Finally I saw a solitary tall young African-American and decided to say hello and share the observation which he no doubt had already made for himself. It happens he was a *Tribune* reporter covering the conference.

There did turn out to be one (and only one) black person attending, Loma Flowers. As I subsequently learned from talking with her and other members, the ASD is well aware of its difficulties reaching minorities. Indeed, the organization acknowledged the problem in its report on this conference (Lewis 1990), but has not so far known how to remedy the situation materially.

The inertia of segregation aside, why should there exist any estrangement of the races in this area where we might rather hope to see the races drawn together?

The dream literature provides little guidance. Race is a topic not often raised, and then almost only from a white (albeit broad-minded) point of view (e.g., Winget et al. 1972; Gregor 1983; Haskell 1985; Young-Eisendrath 1987; Wikse 1988). Otherwise the literature is ostensibly "color-blind"—which, from a minority standpoint, generally means "white." What is more, African-American dream culture per se has hardly been touched upon, by scholars white or black.

So to investigate this problem, I turned to the publications of African-Americans writing on the general topics of black culture and psychology, and subsequently I interviewed a number of these writers, as I did the few black dreamworkers I could find (Shafton 1991). The opinions that follow draw heavily on the comments of these professionals, especially those of Faheem C. Ashanti, William M. Banks, Carole "Ione" Bovoso, Loma Flowers, Gerald G. Jackson, Charles Payne, William D. Pierce, Loudell F. Snow, and E. Bruce Taub-Bynum (undated citations of these persons refer to personal communications). Subsequently I have conducted approximately 100 hours of taped interviews with sixty African-American individuals on the subject of their dream lives. Of course, I don't speak for the professionals or for the informants with whom I spoke, still less for blacks in general.[1]

Those of us who concentrate on dreams can forget that the average person of any race nowadays has an impoverished sense of dream meaning and worth. But I found a consensus that blacks as a rule pay more attention to dreams than do whites in the United States. This interest does not, however, carry them into the settings where most dreamwork takes place. Many of the professionals emphasized that blacks, with their pressing reality concerns, consider dreamwork, as the dream movement conceives of it, a luxury they can't afford—to the extent, that is, that they are even aware of its existence.[2] Dream groups, along with other growth modalities, are viewed as (and distanced as) white middle-class pursuits. Even successful blacks, those most likely to participate, are too busy contending with the real or perceived danger of sliding into poverty to get involved. Dreamwork takes a certain mentality of leisure which they—not to speak of the less advantaged majority of blacks—do not possess (Payne).

What of potential black dreamworkers and dream-oriented psychotherapists? Some choose conventional career tracks which promise more success (Flowers). Although their white counterparts confront the same fact of life, a decision to leave the mainstream comes harder to those who have, as have the majority of black aspirants, earned their way to the status of professional against high odds.[3]

Others choose approaches they believe address issues of survival in a racist society more directly than does dreamwork. When "the real world is the problem," as it is for many black clients, then dreams and dreamwork may seem "less relevant" (Banks). Black psychologists opt for approaches perceived to be more empirical and concrete (Jackson, Pierce).

Anyone with confidence in the peculiar relevance of dreams to life could dispute this attitude toward dreamwork. Bear in mind, however, the urgency of social and economic (on top of emotional) problems often besetting blacks seeking help.

Moreover, this attitude should be seen in the context of a general criticism of Euro-American psychology. Certain black psychologists consider racism "the major impediment to psychological wellness in the Black community." Consequently, when blacks reach out they have a right to expect "social and political advocacy" (White 1984), or even "a social action program" (Pierce 1980). Otherwise, "the professional's mission is oppressively one of getting the client to adjust to the status quo" (Jackson 1980a). Color-blind white psychology suppresses specifically black issues. It lacks a proactive orientation, while implicitly throwing the burden of change onto blacks (Banks 1980). Dreamworkers should be aware that many potential black participants expressly or intuitively share these views articulated by black psychologists.[4]

There do exist currents of social activism in Euro-American dream psychology, notably in the tradition of "culturalism." Alfred Adler (1958), one of the original 'big three' of depth psychology, urged us to reject many values of the culture. Erich Fromm launched a "critical evaluation of the effects of Western culture [on] mental health and sanity" (1955, 11). In *The Forgotten Language* (1951), Fromm's widely read book on dreams, this line was unfortunately left merely implicit. The lapse has in part been made good by Montague Ullman, a "neoculturalist" (1969) who acknowledges (1973, 1988) the influence of Fromm's social ideas, which he combines with Adler's penchant for community outreach. While he has not issued anything like Fromm's political agenda, his discussions of "social myths" are germane to the concerns about racism expressed by black psychologists. He speaks of "the emotional fallout from the social arrangements and institutions around us" (1988), of "embedded kinds of ignorance," and of "power deprivation" (Ullman and Zimmerman 1979, 184). These all entail "social myths" embedded in the "social unconscious" and appearing "inevitably" in dreams, where they are accessible to dreamwork (Ullman 1973). "To the extent that those involved in dreamwork remain impervious to the deceptions and imperfections of the social order, the work itself will collude with the dreamer's waking collusion with that order" (1992). Activism is certainly not the hallmark of contemporary white dream culture, but exceptions exist,[5] and it is hopeful for the future of interracial dream sharing that such ideas are found in Ullman, the foremost advocate of dream groups on today's scene. That said, even Ullman analyzes the majority of dreams, not for social (much less racial) but personal psychological content. In this respect he exemplifies what I was told by various professionals is a difference in how blacks and whites typically think—a difference which renders much dreamwork unattractive to blacks. As it was put by Taub-Bynum, a family therapist, whites tend to view life and interpret dreams in "intrapsychic" terms, blacks in terms of social milieu and spiritual reality, or "field."

Others concurred. Ashanti, a psychotherapist and Voodoo priest, phrased it that blacks are more oriented to the "external," both social and spiritual. Payne, a Jungian, added that blacks identify themselves with community more than do individualistic whites. Jackson, a professor of psychology, said that these considerations pertain also to black professionals and explain in part why more do not practice prevalent styles of dreamwork.

Of course, many whites also think dreams can concern extrapsychic reality, in its consensual and/or spiritual dimensions. That view is prominent in fringe approaches such as Eckankar with its promise of actual "soul travel" (Twitchell 1980), but also in the most solid mainstream dreamwork (Delaney 1991). And it surely remains the naive view among whites that dreams are about the real world if they are about anything. Moreover, almost every dreamworker suggests doing some sort of reality check on dreams before turning in the direction thought usually to be more pertinent, intrapsychic interpretation.

But without question, the drift has long been toward what Jung called interpretation on the "subjective level," whereby "persons or situations appearing in [the dream] refer to subjective factors entirely belonging to the subject's own psyche" (1971). Jung also found an "objective level" of dreams, referring to the immediate milieu, society-at-large, or even real spirits (1965). And he held that "Freud's interpretation of dreams is almost entirely on the objective level, since the dream wishes refer to real objects, or to sexual processes which fall within the physiological, extra-psychological sphere" (1971). But from the perspective of some black psychologists, the contrast Jung drew between himself and Freud leaves both, along with other prevailing dream psychologies, concerned far less with the outer field than with the inner. It was sobering to hear Euro-American dreamwork called uncongenial to the psychology of African-Americans in just this aspect which might well be regarded as its particular genius, intrapsychic analysis.

Unfortunately, African-Americans have historical reasons for associating the intrapsychic approach with racism. "[T]he failure to grasp the social context of behavior results in interpreting behavior as deviant even when it is realistic and normally adaptive. The black man's justified suspicion of white people is mistakenly identified as paranoia pure and simple. His bitter protest against a boss or slumlord is seen as an expression of 'Oedipal hostility'" (Thomas and Sillen 1991, 57–58). This is simply the twentieth-century equivalent of the antebellum Southern diagnosis of "*drapetomania,* literally the flight-from-home madness," diagnosed for runaway slaves (Thomas and Sillen 1991, 2).

What if a dream of "social rebellion" were said to show "upsurging of sexual impulses" instead of desire for social change? As Robert Haskell once pointed out (1985), this is the sort of bias which white treatments of black dreams have in fact shown—dream psychology has not been untainted by general psychology's historical alliance with racism (Guthrie 1976).[6] Few dreamworkers would insist on such a reading, perhaps; yet its standpoint is uncomfortably familiar. It exemplifies the two ways "our" dreamwork fails to satisfy the real-world orientation of blacks: too little focus on society and injustice, and too much focus on intrapsychic process.

It is interesting to find complaints about one-sided intrapsychic analysis beginning to be voiced by whites in the dream movement (Watkins 1992; King 1993 and this volume). However, several professionals framed the matter in ethnic terms, asserting that the African-American traits involved are truly African in origin. They referred to the movement among black intellectuals which finds West African (Nobles 1980; Baldwin 1981) and even Egyptian (or "Kemetic") (Diop 1974; 1990; Karenga 1990) roots for characteristics of blacks in the Americas.[7] In this view, because slavery entailed isolation from white culture, it enabled the maintenance of certain deep traits of Africanity—it was only with television in the fifties that U.S. blacks were brought into something like full contact with Euro-American culture. Prominent among those characteristics is a sense of self based on group solidarity.

"[T]he African philosophical tradition does not place heavy emphasis on the 'individual.' Indeed . . . in a sense it does not allow for individuals" (Nobles 1980). "The main thrust of a child's education [in Africa] seems to be a sort of 'hypopsychologization' combined with a 'hyperculturalization' of individual outlooks and behaviors." (Sow 1980, 145). Certainly the struggle for survival has concentrated the African-American mind outward, and put a premium on social support. Arguably, however, a sense of collective identity or "primacy of the group" conveyed from Africa (Jackson 1980b), as much as the harsh life here, has contributed to the real-world, extrapsychic orientation of African-Americans; whereas Euro-American individualism lends itself to intrapsychic understandings. Moreover, to "do your own thing" is viewed as alien to Africa-based values (Nobles 1980). Hence the general coolness of blacks to the human potential movement (Toldson 1973) and its sequels, including dreamwork in some popular forms.[8]

A traditional African trait claimed to foster collective over individual identity is a time sense emphasizing past and ancestry more than personal future. It contributed to tribal solidarity, which, with the destruction of those bonds under slavery, was transferred to blackness per se as "the final definition of tribe" (Nobles 1980). It also emphasized kinship ties, an area of special sensitivity when blacks encounter white psychological modalities.

Prevailing views of the black family fit the tradition holding blacks to be inferior, if not from genetic, then from societal causes (Banks 1980; Thomas and Sillen 1991). True, black families have "real and definite problems associated with racism and oppression" (Nobles 1978). But supposed "deficits" may actually reflect normal features of the African family, adapted to a harsher setting (Jackson 1980b). Features found on both continents (Nobles 1974) include: horizontal kinship ties (partly replacing the nuclear family); "kin-like" relations ("informal adoption," care for the unrelated elderly); "interchangeable" roles (children take adult responsibilities, genders exchange nurturing and earning); and the prominence of the mother-child bond (note that the white single-parent home has been legitimized, while the black parallel is held pathological [White 1984]).

In the minds of influential black psychologists beginning in the seventies, the intrapsychic, self-centered approach of white psychology is connected with the liberal assumption that blacks will assimilate by overcoming their deficits vis-à-vis white middle-class standards (Banks 1980; Thomas and Sillen 1991). But neither progressive policies nor the ideal of color blindness recognize black mores as valuable in their own right. These thinkers insist that African-Americans derive "unique status . . . not from the negative aspects of being black in white America, but rather from the positive features of basic African philosophy" (Nobles 1980).[9]

This has little to do with dreams directly, but bears on why blacks are reluctant to bring their intimate concerns into white settings such as those where most dreamwork is done. Average African-Americans may not be aware of these anthropological perspectives, but they are sensitive to the dissonance between prevailing attitudes to black life and their own, and are alienated from white mental health by a "history of misdiagnoses and stereotypes" (White 1984; see also Gross et al. 1969).

Are there alternative resources in black communities, contributing to dreamwork segregation? That culture has scarcely been touched in the literature—a fact which in itself should give pause. African-American are comparatively unaffected by Euro-American prejudices against dreams, having remained for so long outside the mainstream. Many regularly consult their dreams. Some share and interpret dreams with trusted relatives and friends, that is, in ad hoc dream groups composed perhaps of varying members, but always of trusted intimates. (Children are seldom instructed directly about these matters, but instead pick up their knowledge by being allowed to overhear adult conversations.) However, few or no formal dream groups exist. Equivalent communal functions are provided by ministers, healers, and spiritualists. These persons do meet with groups; but though they also often interpret dreams, they do so one-on-one, not in group settings. Dreams are sometimes mentioned in church, particularly in the so-called sanctified churches. Some one may testify that God spoke to them in a dream, or the minister might speak of being called in a dream. But dreams play less of a role than they do in many of the so-called independent churches of Africa.[10] So if a dreamer needs interpretive help, she or he may seek out a dreamwise neighbor, relative or co-worker, or visit a minister, healer or spiritualist privately.

Euro-Americans may suppose that spiritualism, "rootwork," "hoodoo," and so forth are confined to lower-class and rural blacks. But not a few middle-income blacks visit spiritualists and healers. "Every community has it," though white associates usually will not realize the fact (Jackson). One of my informants, herself a spiritual reader who mingles traditional African-American practices with adopted Yoruban beliefs, boasted about the judges, entertainers, and other prominent clients who consult her. Especially some lower-class blacks do seek help from dreams for gambling, finding mates, and so on, and such uses of dreams are more common among middle class blacks than whites. Virtually every African-American has relatives or acquaintances who play the lottery (and, formerly, the indigenous lottery called "policy" or "numbers") from dreams, often with the help of dreambooks published for that purpose. All the same, the range of black uses of dreams is imbued with genuine religiosity and aesthetics. Even the numbers (on which Malcolm X provided a good primer in his autobiography [1966, 84–85]), have a spiritual component. One informant told me about a relative who regularly wins at lotto based on dreams. The big prize?, I asked. No, the little ones. Why, if she has such powers, doesn't she play for the big money? Because, my informant explained, then she would be acting out of greed. The prizes she wins are small rewards for her faith from God. It is not implausible that such a use of dreams by African-Americans, which is part of a more general orientation to dreams as spiritually founded warnings or predictors of the future, descends from divination practices in West African cultures.

Parenthetically, none of those interviewed could say that spiritual and religious trends in the dream movement have attracted either spiritualist or more conventionally religious blacks.

Finally, what of blacks who have more completely internalized Euro-American culture? They have a stake in conforming to prevailing attitudes, which are inimical to recent developments in dreamwork as well as to other growth trends (Payne). Therefore they usually turn to styles of individual therapy with more sanction but less interest in dreams (Taub-Bynum).

II

What follows are several examples of African-American dreaming and dreamwork which illustrate some of the generalizations attempted in section I. The dreamers in these anecdotes represent different degrees of assimilation to the dominant culture. Black folk beliefs about dreams will be illustrated by a pair of examples (1a and 1b). The next example (2) shows the work done on a dream by an assimilated black professional in an interracial dream group. These examples are from published sources here edited, and with minor adjustments of wording and punctuation). The final and longest example (3), which reports an interview I conducted, is in some sense intermediate.

This selection should in no way be construed as encompassing the full range of dream-experience of United States blacks, which is of course as diverse as that of any heterogeneous group.

1. The following two anecdotes give an indication of U.S. black folk beliefs involving dreams. Such beliefs are somewhat less prevalent than in previous decades, for the same reasons that folk beliefs of all ethnic subcultures tend to dissipate in this environment. Just how widespread beliefs of the kind remain is difficult to say.

1a. Linda Camino (1986, 229–33) studies "non-orthodox healing practices" among contemporary African-Americans. She attended the visit of James, a man with "jumped-up stomach" (probably gastroenteritis) to a Southern "root doctor" named Joe, who "describes himself as half Black and half American Indian." Joe diagnosed "conjuration":

> Joe: Most people who practice it do so out of a need to show they got control, or because they are scared of losing you. They can do it 'cause they got this knowledge which is power. Witchcraft *is real.* You know they can put stuff in your food—that's the main way of tricking. But they can get a piece of your hair, or your fingernail, or your toenail, or they can even get your picture and work a spell that way. They watch you and find out which way you travel every day and what you do. Do you live alone?
>
> James: No, I got a wife.
>
> Joe: You got any woman friends? You seeing another woman?
>
> James: (looking down at the floor): Yeah. A woman I got to know.
>
> Joe: She the one who got you?
>
> James: Yeah.

Joe: You got a devil spell put on you and put on you good. That spell has got to come off before you ever feel normal again or happy again. You ever eat her cooking?

James: Yeah.

Joe: She's got you good. That's how she got you. Put poison in your food. [Along with fasting, herbal tea and bible readings, Joe prescribed a dream incubation:] You have anybody close to you that has died?

James: One of my brothers.

Joe: You got someone on the other side. He can tell you what to do, but you got to have a way of getting through to him by way of this world. You got a graveyard near where you live?

James: There's one a few blocks off.

Joe: Now you get some graveyard dirt and get it from a newly dug grave. You take that dirt home with you and put a circle of candles around it, just candles you got in the house, light them and say your brother's name. Then go to bed and your brother will come to you in a dream and he'll tell you what to do.

James did as prescribed. His brother appeared in a dream and told him he must break it off with the woman he was seeing on the side. At their session, Joe had already settled on this woman as the probable cause of the "devil spell," which she worked by putting "poison" in her cooking. James followed his brother's advice, and his condition improved (Camino 1986, 234, and personal communication 1994).

"This continued interest on the part of the dead for the affairs of their living kin is," thinks Snow, "one of the strongest links of African-Americans to the African past."[11] Many do or expect to dream about— or to see, or hear, or sense the presence of—relatives who have passed, and these events are commonly regarded as genuine visitations.

1b. To dream for someone else's benefit is known in many cultures (Desjarlais 1991), including our own (Ullman 1986, 388; Windsor 1987, 162) and ancient Egypt (Krippner and Dillard 1988, 13, citing Van de Castle). Dreaming for others by specialists is a practice in Muslim black Africa, where certain clerics perform this service for Muslims and non-Muslims alike (Fisher 1979). Snow (1993, 190–91) describes dreaming for others in the medical folk beliefs of U.S. blacks:

> The message that someone is pregnant is often delivered via a dream and the pregnancy may be that of oneself, a family member, or friend. Fish are a common theme of these dream-messages. Thirty-nine-year-old Jackie

Forde laughed as she reported that her mother had called from Mississippi to see if she was pregnant again. "At my age!" In fact her mother had called *all* her grown daughters with the same question. The older woman had been dreaming of sitting on her front porch and fishing in a small puddle in the yard. Her mother would no doubt continue to check with all the female members of the clan until she located a pregnant woman, said Jackie. And that would "prove" the old belief once again. (East Lansing, Michigan, 1987).

This story once again illustrates the predictive function of dreams in African-American culture. One of my informants, with one foot in traditional and the other in mainstream culture, told me that dreams are about "my own personal experience. Or, I guess, the future related to me."

Many though not all of my informants are familiar with the existence of traditional dream codes or signs, and the one of fish meaning pregnancy seems to be the best known. My impression is, however, that few contemporary Northern urbanites can recite very many of these codes. Other fairly commonly known ones are the reversals of birth meaning death, and death meaning marriage. In spite of the last of these, several informants volunteered that dreams of someone they know dying make them very nervous, on the grounds that such dreams can be directly predictive. Often such dreams are deliberately not communicated to the people concerned, either from fear of causing alarm, or, in some cases, to avoid any implication of oneself being maliciously instrumental in the predicted outcome.

2. One of the few published accounts of dreamwork centering on racial issues is in Ullman's book with Nan Zimmerman (1979, 192–94). It illustrates that dreamwork addressing racial issues can profitably be conducted in an interracial setting with mainstream, educated dreamers. The work concerns the dreamer's conflicts arising from upward mobility:

> [This] is the dream of an ambitious young black lawyer working hard to advance himself. At the same time he feels strongly committed to "being of help to my people." [Edwin dreamed:] "I was playing baseball with a childhood friend in a wooded area. There were two out for the home team. I looked and assessed the situation. I realized that the better team was the one that was out on the field. I felt conflicted. I wanted to be on the winning team but my friend, who was on that team, said that I would

have to play in the outfield. This didn't appeal to me. I wanted to be at bat and the center of the action. I wound up coaching a rundown between first base and home plate. I finally saw the first baseman was going to miss the ball. I encouraged the batter to go. He rounded first and was going to second."

The night before the dream Edwin had been at a meeting where he was called upon to act as a mediator between a group of black workers and their higher-ups. He realized that, as an educated black professional, he was facing choices that would test his resolve to be a leader to his people when such choices might compromise his own ambitions. He [said]: In the dream I was torn. I wanted to be part of the winning team but I knew what would happen if I did. I would find myself out in left field, socially successful perhaps but unimportant, unrecognized, unfulfilled. This is what happens to upwardly mobile blacks. They are co-opted and give up the struggle. The other choice was to do what I could for my own home team. I would have liked to be a hero and save the game by my performance at bat. This is the part of me that wants to make a grandstand play and gain recognition. In the dream I seem to have worked through to a role that will take into account my need to further develop my professional skills and, at the same time, direct those skills toward helping my team."

There were a number of more personal associations to the dream, but one in particular opened the dream up for the dreamer. He became aware that the friend in the dream who warned him of being in the outfield if he joined the winning team was a composite image of two childhood friends. One tended to play it safe and went on to a successful career in the business world. The other took risks, became alcoholic, and died quite young. He could identify with both. The dream seems to be saying that both images would have to be transformed if he was to work toward his ideals and still survive. It also pointed to a strategy that seems to work. Being on the losing side he has to take advantage of the errors of his opponent. He does this in the dream even at the risk of being "run down."

3. The following interview illustrates several trends of African-American dreaming, as I will point out in conclusion. The account also provides an instructive, if unusual, example of how dreams can play an actual part in processes of social transformation.

I first heard about Marion Stamps in a National Public Radio feature concerning the gang truce at Chicago's Cabrini Green housing project after the shooting death of a young boy, Dantrell Davis, in October of 1992. NPR asked her about an open letter she had earlier written to her community which eventually contributed to the truce after the shooting. She mentioned that she had been moved to write the letter by a dream. But her dream experience was more involved than that, as may be seen in the following edited transcript of my own interview with her in February of 1993.

Marion Stamps is a fireplug of a woman, with grey showing on her forehead at the base of her cornrows. A long-time community activist, she has a reputation, as I later learned, for being a tough, accomplished political infighter who doesn't hesitate to put herself forward. Her reception of me was reserved, except that she soon seemed eager to tell a neglected part of her story.

Stamps is presently director of an infant mortality program and president of a community center. When we met at her office, I primed her by recounting two 'big dreams' of modern political figures which had had an impact on their political actions.[12] Then I asked her to talk about her own dream:

MS: I know for myself, having been part of the whole black movement for self-determination, I've had to rely on spirits and dreams and things that might come as I've sat in a chair that I might not necessarily have thought about. I think it has a lot to do with just survival skills, living in the kind of environment that we are forced to live in. So—I tend to always move based on spirit. I have learned that when you don't put God first in what it is that you do, you're going to have some problems. So when I had this dream, it really was just part of a very stressful kind of situation that I was going through, and everything that I had tried and tried to address that stress never worked out. Look at the fact that our children continue to die, whether it's by bullets or books or videos or preachers lying to them, or whatever. To me in this community there exists a dark side of—of Hell! And that is not something that I have felt until recently, until maybe in the last twelve or thirteen months. So when I had this particular dream, it was like I was trying to come up with a way to deal with the violence in the community, you know, the violence had just totally really gotten next to me. And I had gone to sleep, and what I had dreamed about was that the Lord told me he wanted me to plan a four-day feast. The Friday night feast was supposed to be a unity feast where *every*body in the community regardless of who they were were invited. Then on the Saturday night it was only supposed to be certain key people who had certain positions in the community, that they could make a change if they in fact wanted to do that. Then on the Sunday, we would announce this great big unity thing that we had came up with. And then that Monday, it would be a big gala celebration out in the community, okay?

When I woke up, I just like scratched the stuff down, so to remind me the next day what I was supposed to be doing, right? Friday night [first just] the street organizations [gangs], and then we was going to all sit down and break bread together, and then each group would say why they accepted the invitation to come, and what was their commitment, based on what they had heard. And then that Saturday all the community agencies were going to be invited. And we was going to present to them what had came out of that Friday reunion for peace, right? Then that Sunday it was supposed to be like a whole spiritual thing, we was going to have like different choirs from the churches to come and sing and stuff. And we was going to have prayer.

AS: Was this all strictly Christian, or was there other . . .

MS: No, those who believe in Islam, or whatever. We would like drink wine together, we would pay homage to those brothers and sisters who had come before us and all that—you know, the whole thing. And then that Monday we was going to have this big old celebration.

This happened in January of ninety-two when I had this dream, before Dantrell got killed. I talked to my minister, and he was saying that that's what the Lord wants you to do, so you got to do that. Then I talked with the sister Paulette, whom I'm very very close with, and she was saying like, "No, you oughtn't to do that." So I just kept talking to people, to a bunch of people about this dream I had.

AS: So at this point you were thinking in terms of really living out the dream as you dreamed it.

MS: As I dreamed it and as I wrote it down. But: it wouldn't come together. So what happened—this was whenever Easter was—I was playing solitary [cards] and I was like in a different state, I was—you know, it was like a mechanical thing that I was going through. And all these thoughts was running through my head and stuff, right? So I got up, and I say, you know, like I'm tired and stuff so I'm going to lay down. And I—I wasn't really asleep, I was, you know, sort of like nodding off and everything, but I wasn't like in no deep sleep. And all these words came to me, and I got up, and I wrote 'em all out. "This is a open letter to my community. May I take a few minutes of your time. I know you busy," I said, "but I got to say this and I just thought of saying it." And I started writing and I wrote it all out. The next day, I had my secretary to type it. Then that Friday and Saturday, I walked this whole community and I gave all the brother and sisters that I seen a copy of it, and I asked them to please read it, please read it, please read it. Okay? And about a week or so after that, Lu Palmer [black radio personality] called me and he said he had heard about this letter. So I went on his show and I talked about my whole point in writing the letter was just to say to the brothers that they got to stop killing us. And from there, John Davis did a thing on his radio show.

AS: Was the fact that you were motivated by a dream part of these radio discussions?

MS: Yes, uh-huh. And then different brothers started calling me. And that's how I got involved in this whole United in Peace action. From April all the way up to today there has been movement to bring about a united peace among the different tribes in the African-American community. Here on the Near North Side, we were able to bring about a united peace among all the different gangs, seven and a half weeks before Dantrell got killed. In July we marched from this community to City Hall to demand that Richard Daley sit down and talk to us about the violence that exists here in this Cabrini Green Near North community. I'm the president of Tranquility/Marksman Community Organization. We were funded through the Community Trust to work with the different youth organizations in the community, gangs, whatever folks want to call them, Disciples, Vice Lords, Cobras, Stones. This was between June of ninety-two up until October of ninety-two. All of us in Tranquility were providing recreational activities for the young people. We had a social service component, we had family nights, we would have rap sessions and group sessions, we went on all kinds of trips that people would not ordinarily take a group like that on. We reviewed certain movies and [had] discussions on those movies. We had a total holistic approach in terms of reeducating and revitalizing the person, in order to get them to a point were they would think for themselves about what they doing, and why they doing it.

AS: What was the status of your original four-day feast now? Were you still thinking about that?

MS: Everything that I was doing was based on the four-day feast. But it wasn't—see, I thought the dream was telling me to have a four-day feast, like Friday, Saturday, Sunday and Monday. But that wasn't what the dream was saying. The dream was saying that in order for you to bring about the kind of peace that is necessary for this community to survive, there's some other kind of groundwork that must be laid. So the groundwork that was laid was us getting the Community Trust grant, so we would have all the different representatives right there up in one room, you know. Rather than them coming together up under one room for a feast, they came together up under one room for—for a program.

AS: And then what in your mind was the relationship between the original dream and the vision or whatever it was when you wrote down the letter?

MS: The letter—the letter and the dream itself was a blueprint, it was a outline in terms of what God had laid out for me to do to work towards united peace in our community.

AS: So you saw the letter as the continuation of the dream?

MS: Right. See, like I'm saying to you, [back before Easter] I just went out there and organized a four-day whatever, based on what I thought it was, right? But it didn't come like that. It came the other way, it came with different gang leaders from across the city coming to me. It came with me going places in Chicago with people I had never met before, in alleys that I did not know exist. My mind, of course, is still on what it is that I dreamed that I was supposed to do. And we continued to work and build. So, what happened, we had planned this—this four-day feast thing again.

AS: Who's 'we'?

MS: Tranquility/Marksman, along with the different brothers and representatives who was working toward the peace initiative, right? It was the Friday, Saturday, Sunday and Monday of Labor Day. So that Friday, we had this big old get-together. It was primarily sisters. And we danced and we sang and we talked and we ate and we reminisced, and—there was really a lot of soul-sharing that took place. We had something like a testimony, about how glad they were that the shooting had stopped, and giving credit where credit was due, and stuff like that. Then that Saturday we was supposed to have this big fund-raiser, because, see, in the meantime Tranquility hadn't got no water and no gas. We was going to charge people twenty dollars. Man, laid the stuff out, didn't raise a dime. Because what happened, the leader said that he didn't feel that they, the Cobras, were ready to participate in anything that serious until [the other gangs] became that serious, because it was very very serious, to him. So what was scheduled for that Sunday didn't happen. That was when the different nations was supposed to come together and announce that they were moving to another level of consciousness and struggle. So that Sunday, we just ended up partying. But that Monday we had this great big old block party. We had about three thousand people. Everybody, the children, the elders, everybody—it was beautiful.

And after that was over with, we were still trying to deal with this situation. The Vice Lords were still shooting at the Cobras. I was trying to talk to the Vice Lords [about] the importance of their leadership talking to the Cobras. That never really did happen until after Dantrell had gotten killed. And then a week before Dantrell got killed, I was on the second floor of Tranquility, and I was looking out the window at the Vice Lords and the Disciples shooting—at anything that moved. They shot at women and children—it was a trip. And I was saying to myself then, if I had the power to deal with that, I would tell my brothers and sisters, "Let's gun up and go get them. Fuck them, let's go down like we live, we ain't no cowards, we sick of this shit, they been shooting at us now on a regular mother-fucking basis for four weeks." At my babies, you know. That following Friday I left town and went to Mississippi to see my Daddy, and then I get a call that Tuesday that Dantrell had gotten killed. Since that time, I've spent a lot of time trying to maintain the peace initiative and make some sense of this insanity. I know eventually all this stuff will work out, but I'm moving based on what my spirit is.

AS: Was your letter still part of things? And did people know this was the product of a dream?

MS: Yes, the people that I talked to, I told them how came the letter. People asked me, "Well, what made you write the letter?" "I had this dream. And the dream said 'Do this, this and this'."

AS: Do you know other people in this whole episode or in general in your political activism who have been motivated by dreams in the way you're describing?

MS: Most of the brothers and sisters that I associate myself with on a personal and a political basis—they may not necessarily say that a dream came to me but they just say, "I had a thought or "I had this vision."

AS: Do they mean it in a literal sense? Because that's a way of speaking, too . . .

MS: Nn-nn. They mean it in a literal sense.

AS: Could you describe the original dream a little more to me? You said the Lord *told* you about the four-day feast. Was there a visual dream scene too?

MS: Right. On that Friday night, there were all these different representatives of the Stones, the Cobras, the Vice Lords and the Disciples. Each one of them came with fifteen of their top people. The Disciples had on the blue and whatever it is that their colors are, the Stones had on the red and the white, the Cobras had on the green and grey, the Vice Lords had on the gold and black. They were all in their colors, and they were all sitting at different tables. And they were all in Tranquility. I did like a welcome, and explained, you know, why we were here, based on it's nation time.

AS: In the dream you actually did this?

MS: Right, it's nation time, and it's time for us to come together as people. And some of the brothers were saying that they felt like I fronted them off, the way I put the letter out there, because—they felt like I was calling them out. And I was explaining to them, "I am calling you all out . . .

AS: Wait, now wait wait wait. Are you telling me that in the original dream you dreamed about the letter that you were later going to write?

MS: (Pause) Yes.

AS: In that original dream, you dreamed about the letter?

MS: Right! In the original dream, I had put out a letter or a flier or something that invited all of the leadership of the gangs to come to this unity feast. So they all came, representing their different nations to the feast. Right. And—and at the feast, some of the brothers were initially sort of upset, 'cause they said they felt like I had fronted them off. It's probably because I named the gangs, right? When I put the real letter out I named the gangs, so I guess that might have been what they was talking about in the dream. Everything that happened for real happened in the dream, and it came from the dream.

AS: Right. Except unfortunately it didn't work out quite as well as . . .

MS: But it worked out, because see even with Dantrell—it wasn't in the dream, but I believe that Dantrell's death were by divine intervention on the part of God to let people know, "It's time for yo'all to get this bullshit together."

AS: You said the Lord *told* you about this. Now, was there a voice? Or did you simply mean you understood that what you were dreaming was *from* the Lord?

MS: I talk about God in the dream, because the dream came as a result of me sitting and praying for the Lord to show me a way to deal with what was going on in the community.

AS: The Lord wasn't a character in the dream, in other words.

MS: No.

AS: If you don't mind my asking, in your family background what place did dreams have? Did you and your folks talk about dreams? Do you now share dreams with your friends or your relatives?

MS: I've always shared dreams with my children. Always, you know. Dreams I've had have governed how I've dealt with my children.

AS: Did your folks treat dreams with you the same way?

MS: No, nn-nn.

AS: So where did you learn to deal with dreams that way? Was that just something that came to you or did other people influence you in that direction?

MS: No, I think—like I say, I'm a product of the Movement.

AS: In the earlier days in the Movement, did people talk about their dreams among each other?

MS: I always talked about visions. I learned very very early in life that you had to pay attention to your emotions, to what your mind was saying to you. You had to always deal with your subconsciousness. It's about spirit. If the spirit say boycott, you boycott. If the spirit say go to jail, you go to jail. Because the spirit is a collective energy of everybody. It's not your energy, it's a collective energy. You feeling all these forces, pouring into you, saying you got to do what the spirit say do.

AS: So you understand your dreams in the same way, that they're part of collective energy?

MS: They're the same thing. It's not just dreams, either. It's my total environment. I don't invite people to my house that I know that don't necessarily like me or don't necessarily believe in what I believe in. You know, don't have the same spirit that I have. Because, see, they can only bring negative spirit around me—I don't like being around people that are negative. I don't like being around people that ain't where I—where I am.

AS: Do you find that that influences your dreams? The *negative* energy of people?

MS: Nn-nn. My dreams have kept me from the negative energy of people.

AS: So, if the dream represents the collective spirit, it's the collective *positive* spirit . . .

MS: Positive spirit. Right. My dreams protect me from the negative spirit.

Marion Stamps is unwaveringly confident that dreams are relevant for life. She regularly guides family decisions by dreams shared with her children (even though she did not learn dream sharing from her own parents). After she dreamed of the four-day feast, she immediately consulted with her minister about it and with a close friend. These attitudes and actions are consistent with African-American dream culture, as discussed in section I. Moreover, when she circulated her letter she did not hesitate to say it was prompted by a dream. Unusual as that may be, she fully expected—evidently with justification—to be taken seriously by her community on the dream's account, even to be authorized by it for public action. It is hard to imagine a white political activist approaching a constituency on such terms.

Stamps discerns a correlation at depth between her dream and whatever subsequently occurred in connection with it. She was given the dream for guidance and motivation. Further, the dream predicted events, and probably, in her mind, instrumentally caused events to happen, since it emanated from God. In one place she names the source of dreams as "subconsciousness," but elsewhere as "God," as "spirit," and as the "collective energy of everybody"—agencies with no obvious boundaries separating them.[13]

Thus the dream is substantially extrapsychic in causation as well as meaning. Stamps' reading of her dream concerns how she is affected by her real-world social-spiritual environment and how to act in relation to it. During our interview she offered no opening at all to an intrapsychic line of questioning. Her dream-experience is a good example of the extrapsychic orientation of U.S. black dream psychology, as discussed in section I.

Stamps' belief in her dream's objective, prophetic validity gave her latitude to adjust her interpretation in the light of events and even, it appears, to amend the dream itself in good faith, without dishonesty. One can't be absolutely sure where the boundaries lie between her initial four-day feast dream, her conscious efforts to actualize the dream, her vision of the letter and the writing of it—which itself either actualized a part of the dream or else became a part of the dream retrospectively—and her reevaluations of the dream in the light of partial successes, setbacks, and other real-world events.[14]

Something worth noting is that Stamps speaks as naturally of visions as of dreams, and makes little distinction between them beyond the obvious ones. Even imagination ("things that might come as I've sat in a chair that I might not necessarily have thought about") is not sharply differentiated from these other states of consciousness. Dreams and visions are also relatively interchangeable in the African independent churches mentioned earlier (Kiernan 1985; Charsley 1987), but probably also in most other cultures where diverse states of consciousness are believed to come from, and are trusted to reveal, extrapsychic reality. Snow's illustrations of U.S. black folk beliefs (1993) suggest that many blacks are more comfortable with visions than are most members of the dominant culture, which teaches us to mistrust any experience like a waking hallucination (Foulkes 1985, 76).[15]

III

Finally, let me return to the hopeful notion that dreamwork might be a meeting ground for the races. Unfortunately, the existing segregation of dream cultures is not soon likely to change substantially. The dream movement has yet to show that it can catch the attention and address the needs of African-Americans in numbers. While to say that prevailing styles of dreamwork are not relevant to the real world is surely wrong, all the same, our methods and mind sets may not always get to the point as keenly as we like to believe. We should realize that there exist, between the races, real differences not only in social condition but also in psychocultural style. Moreover, the effects of those differences are compounded by today's climate of ethnic separatism.

In addition to the obstacles to cultural exchange mentioned in section I, the very prominence of dreams in traditional African-American culture paradoxically creates further obstacles. Individuals still imbued with that culture often keep it private to protect it and themselves from scorn or skepticism; while assimilated blacks may not expose their interest in dreams so as to avoid becoming identified with old Southern country ways.

Nonetheless, the possibilities of interracial dreamwork remain attractive. Compare family or marital counselling, where a dream can serve as a semi-objective mutual point of reference for the hostile parties, facilitating openness (Markowitz et al. 1968).

Insofar as blacks do appear at white dreamwork venues, white dreamworkers need, as do all white care providers in a broad sense, to be more aware of black traits and perspectives than they generally are (Snow 1974). Equally to the point, whites should be prepared to learn from blacks. The races should meet, if at all, on equal and mutually beneficial terms, respecting differences. Thus I believe that we need not give up a predominantly intrapsychic view of dream meaning, nor too much of what that entails for a view of life, in order to profit from black perceptions of social injustice and inflated individualism in Euro-American culture. And surely the intrapsychic approach holds reciprocal benefits for blacks who do participate in the dream movement.

Notes

1. One of my informants, Loudell F. Snow, an authority on African-American folk medicine (1993), is actually white, as I was surprised to discover long after our interview. She has described to me her own surprise at a meeting of anthropologists to find that all of the prominent figures in her specialty were also white. It is simply another consequence of unequal advantage, that whites are sometimes first to investigate race-related topics which blacks subsequently take up—as was observed to me reassuringly by a black intellectual, the sculptor Richard Hunt.

2. A handful of my female informants mentioned seeing dreams discussed by someone on "Oprah," and most recognized the name of Gayle Delaney when I volunteered it. Several informants had looked casually at recent popular magazine articles about dreaming. One had bought but not yet read Robert Bosnak's *A Little Course in Dreams*, in a mini-pocket edition in a New Age series .

3. For similar reasons, there are more (if not many more) black Freudian than Jungian analysts. Additionally, Polly Young-Eisendrath (1987) has detected "a *de facto racism*" on the part of U.S. Jungian analysts. Their anxiety to establish an identity apart from Freudian depth psychology has led them into "acting and sounding like we are Europeans. Unintentionally we may have developed a psychology that is irrelevant to many Americans, especially to Afro-Americans." This has entailed an evasion of issues involving the "political, social, and psychological diversity" so conspicuous in the United States. "Moreover, we may have rejected certain aspects of our American character that Jung found distasteful, and projected these onto the Afro-American." In 1987 there was only one black Jungian analyst in the United States, who has since died. One of my interviewees, Father Charles Payne, is a candidate, on leave while he serves as president of an inner-city private school. In his opinion, blacks might not become Jungian practitioners because of the extent of education one needs "to feel comfortable in those circles"; while those who *are* sufficiently educated are "in such demand that they don't have the leisure to be Jungians."

4. At the same time, white caregivers need to guard against being "so impressed by the alarming world in which black people live that

they are unable to bring the individual pathology into clear focus" (Grier and Cobbs 1969, 130; see also Baker 1988, 156).

5. For example, a book by Phyllis Koch-Sheras et al. (1983) is strongly feminist. Kelly Bulkley (1991) writes on dreamwork and environmentalism. lames Harrington (1991) relates the dream which led him to become a military objector to the Gulf War. Jeremy Taylor's book (1992, 23, 27) expresses general thoughts on activism similar to Ullman's: dreaming is "inherently 'radical' because it gets to the truth. n Dreams "regularly offer specific creative inspiration for our collective struggles . . ." (118). Taylor overstates the position when he calls "paying attention to our dreams . . . the single best and most reliable way" of priming the mind for "collective liberation and self-determination" (114). Contrast Gayle Delaney's (1990, "7) hard-headed remarks about dreamwork as a vehicle of social change on a national and international scale: "Dreams will not get us there on time; it's going to take much too long. Unless dreamworkers get really smart and go for people in power, and people in power are very afraid to tell their dreams. . . . I try, through individual contacts, to deal with people in power, but it's very hard; they're very inflated. So, I'd love to say: 'This is going to save the world,' but I don't think we can wait for dreams to do it."

6. In answer to a questionnaire in 1930, only 11% of psychologists thought evidence indicated that blacks and whites are mentally equal; the balance thought blacks inferior (25%) or the data inconclusive (64%). These numbers for psychologists were more extreme than for the other professions questioned, educators, sociologists and anthropologists (Guthrie 1976, 64). An early psychoanalytic paper in the United States, "The dream as a simple wish-fulfillment in the Negro" (Lind 1914), argued that because Negroes are mentally childlike, their childlike dreams are "as valuable and more accessible than [those of] the child" for studying Freud's observations about the simple wish-fulfilling qualities of children's dreams (Thomas and Sillen 1991, 9, 11). The racial (and class) bias of the Stanford-Binet IQ test, which has often been employed expressly to reinforce prevailing stereotypes of black inferiority as well as that of other nonwhites, has surfaced once again in Richard L. Herrnstein and Charles Murray's *The Bell Curve* (New York: The Free Press, 1994).

7. 'Kemetic' is from 'Kemet', the hieroglyphic word for 'Egypt', which means 'black'—whether the black of Kemetic skin or of the soil of the Nile flood plain is debated (Karenga 1990). Diop (1974, 1990) argues not only that pharoanic Egypt was black and itself arose from black cultures to the south of modern Egypt, but also that later, sub-Saharan cultures, particularly those of West Africa, whose population provided New World slaves, were directly and determinatively influenced by pharoanic Egypt. In this light, popular New World black beliefs about dreams along with folk healing and spiritualism in various forms including U.S. rootwork, Haitian Voodoo, Cuban Santeria, Trinidadian Shango, Brazilian Candomblé, and so on, are not just quaint survivals from the slave quarter or bits of lore from the jungle. They are, rather, survivals of pharoanic medicine and religion, preserving to an extent the wisdom and spiritual profundity of the ancient culture (Ashanti 1990).

8. Godfrey Lienhardt (1985) comments that "much of what has been written about African ideas of self, rightly putting to the fore the importance of a person's group and status . . . can deflect interest from [the] African concern, also, on occasion, with individuals as individuals." Lienhardt recounts among other proverbs and folktales the West African (probably Yoruban) tale of a prize for dancing awarded to the tortoise by the king, who answers the protests of the other animal dancers by explaining, "it is only I who can see the dance of the tortoise: his dance is entirely inside him." Lienhardt also points to the fact that corporate identity is not incompatible even with self-indulgent individuality. And Africanist Rosalind Shaw (1992) observes that in certain African cultures "secrecy pervades social life and social relationships, particularly power relationships."

9. Historically, liberals have perceived the failure of blacks to assimilate to be a consequence of "negative aberrations" incompatible with the dominant middle-class culture, attributable to a "deficient and pathological" black culture shaped by racism (Banks 1980). Well-meaning people, including Moynihan in his (in)famous report of 1965, perpetuate the picture of blacks as deficient, attributing their condition to the dire consequences of oppression and prejudice. Black thinkers have long voiced something similar. Thus W. E. B. Du Bois in 1903 attributed the instability of black family life to the lingering effects of

slavery's assault on marital bonds, plus difficult economic conditions
(1961, 105–7). Richard Wright in 1940 attributed his *Native Son's* "lack
of inner organization" to "American oppression" (1986, xiii). James
Baldwin in 1955 wrote, "I can conceive of no Negro native of this country who has not, by the age of puberty, been irreparably scarred by the
conditions of his life" (1984, 71). Stokely Carmichael spoke of the
physical, emotional, and intellectual maiming of blacks by institutional
racism" (1967, 4). But all these authors balanced their observations by
emphasizing the positive qualities of African-American culture, and
they held the appropriate remedy to be the strengthening of black identity rather than assimilation to white culture.

    10. There is a literature, largely European, concerning dreams and
visions in African independent Christian churches, that is, those of
indigenous origin, in contrast to missionary and predominantly
European churches (e.g., Turner 1967; Lanternari 1975; Mullings
1984; Kiernan 1985; Charsley 1987, 1992). These churches are called
"Zionist" in South Africa, and "spiritual" or "Aladura" in West Africa.
They are given various designations in the scholarly literature (prophet
movements, separatists sects, etc.). Dreams and visions, and other
extranormal experiences such as clairaudience, are particularly prominent in what Turner calls the "prophet-healing" independent churches,
which have mostly arisen since the 1920s and which incorporate more
indigenous elements than the more orthodox independent churches
which mostly formed around the turn of the century. Indigenous elements include music, symbols, polygamy, and so on, as well as reliance
on dreams and visions, which like healing is fed by both indigenous and
biblical influences.

    11. Hyatt's (1970–1978) inimitable collection of African-
American folklore contains various incubation instructions, including:
to use graveyard dirt as a pillow to obtain a dream of a dead person who
will give advice for playing the numbers (vol 2, 1318); to dream of a
dead person by urinating on a handkerchief, letting it dry in the shade,
then sleeping on it under one's pillow (vol. 2, 1349); and to discover a
murderer in a dream by sleeping in the victim's clothes at the time of
burial (vol. 4, 3268) (Michael E. Bell, Director of the Rhode Island
Folklife Project, called these items to my attention). Incubation of
dreams of the dead by sleeping on or by their graves is reported from
cultures as diverse as the ancient Egyptians (MacDermot 1971, 46),

North American Inuits (Foulks 1992, 200), and Talmudic Hebrews (Lorand 1957, 94). For information about dream incubation in contemporary Christian and Muslim black Africa, see Fisher (1979).

12. The first was related to the Iranian parliament in 1951 by Mohammed Mossadegh after the success of his democratic, anti-imperial movement, and before his assassination by the C.I.A. "In the summer of 1950 preceding the vote for the nationalization of oil, my doctor prescribed prolonged rest for me. A month later, while I was sleeping I saw in my dream a radiant person, who said to me: 'This is no time for rest; arise and go break the chains of the people of Iran.' I responded to the call, and in spite of my extreme fatigue I resumed my work on the oil commission. When the commission accepted . . . nationalization two months later, I had to acknowledge that the person of my dream had inspired me well" (Borges 1976, 139 [my translation]). The second political dream is Cory Aquino's: "When the Filipino people began to turn against Ferdinand Marcos, she was asked to accept the nomination for the presidency. While she was trying to reach a decision, she had a recurrent dream that she was going to church and seeing a casket that she expected to contain Ninoy's (her assassinated husband's) body. But the coffin was empty: Ninoy, she felt, had been reborn in her (Signell 1990, 9–10, citing Cooper et al. 1986).

13. It is my impression that African-American employ the term 'subconscious,' not 'unconscious,' unless they have been educated to European-American psychodynamic theories. The subconscious is sometimes conceived of as the function of mind through which the individual comes into contact with extrapsychic spiritual reality.

14. In the Zulu Zionist Church studied by Kiernan (1985) in South Africa, a vision is not regarded as a single immutable event, but as an approximation of an objective truth, the approximation itself being mutable. "'This happens at group prayers. Someone gets a passing glimpse of a vision or hears a snatch of a voice and this is added to as time passes.'"

15. Vittorio Lanternari, who wrote a valuable book which discusses the function of dreams in the political movements of oppressed peoples (1963), makes this challenging statement (1975): "[A]n important distinction must be made between what is officially know as modern society, i.e. urban and industrial, and traditional societies, i.e. preindustrial, underdeveloped or developing. Rural and marginal

groups and classes in modern society should also be associated with the latter because they have many substantial similarities in experience, cultural attitudes, and value systems. This distinction directly concerns the cultural value of dreams in the two types of society or social groups." Lanternari goes on to contrast the intrapsychic and clinical approach to dreams of modern society to the extrapsychic approach of traditional societies.

References

Adler, Alfred. 1958 [1931]. *What Life Should Mean to You*. New York: Capricorn Books.

Ashanti, Faheem C. 1990. *Rootwork & Voodoo in Mental Health*. Durham, NC: Tone Books.

Baker, F. M. 1988. Afro-Americans. In *Clinical Guidelines in Cross-Cultural Mental Health*. Lillian Comas-Díaz and Ezra E. H. Griffith (eds.), New York: John Wiley & Sons.

Baldwin, James. 1984 [1955]. *Notes of a Native Son*. Boston: Beacon Press.

Baldwin, Joseph A. 1981. Notes on an Afrocentric theory of black personality. *Western Journal of Black Studies* 5: 172–79.

Banks, William M. 1980. The social context and empirical foundations of research on black clients. In Reginald L. Jones (ed.), *Black Psychology*, 2d edition, . New York: Harper & Row.

Borges, Jorge Luis. 1976. *Libro de Sueños*. Buenos Aires: Torres Aguero.

Bulkley, Kelly. 1991. The quest for transformational experience: dreams and environmental ethics. *Environmental Ethics* 13:151–63.

Camino, Linda Anne. 1986. Ethnomedical illnesses and non-orthodox healing practices in a black neighborhood in the American South: How they work and what they mean. Ph.D. diss., University of Virginia.

Carmichael, Stokely and Charles V. Hamilton. 1967. *Black Power*. New York: Vintage Books.

Charsley, Simon. 1987. Dreams and purposes: an analysis of dream narratives in an Independent African Church. *Africa* 57:281–96.

———. 1992. Dreams in African churches. In M. C. Jędrej and Rosalind Shaw, (eds.), Dreaming, *Religion and Society in Africa*. Leiden: E. J. Brill.

Cooper, N. (with M. Liu, W. Lin, and R. Vokey). 1986. The remarkable rise of a widow in yellow. *Newsweek* 107(10), 10 March, 34.

Delaney, Gayle. 1990. An interview with Gayle Delaney. Interview by Helen Roberta Ossana. *Dream Network Journal* 9(3):13, 24–27.

———. 1991. *Breakthrough Dreaming*. New York: Bantam Books.

Desjariais, Robert R. 1991. Dreams, divination, and Yolmo ways of knowing. *Dreaming* 1:211–24.

Diop, Cheikh Anta. 1974 [1955, 1967]. *The African Origin of Civilization: Myth or Reality?* Chicago: Lawrence Hill Books.

———. 1990 [1959]. *The Cultural Unity of Black Africa*. Chicago: Third World Press.

Du Bois, W. E. B. 1961 [1903]. *The Souls of Black Folk*. New York: Dodd, Mead.

Faraday, Ann. 1972. *Dream Power*. London: Hodder and Stoughton.

Fisher, Humphrey J. 1979. Dreams and conversion in black Africa. In Nehemia Levtzion (ed.), *Conversion to Islam*. New York: Holmes & Meier.

Foulkes, David. 1985. *Dreaming. A Cognitive-Psychological Analysis*. Hillsdale, NJ: Lawrence Erlbaum Associates.

Foulks, Edward F. 1992. Reflections on dream material from Arctic native people. *Journal of the American Academy of Psychoanalysis* 20:193–203.

Fromm, Erich. 1951. *The Forgotten Language*. New York: Rinehart.

———. 1955. The *Sane Society*. New York: Rinehart.

Garfield, Patricia. 1974. *Creative Dreaming*. New York: Simon & Schuster.

Gregor, Thomas. 1983. Dark dreams about white men. *Natural History* 92(1):8–14.

Grier, William H. and Price M. Cobbs. 1969 [1968]. *Black Rage*. New York: Bantam.

Gross, Herbert S., Myra R. Herbert, Genell L. Knatterud, and Lawrence Donner. 1969. The effect of race and sex on the variation of diagnosis and disposition in a psychiatric emergency room. *Journal of Nervous and Mental Disease* 148:638–42.

Guthrie, Robert V. 1976. *Even the Rat Was White*. New York: Harper & Row.

Harrington, James Lawrence. 1991. Dreams of war: the unconscious call to initiation. *Men's Council Journal*, February, 6–7.

Haskell, Robert E. 1985. Racial content and issues in dream research. *Association for the Study of Dreams Newsletter* 2(1):7–9.

Hillman, Deborah Jay. 1988. Dream work and field work: linking cultural anthropology and the current dream work movement. In Montague Ullman and Claire Limmer (eds.). *The Variety of Dream Experience*. New York: Continuum.

Hyatt, Harry Middleton. 1970-1978. *Hoodoo, Conjuration, Witchcraft, Rootwork*. 5 volumes. Hannibal, MO: Western Publishing.

Jackson, Gerald G. 1980a. The emergence of a black perspective in counseling. In Reginald L. Jones. (ed.), *Black Psychology*, 2nd edition. New York: Harper & Row.

———. 1980b. The African genesis of the black perspective in helping. In Reginald L. Jones. (ed.), *Black Psychology*, 2nd edition. New York: Harper & Row.

Jung, C. G. 1965 [1961]. *Memories, Dreams, Reflections*. New York: Vintage Books.

———. 1971 [1921]. *Psychological Types*. Princeton: Princeton University Press.

Karenga, Maulana, ed. 1990. *Reconstructing Kemetic Culture*. Los Angeles: University of Sankore Press.

Kiernan, J. P. 1985. The social stuff of revelation: pattern and purpose in Zionist dreams and visions. *Africa* 55:304–18.

King, Johanna. 1993. Let's stand up, regain our balance, and look around before we fall (or melt) into the pool. *Association for the Study of Dreams Newsletter* 10(1):13–15, 17.

Koch-Sheras, Phyllis R., E. Ann Hollier, and Brook Jones. 1983. *Dream On. A Dream Interpretation and Exploration Guide for Women.* Englewood Cliffs, N J: Prentice-Hall.

Krippner, Stanley and Joseph Dillard. 1988. *Dreamworking. How to Use Your Dreams for Creative Problem-Solving.* Buffalo: Bearly Limited.

Lanternari, Vittorio. 1963 [1960]. *The Religions of the Oppressed.* New York: Alfred A. Knopf.

———. 1975. Dreams as charismatic significants: their bearing on the rise of new religious movements. In Thomas R. Williams (ed.), *Psychological Anthropology.* The Hague: Mouton.

Lienhardt, Godfrey. 1985. Self: Public, private. Some African representations. In Michael Carrithers, Steven Collins, and Steven Lukes, (eds.), Cambridge: *The Category of the Person: Anthropology, Philosophy, History.* Cambridge University Press.

Lind, J. E. 1914. The dream as a simple wish-fulfillment in the Negro. *Psychoanalytical Review* I :295–300.

Lorand, Sandor. 1957. Dream interpretation in the Talmud (Babylonian and Graeco-Roman period). *International Journal of Psycho-Analysis* 38:92–97.

MacDermot, Violet. 1971. *The Cult of the Seer in the Ancient Middle East.* Berkeley: University of California Press.

Maguire, Jack. 1989. *Night and Day.* New York: Simon & Schuster.

Markowitz, I., Gwen Taylor, and E. Bokert. 1968. Dream discussion as a means of reopening blocked familial communication. *Psychotherapy and Psychosomatics* 16:348–56.

Mullings, Leith. 1984. *Therapy, Ideology, and Social Change. Mental Healing in Urban Ghana.* Berkeley: University of California Press.

Nobles, Wade W. 1974. Africanity: Its role in black families. *Black Scholar* 5(9):10–17.

———. 1978. Toward and empirical and theoretical framework for defining black families. *Journal of Marriage and the Family* 40:679–88.

———. 1980. African philosophy: Foundation for black psychology. In Reginald L. Jones (ed.), *Black Psychology*, 2nd edition. New York: Harper & Row.

Perls, Frederick S. 1969. *Gestalt Therapy Verbatim.* Moab, UT: Real People Press.

Pierce, William D. 1980. The comprehensive community mental health programs and the black community. In Reginald L. Jones (ed.), *Black Psychology, 2nd edition.* New York: Harper & Row.

Shafton, Anthony. 1991. Why so few blacks in the dream movement? *Association for the Study of Dreams Newsletter* 8(4) :1, 12–14.

Shaw, Rosalind. 1992. Dreaming as accomplishment: power, the individual and Temne divination. In M. C. Jędrej and Rosalind Shaw (eds.), *Dreaming, Religion and Society in Africa.* Leiden: E. J. Brill.

Signell, Karen A. 1990. *Wisdom of the Heart.* New York: Bantam Books.

Snow, Loudell F. 1974. Folk medical beliefs and their implications for care of patients. *Annals of Internal Medicine* 81:82–96.

———. 1993. *Walkin' Over Medicine.* Boulder, CO: Westview Press.

Sow, L. 1980 [1978]. *Anthropological Structures of Madness in Black Africa.* New York: International Universities Press.

Taylor, Jeremy. 1992. *Where People Fly and Water Runs Uphill.* New York: Warner Books.

Thomas, Alexander and Samuel Sillen. 1991 [1972]. *Racism and Psychiatry.* New York: Citadel Press.

Toldson, Ivory L. 1973. The human potential movement and black unity: counseling blacks in groups. *Journal of Non-White Concerns* 1:69–76.

Turner, H. W. 1967. *History of an African Independent Church.* 2 volumes. London: Oxford University Press.

Twitchell, Paul. 1980. *The ECK-Ynari.* Menlo Park, Calif.: Eckankar.

Ullman, Montague. 1969. Discussion. In Milton Kramer (ed.), *Dream Psychology and the New Biology of Dreaming.* Springfield, IL: Charles C. Thomas.

———. 1973. Societal factors in dreaming. *Contemporary Psychoanalysis* 9:282–93.

———. 1986. Vigilance theory and psi. Part II: Physiological, psychological, and parapsychological aspects. *Journal of the American Society for Psychical Research* 80:375–91.

———. 1988. Dreams and society. In Montague Ullman and Claire Limmer (ed.), *The Variety of Dream Experience.* New York: Continuum.

———. 1992. Personal and social honesty and cultural differences. *Association for the Study of Dreams Newsletter* 9(2–3):3–4.

———, and Nan Zimmerman. 1979. *Working with Dreams.* New York: Delacorte Press/Eleanor Friede.

Watkins, Mary. 1992. Perestroika of the self: Dreaming in the U.S.S.R. *Dreaming* 2:111–22.

White, Joseph L. 1984. *The Psychology of Blacks.* Englewood Cliffs, NJ: Prentice-Hall.

White-Lewis, Jane. 1990. Members evaluate the 1990 Chicago conference. *Association for the Study of Dreams Newsletter* 7(5):8.

Wikse, John R. 1988. Night rule: Dreams as social intelligence. In Montague Ullman and Claire Limmer (eds.), *The Variety of Dream Experience.* New York: Continuum.

Windsor, Joan. 1987. *Dreams and Healing.* New York: Dodd, Mead.

Winget, Carolyn, Milton Kramer, and Roy M. Whitman. 1972. Dreams and demography. *Canadian Psychiatric Association Journal* 17 (supplement):203–8.

Wright, Richard. 1986. How "Bigger" was born. Introduction to *Native Son* [1940]. New York: Perennial Library.

X, Malcolm (with Alex Haley). 1966 [1965]. *The Autobiography of Malcolm X*. New York: Grove Press.

Young-Eisendrath, Polly. 1987. The absence of black Americans as Jungian analysts. *Quadrant* 20(2):41–53.

Chapter 6

Sex, Gender, and Dreams

From Polarity to Plurality

Carol Schreier Rupprecht

I

Sex, gender, dreams. A trio of topics touching the very nature of what it means to be human and, at the same time, to be a unique person grappling with the eternal question: Who am I? Taken separately, each topic is guaranteed to evoke the deepest human sentiments and to provoke the most strenuous human controversies. No sensible person enters these arenas without trepidation, and I am no exception. It was my hypothesis in undertaking this chapter, however, that treating these three topics collectively and uncovering their interdependence would release a cumulative, transformative energy capable of propelling me, and my readers, toward greater knowledge about each one. And greater knowledge is urgently, even desperately, needed, as current events as well as the following nightmares, culled from thousands like them, indicate:

She dreamed:

The master of a well-to-do house puts a girl—alive—into his freezer. It's just temporary, as a punishment, as he's old-fashioned. There's a lamp over the freezer. What if the lamp falls? It does fall, and there's a fire, a conflagration. Does anyone know? She'll die! The man opens the freezer as though it's a treasure chest. Where's the girl? Under the food. One large foot is wrapped up. He readjusts it as if it's a treasure. Is there an inspector around and he's trying to hide the foot? (Signell 1990, 147)

He dreamed:

I was kidnapped with two or three other men and taken to a home. We were being held hostage. The only person I knew in the dream was a middle-aged woman, a friend of my mother's. She was the gang leader.

The other guys trying to escape were killed, knifed in the stomach. It was obvious that my turn would come. The woman was trying to be nice to me. I wasn't panicked, but I still knew my time was coming, although she was trying to say things to make me feel I wasn't on her list. (McDonald 1987, 79)

And so the "war between the sexes" continues to be waged even as the level of sleep and dream? The answer seems to be yes; and the power and ubiquity of such dreams calls for attention to their complex intertwining with sex and gender.

To begin with the most loaded term, "sex" is used throughout this chapter to refer to the biologically constituted body which receives at birth the label "female" or "male." This labeling according to sex is the first name with which we humans bestow identity on one of our species. The seemingly benign, or at least neutral, and ostensibly objective description is based on material fact, the presence or absence of specific biological structures.

Simultaneously with the visual register of these structures by the first observer, however, there flows a set of socially constructed interpretations about what it *means* to be female or male; in other words, "gender" arrives on the birth scene as the twin of "sex." Thus our initial act of identification is also one of differentiation into two separate, distinct categories, female or male. Baby becomes instantaneously girl baby or boy baby as the unsuspecting infant is subsumed in the whole complex of perceptions about, behavior toward, and expectations of her or him that make up gender. Already in the very first moments of human existence, even in prior existence in the womb when the sex of the foetus is known, gendering begins.

And this is true in the other way the English language uses the word "sex," as a noun describing a range of activities enacted through these sex-specific biological structures. Such sexual activity, of course, takes place enmeshed in a genderized web of social interaction. Sex is perhaps the most prominent among the ways we humans express love, our deepest yearnings for connection, union, touch, taking and giving care with other humans, our longings for emotional and physical intensity, our urge to be more fully alive at all levels, our desire to procreate and to generate human bonds through marriage, companionship, reproduction, our aspirations to ideal reaches of feeling and action.

At the same time, however, both sex and gender have been and still are the site of some of the most troubling dimensions of human nature and of our alarmingly vicious behavior toward each other. Around sex and gender cluster our obsessions, prohibitions, inhibitions, conflicts, frustrations, delusions, and defenses. In the late-twentieth-century United States, to take only one example from a global pool, sex and gender underlie many troubling social problems, vexing ethical issues, and dramatic public policy challenges. The alphabet that follows could be drawn up from one week's reading of almost any newspaper in the United States, from a few days' viewing of any television newscast: abortion, abuse, Aids, battering, gay bashing, heterosexism, homophobia, incest, murder of abortion providers, rape, and, among some groups of U.S. citizens, even female genital mutilation such as clitoridectomy.

Enter dreams and nightmares, the mentation during sleep which can uniquely provide the revolutionary and revisionist perspectives we need to puzzle out the interface in our lives of the psychological, somatic, and social. I will not claim that dreams offer a panacea for social ills, but I will argue that as long as the imaginal unconscious and its nightly creations are neglected or ignored in collective as well as individual functioning in U.S. society, deeper understanding of our shared human condition, an essential component of lasting social change, will elude us. This is especially true in the operation of what Gayle Rubin has called the sex/gender system: "a set of arrangements by which a society transforms biological sexuality into products of human activity"[1] (Rubin 1975, 179). Yet when we turn to research and scholarship on dreaming to illuminate sex and gender issues, much of what we find is unsettling and can be misleading in its narrowness of scope.

In the West, twentieth-century research on dreaming has focused almost obsessively on those sex/gender differentiations initiated at birth: where there is not open conflict between females and males in dreaming, there is unmistakable contrast.[2] Persistent differentiation has been recorded everywhere in the world of dreams, from research in a wide range of disciplines as well as from the night diaries of ordinary people who are neither patients in clinical settings nor subjects in scientific experiments nor objects of study in the social sciences.

Further, if we explore the available documents from many different cultures across several centuries on theories about and literary representations of dreams and dreaming, we repeatedly encounter one invariable theme, now explicit, now implicit: women and men dream differently. At least they appear to do so, since they differ in their reports of their dream experiences, the effects on them of dreams, their interpretations of dreams and their attitudes toward dreaming.

The preoccupation with difference, then, seems justified. But it remains a formidable obstacle to innovation in thought and action. Difference works like a smokescreen that blurs our visions and blunts our visionariness, our capacities to imagine new ways of being and to transform our common social institutions. In carrying out my exploration of our triad of topics, then, I will first address some of the limitations of difference-based thinking. Then I will review some of the newest dream research on sex and gender and demonstrate that its potential for enlightenment on the relations among mind, body, and society has been underestimated. Finally, I will propose a recasting of the entire discourse on our topics and suggest ways we can fruitfully begin to reconfigure our experience of inhabiting a sex-specific body in a gender-governed society.

I will look only at the United States, although I believe my observations apply cross-culturally, because the United States is where I have lived the first half-century of my life. It is the society in which I have enacted my sexual identity—female—and performed in such gender-marked roles as daughter, sister, wife, mother, mother-in-law, and aunt as well as such ostensibly unmarked roles as author, editor, activist, athlete, professor, scholar, friend, colleague, consumer, and dreamworker.

I want neither to presume the presence of difference nor to demonstrate its absence but to set the subject aside entirely. We know so little about mind/body/society interaction within a single individual, it is premature to be engaged in comparative study of categories of people. And there are at least three other reasons for decentering difference in an inquiry into the relationships among sex, gender, and dreams. While we may be able at this time to confirm differences, one nagging question cannot be put to rest: Are the differences real (has something that actually exists been detected?) or are they the skewed result of gender-biased analysis, commentary, observation, and interpretation? Do they merely reflect the inevitable distortion of the gender-clouded lenses through which we perceive everything around us?

A second reason is that difference is always construed as a polarity, as if sexual identity and even gender roles fit into two neatly prescribed and clearly demarcated forms. These perceived forms then become normative, fixed designations which preclude consideration of sex and gender as a continuum along which individuals move in the course of a lifetime. As long as discussion is carried out in these terms of duality, the only outcome can be the kind of war, of conflict, that we now have, where one side struggles for ascendancy over the other and aspects that differ are assigned differing, and competing, values on a hierarchical scale.

Further, we do not have a language in which we can express sex/gender concerns that is not inherently polarized itself. In English we speak of "the opposite sex" or "the same sex" as if the only options were opposition or fusion, to be separate and opposed or to be merged and identical. Even researchers themselves tend to fall into two camps on difference—Sandra Bem has aptly labeled them maximizers and minimizers—yet her terminology only adds another verbal layer of divisiveness and intensifies the dualism, fueling the tendency toward a split into mutually exclusive extremes. Even the most committed activists for societal change have been forced over the past decade to acknowledge the intransigence of material and social conditions when they are embedded within such polarized, conflictive linguistic and social structures.[3]

A third incentive to de-emphasize difference is that the true challenge lies not in the "fact" or "hypothesis" of difference but in its meaningfulness. That our era's approach to sex and gender studies has foregrounded difference raises the question of what paying so much attention to this phenomenon tells us about ourselves, and about the significance and the meanings we ascribe to difference, real or imagined. Is sexual difference *"the* philosophical problem of our age" as assserted in the publisher's advertisement for the new English translation of French feminist Luce Irigaray's *An Ethics of Sexual Difference?* Or is the real "philosophical question of our age" the fact that we have made difference the hinge of our language and thought about sex and gender? (It is revealing that Irigaray's book is listed in the press catalogue under the rubric "Political Theory.")

II

As soon as we shift focus away from difference, we are freed to explore the ways dreams work to give dreamers access to their own deepest knowledge about what is going on in their bodies and about the way their bodies work to signal what is going on in their minds. In my research I learned of dreams which have "diagnosed" and participated in the healing and acceptance of certain sex-specific diseases like breast and prostate cancer and have offered ongoing, useful insights into bodily processes like impotence and menopause. I found dreams helping reconcile a woman to a necessary, appropriate abortion, uncovering the roots of a man's homophobia, fostering in women and men confidence in their sexual orientation[4] over against all the external forces and unconscious resistances pushing them into conformity with mainstream norms of sexual behavior. I discovered accounts of dreams revealing what was truly at the heart of two people's intimate relationship despite all their often-mutual defenses against such knowledge. And with the help of Arnold Mindell's "dreambody" concept, I learned that it is not only dreams which speak with a truthfulness we can trust, but that the body does, too; the former through symbols, the latter through symptoms. (Mindell 1985, 39)

I first became aware through the dream of the indivisibility of mind, body and society outside of my own personal experience of it just under twenty years ago. As one of the few female professors at a woman's college and one of the even fewer of that group old enough to be married with children, I often became the confidante of my young students. In the early 1970s abortions among the campus population were not uncommon, but they were rarely spoken about in public, or, generally, in private either.

But weeks, sometimes months, after their abortions, women would appear at my office bereft, and embarrassed at being so. They were often driven to see me by memorable, disturbing nightmares which centered, with archetypal force, on the incipient life they had interrupted. Many had never before remembered dreams or given any thought to them. But the students knew of my professional interest in dreaming and so they chose me to hear their nightmare narratives.

Many would begin by berating themselves for weakness in being troubled and seeking help. After all, they were urban, sophisticated, politically active young women; many characterized themselves even then as feminists. They believed in their right to control their own bodies, a right formally reinforced in the law by *Roe v Wade* (1973). They were sexually active and felt very much in control of their destinies as they planned their lives and careers. It was, indeed, the stated mission of the institution they attended to inculcate such sentiments in them .

Nothing, however, had prepared them for the anguishing aftermaths of their decision to abort, aftermaths that initially boiled to the surface only during sleep, in horrifying nightmares. I kept no record of the dream reports, but a few images have stayed with me for two decades. One is blood; there was blood everywhere, even without other evidence of carnage. Another is the victim/perpetrator roles the dream egos often alternated between in the life or death struggles that took place.

As their dream telling gained momentum, my narrators quickly moved from self-chastisement to profound sadness, a sense of loss, and an ambivalence about guilt. Their enactment of legally sanctioned, intellectually defensible and politically correct rights turned out not to be a simple matter of rational decision-making, of being-in-the-world behavior. The experience of abortion had reached deep into primal levels of psyche and body. The opening of the body and the extraction of the fetus seemed to be imaged in many dreams as invasion and violation but since the sexual union resulting in the pregnancy was represented in similar imagery, it was often impossible to distinguish between the two events. The only tangible clue to the students' distress, however, besides the nightmares, was that several looked, and in fact had become, ill, although they usually did not link this illness to the abortion. The dream was their only connection to the event and even that connection emerged for some only very gradually during our conversations as I asked them to reflect on events in their lives preceding the onset of the nightmare episodes.

The subsequent work of our meeting was that of accepting and listening to the voices of their dream selves and of their bodies bringing up into ego processes the unconscious dimension the dreams and illnesses were signaling. The dialogues between self and society, inner and outer, deepened. No judgment was ever passed on their decisions; no position for or against abortion was sought by them or imposed by me or introduced by the nightmares whose primary function, as in many major life events, seemed to be educating the dreamers about the integrated nature of their whole being. Indeed, most of the students were amazed at the encounter with their own multiplicity. And they did gain lasting appreciation for the multivocal and polyvalent dialectic of self that is involved in every human action.

At the time I, too, was impressed by the symbiotic ties of mind and body as they operated within the web of social constructs. I was awed by the dreams' efficacy in overriding all apparently important facts and perceptions to arrive at the true center of meaning for each individual dreamer. I had then no language or thought processes available to articulate the intricacies and implications of the whole series of events. But it all came back to me with force last year in reading an essay by author and Jungian analyst Murray Stein. He corroborated poignantly my students' suffering when he recounted the dream of an analysand with an unidentifiable illness: she is in a church; a gigantic butterfly flies past going outdoors to a winter scene, a landscape familiar to her from her grandfather's stories of his life in Russia, where she had never been:

> The timing of the illness and of this dream was meaningful as well. They occurred precisely during the period when a child would have been born to her had she not aborted it. The decision to have an abortion had been a sound one, practically speaking, but her psyche and her body had not given up the agenda of pregnancy and birth and followed through, after a manner. The dream, with its escaping butterfly and return to the world of the ancestors, charted the course of this unborn soul. It also brought the dreamer, the lost child's mother, to the place of her ancestral origins and roots. (Stein 1990, 36)

Stein ends with the note that such a reach back to a time before one's own origin often anticipates futurity. It prepares the dreamer for acceptance of the past and instils energy for the next motion forward. Stein's account reinforces the sense some of my students reported that their dreams had come out of a preverbal time in their lives. In this regard, his narrative captures a rarely noted dimension of the mind/body melding, its special temporality. Just as body and mind blend symptoms and symbols, obliterating traditional Western dualistic boundaries between them, so conventional notions of time are superseded. The dream ego travels unhampered through past, present and future, both archaic prebirth existence and life yet to be lived. And the body also resonates at the same times with a certain atavistic and anticipatory sensibility.

When I compare my experience and Stein's of this event in the life of women, I realize that we are only approaching the threshold of learning what the study of sex, gender, and dreams together can teach us. What follows is a review of some current work and its ramifications.

III

Let me begin with the "shadow." Jungian theory names as "shadow" all those aspects of self a person is unable or unwilling to acknowledge. Our shadow side, like any part of self from which we are cut off, can sound an alarm to consciousness by manifesting itself through bodily pathology, as physical symptoms and pain. The intensity of such pain can be directly proportional to the strenuousness with which conscious, or unconscious, denial is at work.

Here is one account of such an experience by a young male in therapy who suffered from extreme chronic headaches for which medical treatment had been unsuccessful. He reported the following dream:

> I dreamed I was walking along attending to my own business when wham! I was hit on the head from behind. I turned around and faced the dark figure of the man who had hit me. I woke up with the back of my head pounding. (McDonald 1987, 69)

Subsequently it came out in analysis "that for years he had attempted to *turn his back on* [italics mine] a strong latent homosexuality. Once [this feeling was] brought out, faced, discussed and no longer feared, the pain in his head completely disappeared" (McDonald 1990,

69). The analyst, Phoebe McDonald, further commented that "this is a rare example of the shadow actually attacking the dreamer." It is also a fine example of the mind/body's ingenuity in combining symptoms and symbols to communicate difficult truths.

The analyst does not report the subsequent waking behavior of her analysand, so we do not know if he undertook a lifestyle commensurate with his discovered inclinations. But in the work of National Book Award winner Paul Monette, especially in *Borrowed Time: An Aids Memoir* and his autobiography, *Becoming a Man: Half a Life Story*, we learn both the ferocity of societal repression of homosexuality and the consequent internalization by individuals of this socially constructed inhibition. We also learn about the enlightening and transformative power of dreaming.

> Struggling to be or at least to imitate a straight man, through Ivy League halls of privilege and bohemian travels abroad, loveless intimacy, and unrequited passion, Paul Monette was haunted, and finally saved, by a dream: The thing I'd never even seen: two men in love and laughing. (Monette 1992, book jacket)

In another book about the role of dreams and healing in the lives of men, Jungian-oriented psychotherapist Robert Hopcke traces the paths through therapy of two men, "Pete" and "Nick," one homosexual and one heterosexual, as they struggle with the "anesthesia of male social-ization" (Hopcke 1990, 12). Hopcke's work seriously problematizes the sex/gender/dream research which limits itself to male/female difference by revealing significant variation among males. He shows that the process of coming to psychological maturity by gay men can depart sig-nificantly from the pattern of their heterosexual counterparts despite the shared sexual identity (Hopcke 1990, 122).

Hopcke chronicles perceptively the insistent, often uncanny, metaphorical aptness of the men's dreams. The narratives of the two men remind us that the improbable, impossible, and unthinkable are routine fare for dreams; thus they have the capacity to startle us into recognitions that our waking consciousness would categorically reject or wilfully misconstrue. With Pete and Nick, the dream proves at times uniquely capable of penetrating the wall against feeling which they, like so many males in patriarchal society, have been forced to erect. Only when the vigilant male ego relaxed its guard in sleep could either of the

men "reach through dysfunctional behavior to the underlying unconscious feelings." The figurative language of their dreams encoded powerful, repressed psychic material in such a way that they were forced to
confront certain feelings which they had a great stake in denying and
yet were able to accept these feelings without a sense of incapacitating
endangerment.

Nick's dream of urinating on his baby daughter, for example, thrust
him right up against his unarticulated fears of being an inadequate,
even destructive, father like his own had been. But the dream also
offered him encouragement in his new role by ending with this image:
"I finish and then quickly take her to the bathtub where I begin to wash
her, soaking the sponge full of water and squeezing it over her head and
letting it run down over her body. She begins to laugh and I see her joy
but know I have hurt her, too" (Hopcke 1990, 170). The imagery of
baptism, for both father and daughter, moved the dreamer beyond
guilt, shame, and fear into confidence about his capacity to be a nurturing parent.

Therapist Gregory Charles Bogart further extends our knowledge
about the bases of male sexual behavior, drawing upon both Freudian
and Jungian psychologies in a compelling narrative of dreamwork with
a client who, as a child, had been sexually assaulted by a stranger.
Haunted by homophobia, both hatred of homosexual men and fearful-
ness about his own sexual orientation, "Jim" was locked into frustrating
sexual encounters with women and generally unsatisfying relationships,
including with his family. Gay men, Arnold Schwartzenegger, and
other male figures kept populating his dreams until he began to "get it."
What he "got" was acceptance of a plurality of sexual options, for himself and others.

Eventually Jim came to value and to internalize aspects of those
qualities our culture tends of label "masculine" and "feminine" instead
of splitting them off and projecting them onto hated and feared others.
But he reached this understanding only with the dramatic presentation
to him in a nightmare of how impossible, how threatening (and, of
course, how, therefore, essential to his development) such a psychosex-
ual flexibility could be:

> I met a woman at a party, and went home with her. When we got to the
> door of her apartment she turned around and I realized that she was actu-

ally a black transvestite[5] —a flaming fairy with jewelry, thick makeup, and false boobs. Then I couldn't tell if it was a man or a woman. He or she seemed to be both. I woke up screaming. (Bogart 1993, 205)

Jim concluded that his dreams were saying that "to be sexually mature means to be wise about the full range of sexuality and sexual choices. Then I can make my own choices and respect other people's choices" (Bogart 1993, 204). The experiences of all these men and those who work with them suggest some modification is needed to the view expressed in two different works by one popular and insightful dream writer that "we don't need dreams to learn our sexual orientation" (Delaney 1991, 109; 1993, 290).[6]

Dislodging of the dualistic model of sexual difference and sexual attraction can also result from work with the dreams of transsexuals. Here dreams are an especially effective medium because they operate at the margins as well as at the center, at the surface as well as the depth (Perera 1990, 39–79). Transsexuals' reports show dreams maneuvering easily across a full spectrum of human behavior, censuring nothing as out of bounds or beyond representation in words or images, including a mismatch in a single person between biological sex and psychological gender.

Psychologist Stanley Krippner describes the dismantling of sex/gender expectations and the destruction of stereotypes one experiences in studying the dreams of transsexuals. He reports that comparison among transsexuals, "standard" males, and "standard" females reveals unpredictable variants. Among individuals with male-to-female crossing, some dream content was congruent with that of the standard male control group and some was sharply contrasting. Such direct and inverse variation held true for comparison of these same individuals with the standard female group. And transsexuals had some dream content that was shared only within their own group of subjects.

Despite such a range of variation in other regards, however, the transsexual group generally held in common the sentiment that dreams are important and had meaningful functions in their lives. Krippner observes that preoperative dreams of people planning gender reassignment surgery, as it is called, seem to hold clues about outcomes of this procedure. And, in fact, candidates for such surgery sometimes cited their dream content over long periods of time as proof to themselves of the inappropriate match between their sex and gender (Krippner 1991, 131–33). Many would say, I felt like a woman in a man's body, or vice versa, indicating self-perceptions more shaped by states of mind than by biological structures.

Dreaming continues to educate us if we look at one complex bodily process—pregnancy—which involves material from both sexes, though no longer necessitating contact between two people. Among even the earliest studies of dreaming done in the United States, we find research on the dreams of pregnant women. Valuable discoveries have been made, ranging from the way anxiety dreams may prepare a woman for easier childbirth to dreaming's role in postpartum recuperation.

I will not address that subject here because so much quality work is in print and quite accessible. But I do want to look at a special version of investigation into dreams and pregnancy: Alan Siegel's work on expectant fathers' dreams. He found that dreams of men anticipating the birth of children they had fathered were performing a function similar to that of couvade rituals in primitive cultures: providing "role models and rites of passage to help them understand and integrate their experience of becoming a father" (Siegel 1984, 281).

Many of the dreams he collected were objective representations of childbirth and the expected baby. Yet others spoke more symbolically and appeared unintelligible to the dreamers and unrelated to their status of imminent paternity until the imagery was connected to the actual birth process. All of the men, of course, had had the experience of being born themselves, and it was to this long distant process, the sole direct participation in birthing available to males, that the unconscious seemed to reach for its dream metaphors. The men experienced themselves as if emerging from their own mother's wombs: a large underwater bubble rises up and spawns a furry animal; the dream ego "escapes from a cave through a hole that opened up during an earthquake"; the dream ego "swims downhill in a race to surface in a locker room and be wrapped in a towel" (Siegel 1984, 280).

Thus the dreams bonded the men both to the women who would be giving birth and to the developing fetus. Often accompanied by physical symptoms like nausea and fatigue, yet more evidence of the embodiedness of the psyche, such indices of their intense involvement in the pregnancy fostered in the men an early attachment to the child. The dreams also relieved feelings of exclusion from the process of pregnancy and birth and even served as vehicles for enhancing the male dreamers' overall openness to their emotions.

Work like Siegel's which homes in on the intersection of sex, gender, and dreaming continues to appear and carries usually unexploited information to us about the merging of psychological and somatic phenomena. A function of this chapter is to alert readers to such resources and to instigate deeper readings of them. But one more example of work in the therapeutic community needs more than mention here.

It is the exquisite meditation by Patricia Reis on ancient representations of the female body as they illuminate living women's bodily health and disease, especially of the female organs: breasts, uterus, vagina, ovaries.

And Reis, an artist as well as a therapist, works through dreams like this one of a woman ready to speak out about prior sexual abuse:

> A man tries to steal my purse. I fight him off but he punctures my throat. No one will help. I walk to my apartment holding cloths over my throat. Other girls are there. Women doctors and healers come to care for me. (Reis 1991, 144)

She reports another dream, from a woman with breast cancer who needed to find within herself the energy and aggressiveness to insist that her own opinions be respected in the complex medical and technological processes that lay ahead:

> I am on a rocky coastline. I have found lobster cages, which have surfaced from a very deep part of the ocean bottom. I find, to my horror, that they contain the body parts, arms, and legs of a man. I wonder what to do, who to tell, how to respond. (Reis 1991, 196)

This dream, like the female's dream that opens this chapter and like so many dreams of men and women I have read and heard, contains imagery of bodily dismemberment. Such imagery suggests that the psyche does not experience the body necessarily as a unitary phenomenon, either literally or symbolically. The body appears from the psyche's perspective to be far more fragile and flexible and multiple than we consciously perceive it to be. The body comes through as truly polymorphous, quite adaptable in the possible relationship of its parts to each other and to the bodies of other humans. And sexual identities become dispersed and diffused among dreamers and their dream egos and figures.

When such dream images of multiple parts in diverse arrangements become explicit occurrences in waking life in the actual human body, a concomitant impact on psyche's perceptual processes takes place. This can happen, as we have seen, with abortion; it also happens with pregnancy (the woman's body has another body, either female or male or multiples of each, within it), with loss of limbs through accident, disease, or assault, including surgical procedures, and with organ transplantation. Arnold Mindell has observed that "the dying and diseased are chopped up by medicine men as if the flesh had no soul in it" (Mindell 1985, 2), while dreams reveal unmistakably the interpenetration of body and mind.

As Jungian analyst Robert Bosnak's work on the dreams of heart transplant patients has shown, when body parts of a dead human being are placed in another living one, deeper attachments are made than those between vessels, arteries, ligaments and such. The psyche, which increasingly we can see as infusing the physical body, is also altered, often profoundly, and the effects can appear in dreams. For our purposes it is important to note that the sex of donor and recipient in organ transfer is not a significant consideration. There are women walking around now with some life-giving internal organs of men and vice versa. Clearly old dualisms have given way to new multiplicities even if we currently lack the linguistic range to articulate these changes or the daring to expand our cognitive processes to encompass them.

While some of the dreams presented in this chapter seem to be working only intrapsychically, and most are taken from psychotherapy practices, they are all pushing the outward boundaries of the private sphere. And it would have been possible to select an equally rich set of dream samples from the writing of dreamworkers like Jeremy Taylor and Montague Ullman who have worked with families and informal and facilitated dream groups. The story of "Barbara" from Taylor's *Where People Fly and Water Runs Uphill* is an exemplary one. She dreamed of attending a party in her own basement where she was invisible and carrying a handbag with rotting meat in it that no one could see. Supported by her own intuition and by associations to the dream from members of her dream group, Barbara persisted in medical testing after conventional methods failed to detect a pathology accurately imaged in the dream. The collaboration of the individual's body and mind in creating the warning and of the individual dreamer and her group in translating it into real-life terms allowed Barbara to have life-saving surgery just in time to avoid a fatal spread of a disease.

Just so in many of the cases cited in this chapter, the dreamers were motivated to take action: to become more involved fathers, to challenge the medical establishment, to make public their hidden sexual orientations and thus link themselves to broader communities, to write about their diseases and insist upon public recognition and response.

But people in U.S. society still scorn dreams, consider them frivolously irrelevant in these times of social, indeed global, crisis. In several large bookstores I visited recently, dream books were often still consigned to the section marked "Astrology and the Occult." In the early 1980s I was working on a book on feminist archetypal theory, revisioning Jungian concepts to fit the realities of women's lives, and specifically on a chapter, "The Common Language of Women's Dreams." Many people, including close friends and friendly associates of both sexes, objected to the project. They took me and my co-editor to task for wasting our time dealing with dreams when there were so many crucial issues in women's daily lives to which we should be devoting our energies and professional expertise. What did women's dreams have to do with battering, rape, sexual abuse, the economics of divorce which so often impoverish women, gender-based pay inequities, the absence of female subjects from medical research? I felt confident then that our call for valorizing dreaming and other unconscious processes in the search for social reforms would be heard. In the decade since the publication of that book, my confidence has been confirmed. And I was especially heartened to see new regions of research and public awareness opened up through the work of women like Margie Profet, who recently received a five-year McArthur Foundation award.

An evolutionary biologist, Profet has drawn on dreams to further her scientific projects. The latest, reported in *The Quarterly Review of Biology*, involves explaining the functions of menstruation. The novel explanation she now advances came to her in a dream, with ovaries and fallopian tubes in yellow and a bright red uterus filled with flowing black triangles (Seligman 1993, 86). Perhaps sex-based neurophysiology manifests itself in dreams, suggesting that our minds do know our bodies best experiencing them through unconscious rather than conscious cognitive processes.

Still other critics of the feminist archetypal theory book, however, opposed the introduction of dreaming into feminist discourse because they saw a strong potential for misuse. The very indeterminacy that makes both dreams and dreaming so valuable, also makes them more susceptible to distortion and manipulation. It is no doubt true that whatever has the potential to help can be used to harm. The very systems of psychiatry and psychology, which almost alone among professions throughout this century in the United States have made dreams a central feature of their theory and practice, also took control over the meaning of dreaming. Power-brokering within these systems which offered dream interpretation and application made them very specialized, and expensive. And the process of determining dream meaning became infused with gender, race, class and culture biases; dream interpretation came to be used as an instrument of social control. The only interpretive paradigms that gained professional sanction became traps for the imagination and enforced dominant attitudes and behaviors, many of which were products of a patriarchal order.

Such distortions occurred, for example, when dream content which should have been treated subjectively (as aspects of the dreamer's self) was treated objectively (taken literally as what/whom it appeared to be) and vice versa. Especially vulnerable to manipulation were dream contents dealing with issues, such as sexual orientation, which can be threatening to the social values or self-perceptions of the dreamer or therapist or both.

Take the case of gender-role expectations and male/female figures in dreams. The feminist archetypal theory book contains one anecdote about a woman questioning her sexual identity and orientation. Her dream of a relationship with a much younger male was construed by her male therapist to signify her progress toward what he saw as the desirable goal of heterosexuality. This literal interpretation of the sexual identities in the dream did not resonate with the woman's felt experience during dreaming, however. Later, "in retrospect, she felt the dream had been symbolic of her having gained enough strength (represented by the young man) to act on her intuition and desire by choosing a lesbian relationship despite the difficulties it would bring to her life in society" (Rupprecht 1985, 214).

Therapist-interpreters have also insisted that a client's problem is intrapsychic and personal when the client's suffering directly results from destructive external social conditions which should be changed. But dreams have built-in safeguards against such misappropriation. Unlike the DSM (Diagnostic and Statistical Manual of Mental and Physical Disorders), for example, dreams are not static hard copy. They will return and return with shifting shapes and new insistences until recognized for what they are, until dreamers "get it." And happily there are enlightened therapists, like Phoebe McDonald and Robert Hopcke, who are prepared to follow the mind/body complex wherever dreams may take it.

I want to end my examples with one account of an explicit role for dreaming in addressing social pathology. It was one of the earliest studies to use dreams as a way to understand and rehabilitate a criminal. Although conducted over thirty years ago, the experiment is a heuristic model for future work. This analysis of 1,368 dreams of a single pedophile convicted for child molestation was carried out in the late sixties and early seventies by a social worker, Alan Bell, with psychologist Calvin Hall: *The Personality of a Child Molester: An Analysis of Dreams* (1971).

Several themes were repeated throughout the dream series, including yearning for enclosure and confused sexual identity, the man's and others'. Two dreams seem particularly pertinent. The first has imaged desire of a return to the womb which contrasts noticeably with the dreams of the expectant fathers where similar imagery represented the opposite impulse, leaving the womb.

> I was swimming in a pool. I made large bubbles by clapping my hands in the water. One was big enough for me to get inside. It felt like plastic. I prepared to get inside the bubble. (62)

The second dream took the dreamer back to the earliest assignment of sexual identity with which this study began except that for this man the clarity of that initial separation of the sexes was missing.

> There was a flooded room. An infant was there, and was crying and saying that a snake had bitten it. I picked it up and examined the bite on its foot. I looked for a nurse. People were around. Then I wondered whether it was a boy or a girl. I started to open its clothing, but stopped because I was embarrassed. (37–38)

Bell and Hall learned from their work the special value of dreams in providing "visualizations of psychic phenomena that can only be imperfectly described verbally in waking life" (Bell and Hall 1971, 118). From the man's dreams they were able not only to identify and explain his "personality traits, complexes and conflicts" but also to "assess their strength." Thus they ended up with a possible prognosis for future behavior and a sense of which treatments were likely to be effective for certain kinds of sex offenders (Bell and Hall 1971, 123).

IV

Where do we go from here? These compiled narratives of men's and women's lives and dreams pulsate with an energy that cannot be contained within existing modalities of thought or language. The narratives insist they can only be fully accessed if we recast our discourse and reconfigure our thinking. The insights about how to do this are dawning gradually. One understated but striking sample of such insight appears in Sandra L. Bem's *The Lenses of Gender*. Among many excellent recent studies on the U.S. sex/gender system, Bem's is one of the most lucid and convincing.

She identifies androcentrism, biological essentialism, and gender polarization as root causes of many contemporary social conflicts. At different points in her argument, Bem hints at, but does not develop, the hypothesis that as long as the basis for people's behavior is unconscious, they cannot be changed by cognitively driven social programs, by campaigns of rational persuasion, or even by legislation or coercion from social agencies, schools, governments, churches, courts and other institutions.

Bem's subtext that unconscious forces drive much gender-marked behavior, brings her at the very end of the book to this final assertion, startling and unexpected in the work of a self-proclaimed feminist activist:

> Ultimately gender depolarization would require even more than the *social* revolution involved in rearranging social institutions and reframing cultural discourses. Gender depolarization would also require a *psychological* revolution in our most personal sense of who we are as males and females,

a profound alteration in our feelings about the meaning of our biological sex and its relation to our psyche and our sexuality. (Bem 1993, 139)

Bem, unfortunately, having sharply articulated the problem areas offers no guidance about the psychological revolution she advocates.[7] But the material presented in this chapter provides evidence that the dream can be a very effective instrument of revolution. It will not be enough, however, to start listening to dreams with our current frame of mind, as we so revealingly call it, for we will simply replicate in dream-work all the currently constricting attitudes and assumptions of our consciousness. For example, the United States has experienced in the past decade a resurgence of interest in the role of the mind in health, a turn toward holistic alternative medicine. This apparently positive development, however, has had a negative consequence for the sick: they are now held responsible for their own illnesses.

Such perversion of a potentially valuable sensitivity to the intricate interplay of mind and body in health and illness, however, is the pre- dictable outcome for people trained in cause-and-effect thinking. *If* the way we think and feel is related to the way our bodies behave, *then* it must be that certain thoughts and feelings *cause* certain bodily states: you are an anxious person, *therefore* you have eczema. You have heart trouble *because* you have a troubled heart.

Especially in cancer, that great threatening and uncontrollable dis- ease of our time, blame has been heaped on hapless sufferers in the belief that psychosomatic connections invariably mean that a patient can readily effect a self-cure simply by changing his or her attitudes or outlook or belief system. We identify the problem: "You have cancer of the prostate because you have repressed your sexuality." We tell the patient how to solve the problem: "Change your mind set; save your life."

In the case of AIDS, a perhaps greater epidemic that is more obvi- ously linked to the sex/gender system, the overriding responses are also often shame and blame. "You chose to be homosexual; you should suf- fer the consequences." These condemnatory reactions are rooted in ignorance about the full interrelationship of psychological, biological, and social components in the lives of lesbians and gay men, as well as of heterosexuals, bisexuals, transsexuals, and others. Such perversely per- sonalistic and moralistic misreadings of the reciprocity among mind, body, and society will continue unless we allow the dream full play for its inexhaustible store of information and are prepared in turn to radically re-form our ways of thinking and being.

To fully valorize dreaming will force us to venture outside the usual modalities through which we structure our world: chronological time, dualism, causality, and linearity. For dreams, though they are certainly shaped in part by contemporary social conditions, are not rigidly time- or culture-bound; they operate within different paradigms which require a similarly unshackled discourse which we have yet to generate. None of our current terms—isomorphism, interdependence, symbiosis, complementarity, reciprocity—comes close to depicting the subtle dynamism of the mental-physical, conscious-unconscious, individual-social continuum. But there are at least two concepts, rising out of dreamwork, which begin to translate that complex dynamism into new, more comprehensible forms: Jung's synchronicity and Mindell's dreambody.

Synchronicity is "an acausal connecting principle" that brings together two or more elements in a felicitious but not logical way. Jung described it as "a meaningful relationship between two or more events which have no apparent causal connection" (Mindell 1982 ,7). These events can vary widely in ontological status: a memory with an object, a person with an animal, a name with an apparently unrelated object, an event with a state of mind. Mindell cites one case of a mind/body/dream synchronicity in a man who consulted him for persistent hypertension and an accompanying earache, both unresponsive to medication. No problems of daily life, "except for an occasional feeling of being rushed in his work," could be identified as possible causes for these complaints. (Mindell 1982, 181-182) Then the man remembered a dream, about policemen trying to arrest Mafia leaders and the dream's emphasis on the "incredible pressure" they were under; he related this to his blood pressure and the pressure in his ear and was forced to acknowledge that the stress from his work far exceeded his earlier estimate of its effects. By modifying his work schedule, the man reduced his job-related stress with the result of a commensurate decline in blood pressure and the disappearance of the pain in his ear (Mindell 1982, 181–82).

Synchronicities happen all the time, Jung felt, but we overlook this organizing principle in our lives because we are locked into what we consider more rational ways of ordering our experience. After studying synchronicity many years ago, I began to observe its atemporal inclusivity and its fluid interconnection of diverse phenomena. Once, stuck in a maddening impasse and boiling over with characteristic impatience, I saw on my walk home from work a ponderous turtle making his slow way across a road. A few miles later I passed a familiar shop window and unaccountably glanced at the display which I noticed for the first time. It featured several small hand-blown glass turtles. Arriving home I received in the mail a letter from a former student, on turtle stationery, asking my advice on getting out of a trough of indecision about career change. These temporal, spatial, personal, social, affective, and objective congruences were not, Jung would argue, coincidences. They were a reflection of an order beneath the apparent order of things and they carried a special meaning. For me the turtles taught patience, a reminder that slow and steady increments of movement that seems to be getting nowhere could be beautiful, natural, and ultimately effective.

Similarly the "dreambody" functions to dissolve boundaries we impose between inner and outer worlds, expressing eloquently what the term psychophysical really entails. Like synchronicities, dreambody communication occurs all the time; it is just that no one is listening. It "hovers between body sensation and mythical visualization" (Mindell 1982, 8). The "dreambody" is defined as "a multi-channeled information sender asking you to receive its message in many ways and noticing how its information appears over and over again in dreams and symptoms" (Mindell 1982, 8). It is the term for the total, multichanneled personality and thus makes no distinctions or value judgments between the signals from the body and from the mind: symptoms and symbols are both equally part of the dreambody's language which encompasses the organic and inorganic. It is not only the mind that dreams and individuates, seeking development; the body, too, wants to become all that it can be (Mindell 1982, 3).

The special virtue of these two concepts is that they were generated from, not imposed upon, the processes they seek to express and that they situate the individual mind/body/dream complex in the universal in an ecologically satisfying way. Mindell says, "Your dreambody is yours, yet it's not yours. It's a collective phenomenon, belonging to nature and the world around you" (Mindell 1985, 71).

Synchronicity and dreambody form a threshold upon which we can now stand as we contemplate a burgeoning expanse of sex, gender, and dream issues and see their potential for illuminating other profoundly human issues such as the body/mind relation. Instead of continuing to chase after the elusive chimera of male/female difference, further study on our triad of topics will serve society best and will move us most adeptly from polarity to plurality when it digs beneath the very ground upon which the war between the sexes is being fought.

In *The Mystique of Dreams* (1985) William Domhoff showed that belief in a dream-governed society of the Senoi Temiar in West Malaysia spread throughout the United States in the sixties because it fulfilled our collective fantasy of utopianism. Just so our current obsession with sex and gender difference exposes our pessimistic fantasy for the eighties and nineties of a dystopia of inevitable, interminable, ever escalating, human conflict. In the face of this, we as individuals feel overwhelmed, are rendered helpless, turn against each other or turn solipsistically inward.

I hope in the first decades of the coming millennium we will create together a new fantasy, placing dreaming at the center of our inquiry and concern, yet resisting an unrealistic inflation of its value. I hope we can use the energy of dreaming not to envision utopias or their opposite but to imagine and enact humane, practical forms of social transformation, especially in our country's sex/gender system. I hope this chapter provides one small window on that possible world by reminding us to stay rooted in the body, to honor the unconscious, to weigh carefully our social contexts and to enter into the dynamic among all these equally valuable dimensions of our lives with courage and imagination.

Notes

1. Rubin later repudiated her conflation of sex and gender. In "Thinking Sex: Notes for a Radical Theory of the Politics of Sexuality," she writes: "I am now arguing that it is essential to separate gender and sexuality analytically to more accurately reflect their separate social existence." She also states that "although sex and gender are related, they are not the same thing, and they form the basis of two distinct arenas of social practice" (1984, 307–8). Rubin's more extended definition

of the "sex/gender system" is "a socio-historical construction of sexual identity, difference and relationship; an appropriation of human anatomical and physiological features by an ideological discourse; a culture-specific fantasia upon Nature's universal theme (1984, 62).

2. Some sense of the virtual obsession with difference which drives so much current research and experimentation in dreams can be found by reading widely in two publications of the International Association for the Study of Dreams: a quarterly journal, *Dreaming*, and a bimonthly *Newsletter*. A summary of findings follows, accompanied by dates, title of publication, and authors' names. Readers are referred to these publications for further source information.

A 1933 article has been identified by Winget and Kramer (1979) as the first U.S. study of sex/gender difference in dreams. Since then, claims have been made that men appear more in men's dreams than women do; men and women appear equally in women's dreams (Hall and Domhoff, *Dreaming* 1992). Women dream more than men do about being involved with negative events and/or having negative self-perceptions (Cartwright, *Dreaming* 1992). Men and women have different ways of processing information and are differently affected by stress, leading to gender differences in dream recall (Fitch and Armitage, *Dreaming* 1989; Armitage, *Dreaming* 1992). Women share their dreams more with others and apply their dreams more in their waking life than men do (Pagel and Vann, *Dreaming* 1993). Women have "lucid" dreams more often than men do (Gackenbach, *Dreaming* 1993; Gackenbach and Hearne, *Newsletter* 1978; Dane and Van de Castle, *Newsletter* 1991).When seriously ill, men dream of death, women of separation (Smith, *Newsletter* 1985). Some cross-cultural studies suggest that these sex/gender differences are stronger than differences in culture: e.g., Chinese and North American male students' dream content resembles each other's more than it does the dream content of the female students who share their culture (Walls, *Newsletter* 1982).

3. Throughout *Dreams, Illusions and Other Realities* (1985) on classical texts from India, Wendy Doniger (O'Flaherty) contrasts ideas of what is real in Indian and non-Indian (Graeco-Roman, psychoanalytic) views of the world. Chapter 1 provides a thorough critique of Western dualism and Freud's relation to that mindset.

4. There is debate among many people, including gay men and lesbians, over which term is more appropriate, orientation or preference. I have chosen to use the latter throughout because I think it conveys the idea of the direction of attraction without implicit judgments about whether that attraction is voluntary or involuntary.

5. Race is another of those crucial elements for dream study which has been neglected in U.S. research.

6. Delaney expands on her opinion in *Breakthrough Dreaming* (1991): "Most humans have some attractions to both sexes, but most of us know what our primary sexual orientation is without the help of our dreams" (290). She touches upon but does not investigate a central problematic in dream interpretation: how can you tell when a dream is speaking objectively, i.e., literally (the same/opposite-sex lover in your dream speaks to your manifest or latent sexual desire), or subjectively, i.e., figuratively (the same/opposite-sex lover in your dream speaks to a certain undeveloped side of your self which needs your loving attention).

7. Archetypal psychologist James Hillman, in a collection of his conversations with journalist Michael Ventura, proposes a radical deconstruction of the therapeutic discourse and urges making the consulting room into a kind of command post for social revolution. The thrust of his exhortation is captured in the title: *We've Had a Hundred Years of Psychotherapy—And the World's Getting Worse* (HarperCollins 1992). Yet a disturbing irony of the whole frame of this conversation between two middle-class white men seems to escape them altogether. Throughout a long section of dialogue, which they record on tape, the men sit and talk several yards away from a "fat homeless woman." Her presence is noted, along with that of a variety of other evidence of deteriorating social conditions which clutters their site and view. Yet once they return to the car at the end of their chat, no further mention is made of the woman except for noting, as they leave, that the woman "is wrapping herself in plastic garbage bags" as protection from the night and the elements. No more revealing metaphor for sex, gender, and class inequities in U.S. society could have been created by the most outraged of feminist activists than this scene as cooly observed, commented upon, and then abandoned by Hillman and Ventura.

References
(With suggested readings)

ASD Newsletter. 1982–Present. Newsletter of the Association for the Study of Dreams. Alan Siegel, Ed. Vienna, VA: Association for the Study of Dreams.

Baraff, Alvin. 1991. *Men Talk: How Men Really Feel about Women, Sex, Relationships, and Themselves.* New York: Penguin Books.

Bell, Alan P. and Calvin S. Hall. 1971. *The Personality of a Child Molester: An Analysis of Dreams.* Chicago: Aldine, Atherton.

Bem, Sandra Lipsitz. 1993. *The Lenses of Gender: Transforming the Debate on Sexual Inequality.* New Haven: Yale University Press.

Bogart, Gregory Charles. 1993. Seven dreams in a case of childhood sexual abuse and adult homophobia. *Dreaming: Journal of the Association for the Study of Dreams* 3.(3). (September): 201–10.

Bosnak, Robert. 1989. *Dreaming with an AIDS Patient.* Boston: Shambala.

————. 1988. *A Little Course in Dreams.* Boston: Shambala.

Delaney, Gayle. 1991. *Breakthrough Dreaming: How to Tap the Power of Your 24-Hour Mind.* Foreword by J. Allan Hobson, M.D. New York: Bantam Books.

————. 1988. *Living Your Dreams.* Rev. and expanded edition. San Francisco: Harper & Row.

Dombeck, Mary-Therese. B. 1991. *Dreams and Professional Personhood.* Albany, NY: State University of New York Press.

Domhoff, G. William. 1985. *The Mystique of Dreams: A Search for Utopia through Senoi Dream Theory.* Berkeley: University of California Press.

Dreaming: Journal of the Association for the Study of Dreams. Ernest Hartmann, Ed. New York: Human Sciences Press.

Gackenbach, Jayne and Jane Bosveld. 1989. *Control Your Dreams.* New York: Harper & Row.

Garfield, Patricia. 1988. *Women's Bodies, Women's Dreams.* New York: Ballantine Books.

Hopcke, Robert H. 1990. *Men's Dreams, Men's Healing.* Boston: Shambala.

Kimmel, Michael S. 1993. Clarence, William, Iron Mike, Tailhook, Magic, and Us: Issues for men in the '90's. Talk at Hamilton College, Clinton, New York.

Kimmel, Michael S. and Michael A. Messner. 1992. *Men's Lives.* 2nd. ed. New York: Macmillan Publishing Company.

Koulack, David. 1991. *To Catch a Dream: Explorations of Dreaming.* Albany, NY: State University of New York Press.

Krippner, Stanley, ed. 1990. *Dreamtime and Dreamwork: Decoding the Language of the Night.* Los Angeles: Jeremy P. Tarcher.

Lauter, Estella and Carol Schreier Rupprecht. 1985. Feminist archetypal theory: A proposal. In Estella Lauter and Carol Schreier Rupprecht (eds.), *Feminist Archetypal Theory: Interdisciplinary Re-visions of Jungian Thought* (pp. 220–37). Knoxville: University of Tennessee Press.

McDonald, Phoebe. 1987. *Dreams: Night Language of the Soul.* New York: Continuum.

Mindell, Arnold. 1982. *Dreambody: The Body's Role in Revealing the Self.* Santa Monica, CA: Sigo Press.

———. 1985a. *River's Way: The Process Science of the Dreambody.* London: Routledge and Kegan Paul.

———. 1985b. *Working with the Dreaming Body.* London: Routledge and Kegan Paul.

Monette, Paul. 1992. *Becoming a Man: Half a Life Story.* New York: Harcourt, Brace, Jovanovich.

———. 1988. *Borrowed Time: An Aids Memoir.* New York: Harcourt, Brace, Jovanovich.

Nadelson, Carol. 1993. Ethics, empathy, and gender in health care. *American Journal of Psychiatry* 150: (9) (September): 1309–14.

O'Flaherty, Wendy Doniger. 1984. *Dreams, Illusions, and Other Realities.* Chicago: University of Chicago Press.

Perera, Sylvia Brinton. 1990. Dream design: Some operations underlying clinical dream appreciation. In Nathan Schwartz-Salant and Murray Stein, (eds.), *Dreams in Analysis* (pp. 39–80). Wilmette, Ill: Chiron Publications.

Reis, Patricia. 1991. *Through the Goddess: A Woman's Way of Healing.* New York: Continuum.

Rubin, Gayle. 1984. Thinking sex: Notes for a radical theory of the politics of sexuality. In Carole Vance (ed.), *Pleasure and Danger: Exploring Female Sexuality* 267–319. Boston: Routledge & Kegan Paul.

———. 1975. The traffic in women. In Rayna R. Reiter (ed.), *Toward an Anthropology of Women* p. 159. New York: Monthly Review Press.

Rupprecht, Carol Schreier. 1985. The common language of women's dreams. In Estella Lauter and Carol Schreier Rupprecht, (eds.), *Feminist Archetypal Theory: Interdisciplinary Re-Visions of Jungian Thought,* (pp. 187-219). Knoxville: University of Tennessee Press.

———. 1990. Enlightening shadows: Between feminism and archetypalism, literature and analysis. In Karin Barnaby and Pellegrino D'Acierno, (eds.), *C.G. Jung and the Humanities: Toward a Hermeneutic of Culture,* 279–93. Princeton: Princeton University Press.

Schwartz-Salant, Nathan and Murray Stein. 1990. *Dreams in Analysis.* The Chiron Clinical Series. Wilmette, IL: Chiron Publications.

Seligman, Jean with Karen Springen. 1993. Rethinking women's bodies." *Newsweek* 4 October 86.

Siegel, Alan. 1983. "Pregnant dreams: Developmental processes in the manifest dreams of expectant fathers." Ph.D. diss., California School of Professional Psychology, Berkeley, CA.

————. 1990. *Dreams That Can Change Your Life.* Los Angeles: Jeremy P. Tarcher.

Signell, Karen. 1990. *Wisdom of the Heart: Working with Women's Dreams.* New York: Bantam Books.

Stein, Murray. 1990. On dreams and history in analysis. In Nathan Schwartz-Salant and Murray Stein, (eds.), *Dreams in Analysis,* (pp. 17–38). Wilmette, IL: Chiron Publications.

Stockard, Jean and Miriam M. Johnson. 1992. *Sex and Gender in Society,* 2nd. ed. Englewood Cliffs, NJ: Prentice-Hall.

Stoltenberg, John. 1989. *Refusing to be a Man: Essays on Sex and Justice.* Portland, OR: Breitenbush Books.

Suleiman, Susan Rubin, ed. 1986. *The Female Body in Western Culture.* Cambridge, MA: Harvard University Press.

Ullman, Montague and Nan Zimmerman. 1979. *Working with Dreams.* Foreword by Richard M. Jones. Los Angeles: Jeremy P. Tarcher.

Whitmont, Edward C. 1990. On dreams and dreaming. In Nathan Schwartz-Salant and Murray Stein, (eds.), *Dreams in Analysis,* (pp. 1–16). Wilmette, IL: Chiron Publications.

III.

Dreams,
Spirituality,
and
Modernity

Traversing the Living Labyrinth

Dreams and Dreamwork in the Psychospiritual Dilemma of the Postmodern World

Jeremy Taylor

> *Asleep, we turn our attention to the reality of our interconnectedness as members of a single species. In this sense, we may regard dreaming as concerned with the issue of species interconnectedness. . . . Perhaps our dreaming consciousness is primarily concerned with the survival of the species and only secondarily with the individual. Were there any truth to this speculation it would shed a radically different light on the importance of dreams. It would make them deserving of higher priority in our culture than they are now assigned.*
> —Myron Glucksman and Silas Warner
> *Origins in New Perspective—The Royal Road Revisited*

As a species, Homo sapiens is in trouble. The toxic by-products of our voracious technologies are polluting the soil, air, and water to such an extent that the ability of the planet to continue supporting complex mammalian life appears to be in jeopardy. Our social, political, religious, and cultural institutions, East and West, are breaking down at a rapid rate and everywhere men, women, and particularly children seem filled with an increasing sense of hopelessness, coupled with a feeling of spiritual emptiness and an absence of broader vision, purpose, and connection with anything worthy of the name divine.

Even the numerous religious and political fundamentalisms that appear to be so militantly on the rise everywhere in the world are, in my view, also the result of this increasing loss of felt harmony with higher realities, purposes, and meanings. In all the instances I have met, rigid ideological and doctrinal fundamentalism is a direct consequence of neurotic denial of the anguish and anxiety of lost communion or harmony with something once experienced (often in childhood) as greater and more important than the "merely" personal feelings, opinions, and experiences of individual life. The "fundamentalist attitude" is an effort to regain, by an act of sheer will, the lost sense of harmony and communion with the divine.

One major reason for the intensity of our particular contemporary crisis of confidence and perceived meaning is our fumbling sorcerer's apprenticeship in science and our unfeeling manipulation of nature and the physical world. The stunning short-term economic and political success of our narrowly focused, conscious, abstract, linear, time-limited, technological thinking has produced the secondary effect of distracting us from our deeper, seemingly less rational unconscious psychospiritual experience. In the process of "conquering" the physical world, we have become alienated from two of the oldest and most important and reliable sources of balance, sanity, and evolving self-awareness: myth and dream. (It is worth remembering that "myth" is simply a name for somebody else's religion.)

Dream and myth always address the deeper realities of our lives below the surface of appearance. Appearances can be measured; it is the *immeasurability* of the patterns of meaning that lie beyond appearances, beyond the ability to be "objective" and stand separate and quantify, that has tended to make myth and dream seem so foreign and irrelevant to the lives of people in postmodern industrial societies.

A "mythic" story from the Sufi tradition may serve to elucidate the dilemma. Although it is apparently about a distant, nontechnological world of donkeys and camels and rural villages where everyone knows everyone else, it is also an ironic and exquisitely accurate commentary on our own contemporary Western psychospiritual dilemma.

It seems that the incomparable Mullah Nasrudin has lost his precious gold ring. He wanders through the streets of his village staring at the ground, searching for his lost treasure. His friends and neighbors notice his concentrated efforts, and soon they all become involved in the search.

Finally, it occurs to one of them to ask Nasrudin, "When do you last recall having the ring on your finger?"

Nasrudin casually responds that the last time he can remember actually having the ring on his finger was a while ago, when he was shovelling dung in the course of cleaning the stable behind his house.

"Oh?!" says his friend, "Then we should concentrate our search there, don't you think?"

"Oh, no!" says Nasrudin, "The light's *much* better for looking out here!"

That which was lost in the dark will also be recovered from the dark: the solution to the escalating crisis of global culture and ecological imbalance will not be found in increasingly urgent and desperate efforts to dominate and manipulate the environment even more effectively—it will be found in a deeper exploration of the unconscious depths of humankind that have brought these problems into being in the first place. Our current predicament stems in greatest measure from the dramatic disproportion between our limited and relatively static knowledge of our own intrinsic (unconscious/archetypal) nature as human beings, and our vast and cancerously increasing knowledge of how to manipulate and exploit the physical environment for our short-term gratification.

In the past, human beings were collectively protected to some extent from the full consequences of our ignorance, greed, hubris, and fear by our relative weakness and ineffectiveness. The advent of modern science and technology has made the consequences of our stupidities and self-deceptions much more vast and terrible, but it has not changed the basic source of the problem(s): human consciousness, and *un*consciousness itself.

The Mullah Nasrudin, a universal archetypal fool/trickster representing human consciousness itself (dressed in the "homespun" of Sufi tradition), prefers to look for the archetypal "lost treasure," (the "gold ring" which has always symbolized the depth of commitment to and relationship with something larger than one's self), in the relatively clean and brightly lit public street, rather than in the nasty, smelly depths of his own stable. One clear symbolic message of this story is that we human beings are predisposed to shy away from the work of looking at the "nasty," "dark" (unconscious/emotional) aspects of our individual and collective problems, preferring to engage in repetitive intellectual examinations of the external technical details of our problems, "where the light is better"—where consciousness has less difficulty "seeing," but where the lost treasure will not be found.

An ironic contemporary example of the "logic of Nasrudin" can be seen when Harvard professor J. Allan Hobson uses exactly the same metaphor in his book *The Dreaming Brain*: "In science we often have to look where the light is."[1] He resorts to this metaphor in an attempt to justify his all but exclusive emphasis on the neurophysiology of dreaming, and his dismissal of other methodologies for and perspectives on examining dreams with an eye to their possible meaning and significance.

Even the religions of the world, which profess to know better, generally collude in the suppression of attention to the unconscious, symbolic aspects of human experience (at least in their public, exoteric practice). The sacred/mythic narratives of the world are in startling agreement that human beings have more direct access to the divine and "the Will of God(s)" in our dreams than any other ordinary state of awareness. Despite their numerous and bloody disagreements about so many other things, the sacred texts of the world's religions offer astonishingly unified testimony on this point. Despite this (and indeed, to a great extent, because of it), the actual practice of organized religions today uniformly discourages, or even prohibits paying attention to our dreams.

Judeo-Christian scriptures, for example, are filled with references to the divine revelations that come in dreams, and yet only recently, and with noticeable reluctance, have Christian and Jewish congregations approved of their members examining their dreams, and then only in the "private" context of secular therapy, rather than the traditional public context of collective spiritual debate and discernment.

There have always been moments of historical crisis (not unlike our own), when a return to the primary revelations of the unconscious and the divine in dreams, waking visions, and reassessment of original sacred narratives has been attempted. The Protestant Reformation turned the attention of many believing Christians back to canonical scripture in the effort to replace the traditional authority of the Roman popes and bishops with a "purer" and "more reliable" source of spiritual guidance. In so doing, the early Protestants rediscovered the same dilemma that faced the earlier Church Fathers with regard to the many, unambiguous scriptural assertions and stories pointing to dreams as a direct source of revelation of divine guidance and intervention in the lives of human beings.

Like the established Roman Church against which they were "protesting," the early Protestant theologians were quickly forced by administrative necessity to adopt the same negative stance toward dreams and paying attention to dreams that their predecessors had done: that is, that although dreams had once been a primary source of direct revelation of "God's Will" (in the spiritual "golden age" in which the scriptures were first revealed and recorded), the "book" of such direct revelations was now definitely and firmly closed. Even though there was no scriptural precedent for such a change of attitude, one by one the early Protestant leaders adopted the position that any attention to dreams in the current "common" era was "deviant" and "unacceptable."[2]

In one sense, this recapitulation of the earlier Roman suppression of interest in dreams was historically and politically "inevitable," in large measure *because* the scriptural precedents for the authority of dream revelations was and are so unambiguous and strong. Without such an "administrative" prohibition, it would be all too easy for anyone (the scruffier and more malcontent the better, since social deviation and marginality is a clear and repeating element in the makeup of archetypal figure of the "divinely inspired prophet") to speak up and say, "I had a dream last night, and in it God told me to tell all of you. . . ." Given the undeniable authority of direct dream revelation in the biblical narratives themselves, it would be all but impossible for any merely local authority to maintain order and discipline in any congregation in the face of such a challenge, unless the whole area of dreamwork were collectively prohibited.

The Prophet Muhammad, "God's Holy Messenger," shared his own dreams and listened to and interpreted the dreams of his followers on a daily basis, and the same evolution—from the enthusiastic embrace of daily practice through to discouragement and outright prohibition—has taken place in the history of Islam as well, and for essentially the same reason. The same story repeats itself in the history of Buddhism, and even in the development of modern psychoanalysis. The emphasis placed on dreams as "primary revelations of the unconscious" by the great founders of psychoanalysis (Freud, Jung, Adler, et al.), is being slowly replaced in the succeeding generations by increased attention to other techniques of intervention (ranging from "guided imagery" to the increased reliance on psychoactive drugs), all of which tend to minimize the importance of dreams and put the therapist and the analyst more firmly and directly in charge of the process.

However, when the dreamer is encouraged to take primary direct responsibility for the assessment and interpretation of his or her own dreams, then a more appropriate and healthy balance of authority and autonomy is restored. When dreamers feel genuinely free, and are encouraged to explore the multiple meanings of their own dreams, particularly in on-going, egalitarian, participatory dream groups, then their creative and decision-making powers are enhanced, and their social bonds of intimate relationship, responsibility, and mutual support are strengthened and deepened. The continuing proliferation of such "leaderless" and "lay-led" dream groups is one of the most interesting and potentially important contemporary developments in dream-related studies.

Ironically, it is secular psychology's ongoing demonstration that dreams have such undeniable value in the unravelling of neurosis that has made it possible for dreamwork to be reintroduced into the public collective life of organized religion. The extension of the psychoanalytic implications of dreamwork into the spiritual realm has been generally limited to fairly nervous, defensive, and tentative discussions of the value of psychotherapy and the resolution of personal neurotic dramas as a seemingly necessary preliminary step for truly authentic spiritual development. The understanding that dreams might also have value and worth, not only in the diagnosis and treatment of mental and emotional disorders but also as guides for spiritual unfoldment, did not emerge again until relatively recently.

It is only within the past twenty years or so, with the constellation of a genuine, broad-based popular movement devoted to "lay dreamwork" (pioneered by Ann Faraday, Patricia Garfield, Montague Ullman, John Sanford, and others), that the Western Christian world has begun once again to recognize that dreams can and often do play a potentially crucial and profound role in the unfoldment of spiritual experience and perspective, not just for characters in biblical narratives, but for the lives of contemporary people, as well.

It is the establishment of this broad-based, egalitarian lay dream-work movement has also played a key role in bringing together academic and medical dream researchers with widely differing theoretical perspectives in a vital and creative dialogue. Despite the inevitable class, gender, cultural, generational, ideological, and professional conflicts that divide this burgeoning movement, contemporary dreamworkers are united by a shared conviction born of experience that paying serious attention to dreams and dreaming is a valuable enterprise.

At the individual and personal level, dreams regularly provide encounters with primary archetypal intuitions of the patterns of meaning and "divine presence" that address the specific details of the dreamer's own life and unresolved psychospiritual dilemmas. Let me offer an extraordinary dream narrative from the twentieth-century British author J. B. Priestly as a case in point:

> I was standing at the top of a very high tower, alone, looking down upon myriads of birds flying in one direction; every kind of bird was there, all the birds in the world. It was a noble sight, this vast aerial river of birds. But now in some mysterious fashion the gear was changed, and time speeded up, so I saw generations of birds, watched them break their shells, flutter into life, mate, weaken, falter, and die. Wings grew only to crumble; bodies were sleek and then, in a flash, bled and shriveled; and death struck everywhere at every second. What was the use of all this blind struggle toward life, this eager trying of wings, this hurried mating, this flight and surge, all this gigantic, meaningless, biological effort? As I stared down, seeming to see every creature's ignoble little history almost at a glance, I felt sick at heart. It would be better if not one of them, not one of us all, had been born, if the struggle ceased forever. I stood on my tower, still alone, desperately unhappy. But now the gear was changed again, and time went faster still, and it was rushing by at such a rate that the birds could not show any movement, but were like an enormous plain sewn with feathers. But along this plain, flickering through the bodies themselves, there now passed a sort of white flame, trembling, dancing, then hurrying on; and as soon as I saw it, I knew the white flame was life itself, the very quintessence of being; and then it came to me, in a rocket-burst of ecstasy, that nothing mattered, nothing could ever matter, because nothing else was real but this quivering and hurrying lambency of

beings. Birds, men [sic], or creatures not yet shaped or colored, all were of no account except so far as this flame of life travelled through them. It left nothing to mourn over behind it; what I had thought was tragedy was mere emptiness or a shadow show; for now all real feeling was caught and purified and danced on ecstatically with the white flame of life. I had never felt before such deep happiness as I know at the end of my dream of the tower and the birds.[3]

This is clearly a deeply emotional dream, addressing both psychological and spiritual issues, although it does not immediately reveal any particular "brand" of institutional religion. Priestly was raised in the Church of England, but his dream is immediately recognizable and communicative to anyone who encounters it, regardless of cultural background or religious heritage. It speaks a universal, archetypal language of symbolic form that appears spontaneously in myths and dreams at all periods of history in all parts of the world. The "white flame" that Priestly apprehends so clearly in his dream, and which fills him with joy and acceptance of life and the inevitability of death, could be equally called "a felt sense of the presence of the divine," or "Baraka," or "the descent of the Paraclete," or "Buddha mind," or "The Shekinah," or any number of other technical names that are found in the world's abstruse theological pronouncements.

Priestly's dream addresses "the problem of evil," and offers a solution that "reframes" the problem in a broader context and lifts the spirit without disparaging or minimizing the pain of the initial encounter. It is precisely the kind of *primary* symbolic revelation of the archetypal energy of the divine that the sacred narratives of the world memorialize and celebrate.

It is interesting to note that even in such an overtly "spiritual" dream, the details still reveal a "psychological" consistency of archetypal imagery. The "tower" suggests the structures of abstract and scientific thought that contemporary human beings have erected to get "an elevated perspective" on our existential dilemmas and the painful paradoxes of our lives. The dream implies that for contemporary Western intellectuals like Priestly (and ourselves), there is still a genuine possibility of primary spiritual experience, informed, shaped (and I would even say, enhanced), by the modern "antireligious" intellectual frameworks of evolution and scientific inquiry. In addition to offering a primary experience transcending the fear and anguish of inevitable death, the dream proposes that it is not necessary to "check our brains at the door" in order to have a profoundly moving and important spiritual experience of this kind. In fact, the dream suggests that the elevated perspective provided by the "tower" provides an even better and broader view of this transcendent reality. Once again, the ancient and radical message is repeated: it is only when the *whole* personality, specifically including the unfettered intellect, is vitally and fully engaged in the messy business of living that authentic spiritual experience is likely to manifest in any conscious and communicable form.

It is worth noting that the archetypal image of the "tower" as a symbol of intellectual perspective and the philosophical assumptions that underpin conscious attitude is the same "tower" that is "struck by lightning" on the Tarot card of the same name. "The Tower Struck by Lightning" symbolizes (among other things) the direct experience of unconscious emotional and spiritual realities bursting in on the complacent assumptions of conscious life and shattering them, in order to open up a broader and more whole and authentic horizon of awareness. In this image, the "lightning" is closely related to the "white flame" of Priestly's dream, only in this instance, the dreamer's conscious attitude already includes a radically open spiritual perspective, and thus does not need to be "shattered" by the "white flame/lightning" in order to "see" it and open to it more deeply.

The fact that it is "birds" that Priestly views echoes with the universal figure of the "Spirit Bird," the divine messenger in bird shape that has always brought revelations of the divine to "middle earth," the realm of conscious human awareness. Priestly's "aerial river of birds" is a twentieth-century cousin of the Dove of the Holy Spirit, Vishnu's Garuda, Odin's ravens, Zeus' eagle, the Great Goddess' sacred goose—the list is virtually endless. The dream might as easily have offered a vision of tigers, or butterflies, or human beings, whose pulsing life might have revealed the same transcendental "white flame," but the dream chose the "classic" image of the bird to deliver the message of hidden relationship with the energies of the divine, below and beyond the surface of tortured physical appearance.

Priestly's dream is only one example of a dream that offers primary spiritual experience to those who take the trouble to turn their gaze inward to the experiences. All human beings dream, and this form of inspiration and encounter with the deep collective layers of the human unconscious is equally open to all, even in this contemporary "fallen" age. As Emerson says, "Within is so great as to be Beyond."

Spiritual intuitions and concerns underlie virtually all dreams, even when their manifest content appears to be completely mundane, or even nightmarishly "unspiritual." The dream of a student in an extracurricular dream group at the University of Toronto may serve as an example of a dream that may not appear at first glance to have any particular spiritual meaning, but which by the dreamer's own associations and "aha's" of recognition demonstrates a profound spiritual message.[4]

> I am walking down to the ravine by Summerhill Avenue. . . . The surroundings now become more lush and tropical. It is a huge jungle. In the middle of it is an enormous wooden ladder which goes up, up, up. I don't recall seeing the top of it though there may have been one. It disappears into a fog or clouds. . . . As I approach the ladder I notice a snake in the path below me. I stop to allow him to pass. I am relieved that I saw him. But to my surprise another snake is coming down the ladder. I realize that if I stop for the first, the second will descend and get me. I panic but am frozen to the spot. I have a BB gun in a stapler and attempt to shoot the snake. I wonder if I should use the kitchen knife but figure it would be too messy. I shoot the snake but hit him only in the body. This does not stop him. I think he may bite me when he squirms in pain. He is *really* close. I shoot him again and again but still he descends. I cannot move. I awake in a panic. That's the dream. Weird, eh?

In this group, all the participants were encouraged to draw the images in their dreams whenever possible. The young man followed this suggestion and was surprised (as is so often the case when the visual elements of the dream are explored in their own terms) by the insights that followed.

> As I was sketching the ladder, I was struck by a thought about the biblical story of Jacob who dreamed that he saw God's angels ascending and descending a ladder from heaven to earth. Like Jacob's ladder, my dream ladder reaches into the heavens- But instead of an angel of God, a snake descends! In the Garden of Eden, Lucifer, God's brightest (and proudest) angel takes the form of a snake. This suggests to me that when an angel becomes flesh I can only see it as evil. I am very afraid of this snake. I do not see it as in fact from God, that what it represents, this-worldly matter,

flesh, is also from God. I have created or acquired a dualism which associates this world with evil.

I stopped painting for a minute and found my Bible. I looked for the passage with Jacob's ladder in it. After Jacob's dream, he said, "Surely the Lord is in this place, and I did not know it. . . . How awesome is this place! This is none other than the house of God, and this is the gate of heaven (Gen. 28:16–17). For me this is a very powerful passage. If I am the ravine then I am the holy ground in which "Jacob's ladder" is rooted. This means the Self is "the house of God." This ties in with a Christian doctrine I learned very early at school, that each of us is a "temple" in which the Holy Spirit dwells. This ravine, the Self as total organism—*the body as holy ground*—is where God lives.[5]

Figure 1. Jacob's Ladder, with snakes descending.

Although this insight by no means exhausts the meanings and spiritual energies lying below the surface of the manifest content of this dream, the dreamer's own "aha" of recognition (the only truly reliable indicator of the symbolic truth of a dream), stimulated by his sketching the scene of the ladder and the snake, specifically demonstrates how even the most distressing images and emotions in a dream can have profoundly spiritual implications.

The figure of the ladder itself which the young man equates to "Jacob's ladder" is in itself and archetypal image. Edward Edinger has named this class of images "the Ego/Self axis."[6] By this he means to suggest the class of images that symbolize the psychospiritual function that brings the seemingly separate and sometimes fearful and defensive world of the mundane waking-life ego-self into direct communion and harmony with the transformative energies of the greater divine Self that resides at the core of all experience .

This ladder is made of "wood" in the young man' s dream, and once again there is every reason to believe that at one level of symbolic depth there is a pun pointing to "would." The "would ladder" that connects the fear filled and clumsily violent ego with the profound energies of self-acceptance and transformation of the "dualism" of body and spirit is made up in great measure of the young man' s profound *desire* for spiritual clarity, and his deep longing the sense of being "right with God." This sense of well-being and spiritual harmony is deeply connected to deeper emotional and psychological self-acceptance.

The "dualism" he discovers in himself is something we are all heir to. Many sectarian spiritual traditions (particularly the patriarchal ones) have disparaged the body, and the physical world in general, in contrast to the "pure," "disembodied" world of the spirit. Because *wholeness* is ever and again in the key to spiritual development, the body can not be left behind any more than the mind. The dreams, which always come to serve our evolving individual and collective health and wholeness, also serve our spiritual development by bringing us closer to whatever elements of our whole being we have ignored or undervalued—aspects of our wholeness which have spiritual gifts to offer, if we only pay attention.

To return for a moment to the work of Professor Hobson, in his book *The Dreaming Brain* he also recounts one of his own dreams, involving a waking-life colleague who accepted a post at another Ivy

League school in "psychoanalytic psychology," abandoning the neuro-biological approach that characterized their work together at Harvard.[7] Hobson sees his waking-life annoyance with this colleague having "left him in the lurch" taking shape in the dream. The dream itself concludes with the dreaming Hobson observing somewhat sarcastically, "That is why you have such beautiful buildings and why there is nothing in them."

Although only Hobson's own "aha's" of insight and recognition can confirm any of the meanings in this dream, the image of "beautiful academic buildings" with "nothing in them" invites the thought that it is, among other things, a spontaneous symbolic representation of his "elegant" academic, scientific research into the neurobiology of the dreaming process, which, despite its elegance, is "empty" in the sense of being devoid of the sense of human meaning and importance it is supposed to illuminate. Whether this image is in fact "a minority report" from Dr. Hobson's unconscious pointing to a shadow aspect of his research work or not, it is at least a theoretical example of the way in which dreams, in the service of health and psychospiritual wholeness, convey their meanings symbolically, most often revealing uncomfortable truths to the waking ego—psychological and spiritual truths which the waking ego/persona aspect of the whole being would much prefer to deny and ignore. We can see this tendency clearly in the Canadian student's dream of the "snakes and ladders," and the same basic symbolic strategy can be inferred in Dr. Hobson's image of the "beautiful but empty university buildings."

The understanding that the symbolic statements of dreams have relevance for the development of individual consciousness, personality, and psychospiritual awareness has been generally shared by all dream analysts and "interpreters" throughout history. Contemporary Western technological society appears to be the only society in the history of humankind that has attempted to promote the idea that dreams are meaningless.

One of the most interesting developments of the contemporary dreamwork movement is a growing awareness of the collective, social layers of significance in dreams. Exploring dreams, particularly in the setting of an ongoing, egalitarian dream group, can and often does provide exactly the sort of spiritual insight and perspective that postmodern, industrial people so desperately need.

Authentic spiritual experience is a form of self-knowledge. It tends to awaken people more fully, both to themselves and to the world, drawing them into deeper relationship(s) and into more expression of their creative energies. There are numerous examples of people discovering energies and specific possibilities for collective transformation and change as they turn their attention back to their dream experiences and begin to share them with one another, publicly, on a more or less regular basis.[8]

The psychological process at the root of virtually all forms of human oppression is the so-called repression/projection phenomenon. Whenever a person represses and denies some aspect of his or her own authentic being, that very energy will begin to "appear" (as hallucinated projections) in his or her apprehensions of the other people in the neighborhood. Having denied the humanity of some aspect of his or her own authentic being, it becomes inevitable that this person will deny the humanity of other people, particularly those who overtly express something like the energies being repressed.

Dreams regularly offer symbolic images of the aspects of the psyche that are being repressed and projected. For this reason, working with dreams provides an unrivalled opportunity to recognize and withdraw these projections. Whenever projections are withdrawn, not only is the life experience of the individual clarified and deepened, the collective social situations in which that person previously participated less consciously—situations characterized by projection and its attendant prejudices and oppressions—are also transformed.

In this way, among others, dreams carry information of interest and value for the dreamer's whole community and society. In traditional, nontechnological cultures, dream sharing is most often a regular part of social contact. In such societies, dreams have always been, and often still are discussed and analyzed publicly with an eye to their relevance for the whole community.

Contemporary scientific research into the content of dreams, as well as modern experiments in regular group dream sharing, confirm the value of this ancient practice. Just as there are "leading indicators" of economic and political life that can be examined to anticipate trends and changes in business, education, and government, analysis of dreams from a whole community can provide "early indications" of changes and transformations in our collective cultural and spiritual life.

Let me offer one specific, concrete example of how such collective information can be discovered in the collective, longitudinal analysis of multiple dream reports from a single society.

Statistical research into the content of contemporary dreams in industrial society has shown over and over again that "women dream in color more than men." There is substantial reason to believe that this collectively demonstrable phenomenon is directly related to sex role stereotyping in these societies.

There is an archetypal resonance between "color" and "emotion" in the symbolic archetypal world of myth and dream. Because little girls are consistently encouraged and directed by society to pay minute attention to the aesthetic side of life, and to their own and other people's emotions, while at the same time little boys are consistently discouraged from doing so, it is not surprising that collective content analysis of multiple dreams from many different dreamers should show a consistent pattern of "women dreaming in color more than men."

My own conviction is that this observed pattern is related to habits of *remembering* dreams, rather than primary dream experience. When "black-and-white dreamers" undertake serious and sustained work with their dreams, they invariably become more consciously aware of the subtleties and significance of their own and other peoples' emotions. This expansion of conscious attention to the realm of feeling is invariably accompanied (in my experience of working with more than 80,000 dreams in the last twenty-five years), with an increased awareness of the *colors* present in their dreams, almost always beginning with the color "red," the color symbolically associated most consistently with the strongest emotions, felt in "hot blood."

If one were interested in an objective relative measure of whether or not the sex-role stereotypes of more traditional Western industrial society were actually beginning to break down and transform in response to the contemporary movement for women's rights and the overthrow of sexism, then one might well look to see if the seemingly consistent differential between the reported incidence of remembered color in men's and women's dreams were changing, particularly in relation to the results of similar research in this question carried out earlier in the century.

This is just one, clear, concrete example of the kinds of "objective" information about the psychospiritual depths of our collective experience that would, I believe, be made more available by the pursuit of research into the patterns revealed in the regular, ongoing examination and comparison of many people's dreams.

This process of paying attention to dreams not only reflects the transformations of heart and mind that relieve oppression, it also actively promotes those transformations. When people gather together to explore their dreams together, they enter into a process which challenges and promotes withdrawal of the projections, denials, and self-deceptions that fuel the collective dramas of gender, race, class, and other oppression. The emotional, psychological, and ultimately spiritual information revealed by the successive layers of "aha" recognition of the multiple meanings that are woven into every dream inevitably brings the people involved in the process closer to their wellsprings of archetypal creative energy.

My own experience in working in prisons, community organizing projects, and the like, has convinced me that all dreams serve evolving health and wholeness, not only for the individual dreamer, but for the society, the species, and the cosmos as a whole. The projection of disowned and rejected aspects of the whole self out onto others is an act of self-hatred. When the dreams repeatedly offer and show us symbolic examples of these denied aspects of our being, we have the opportunity to re-collect ourselves, and in so doing, radically alter our relationship with the world and a whole. It is truly said that the truth shall set us free, and our dreams serve the deeper truths of our lives, both individual and collective, on a regular, nightly basis. The exploration of dreams actively promotes the insights and creative energies that are instrumental in the "reconciliation of each with all."

In this connection, it is interesting to note that as of this writing (12/93), the professional Association for the Study of Dreams is currently considering a proposal to establish a computer data base, connected to a large sample of dreamers who are in the habit of recording their dreams by writing them on their personal computers, and who would agree to log their narratives into the system on a regular basis for word-frequency analysis, in order to begin to assess the feasibility and value of such broad-based, ongoing research into the collective "trends" of statistically measurable dream content.

If (and I suspect when), such an ongoing research effort is inaugurated, the data itself will also suggest many new lines and directions of inquiry that simply are not clearly imaginable before the initial information is gathered. This is a new and potentially transformative field of inquiry and investigation into the collective significance of dreams and dreaming.

Notes

1. J. Allan Hobson, *The Dreaming Brain* (New York: Basic Books, 1988), 232.
2. For an extensive discussion of this parallel development in Catholic and Protestant thought, see Morton Kelsey's *Dreams—God's Forgotten Language* (New York: Lippincott, 1968), and *God, Dreams, and Revelation* (Minneapolis: Augsburg Publishing, 1974). The latter is a revised edition of his earlier work, *Dreams, Dark Speech of the Spirit*.
3. J. B. Priestly, *Man And Time* (New York: Dell, 1968), 352–53.
4. Quoted from James Gollnick, *Dreams in the Psychology of Religion* (Lewiston/Queenston: 1987), 146–47.
5. Ibid., 158.
6. Edward Edinger, *Ego and Archetype* (Baltimore MD: Penguin Books): 1973.
7. Hobson, Ibid., 233.
8. This collective aspect of dreamwork has been a central focus of my work for more than twenty-five years. It is discussed in much greater length and detail in my two books: *Dream Work—Techniques for Discovering the Creative Power in Dreams* (Mahwah: NJ: Paulist Press, 1983) and *Where People Fly and Water Runs Uphill—Using Dreams to Tap the Wisdom of the Unconscious* (New York: Warner Books, 1992).

Suggestions for Further Reading

(In addition to the works cited earlier, the following may be of interest in pursuing the ideas discussed here, particularly the possibilities of nonviolent collective/social/cultural change that are promoted by group dreamwork.)

Beradt, Charlotte. 1968. *The Third Reich of Dreams.* Chicago: Quadrangle Books.

Berne, Patricia, and Louis Savary. 1991. *Dream Symbol work.* Mahwah NJ: Paulist Press.

Bulkeley, Kelly. 1994. *The Wilderness of Dreams.* Albany: State University of New York Press.

Mahoney, Maria. 1970. *The Meaning in Dreams and Dreaming.* New York: Citadel.

Neu, Eva. 1988. *Dreams and Dream Groups.* Freedom CA: Crossing Press.

O'Nell, Carl. 1976. *Dreams, Culture, and the Individual.* San Francisco: Chandler & Sharp.

Siegel, Alan. 1990. *Dreams that Can Change Your Life.* Los Angeles: Jeremy Tarcher.

Signell, Karen. 1990. *Wisdom of the Heart.* New York: Bantam.

Ullman, Montague, and Nan Zimmerman. 1979. *Working with Dreams.* New York: Delacorte.

Ullman, Montague, and Claire Limmer, eds. 1987. *The Variety of Dream Experience.* New York: Continuum.

von Grunebaum, G. E., and Roger Caillois, eds. 1966. *The Dream and Human Societies.* Berkeley: University of California.

Chapter 8

Invitation at the Threshold

Pre-Death Spiritual Experiences

Patricia Bulkley

Aunt Jo lay dying in the hospital. She had lived 103 "wonderful years" as she described them, and had told us many times that she was "ready to go." My cousin Richard was sitting at her bedside watching over her as she slept. Slowly her eyes opened and with growing recognition she looked at him first with astonishment and then a gathering sadness filled her eyes. "But you can't be here, you can't," she whispered.

Richard, now feeling her concern himself, leaned closer and said, "But I am here, right here next to you. What's the matter?"

"Grandpa Will, Charlie, Aunt Kate and Aunt Francis are all here, come to get me. But it's not your time yet. Why are you here with us?"

Richard smiled at her, thinking to himself that the old dear had become even more confused in these past few days. He patted his chest with his hands and said, "Look, it's me. I'm the only one here." Then taking her hand in his he added kindly, "You're fine. Everything's just fine."

Richard told me this story a week later at Aunt Jo's funeral and I was fascinated. What had been going on? It appeared that Aunt Jo was dreaming about deceased family members who had come to do what? Accompany her to the next world? And then, upon awakening, she saw

Richard in their midst. Had she somehow mixed her dream world and her real world together?

About a year later I joined the patient care team at Hospice as spiritual care provider. As I began my work at Hospice and spent my days with dying people, I began hearing stories akin to the one Richard had told me about Aunt Jo. In some ways they were quite different, in other ways they were remarkably alike. Let me cite some examples:

- One woman saw a halo of shimmering golden light around the framed picture of her deceased husband which sat on her bedside table.
- A man dreamed that the Virgin Mary, about the size of a small statute, was standing at the foot of his bed with her hand out saying, "Come." It was a tradition in this family for the Virgin to appear at the time of death.
- A young cancer patient named Ashley dreamed of a classmate who had died recently in a car wreck. He was sitting in a red convertible and offered her a ride.
- Susan, who was dying of a brain tumor, dreamed of little Kathy, a friend of her son's, who had died the year before in an accident. Susan was able to tell the dead child's mother that she had seen Kathy, would be with her soon and would tell Kathy how very much her family missed her.
- An elderly gentleman from China saw his parents and grandparents standing in the doorway holding orchids. This vision had a profound spiritual significance for him. At his memorial service his picture was surrounded by orchids.
- A man who had been a merchant marine captain in the Far East in the 1930s dreamed that he was setting sail into uncharted waters. He said the dream brought back the old excitement he had felt as a youth when "the sea called." Because of this dream his near paralyzing fear of impending death was transformed into a sense of adventure and expectation.

Pre-death dreams and visions are often religiously significant and transformative, that is, spiritual reality for the patient is reconstructed.

The person's perception of death is altered in such a way that fear is reduced.[1]

The pre-death dream or vision manifests itself in a variety of ways. Some are dreams, some visions and some a bit of both, especially for people very close to death. People report seeing family members and friends who are already dead. Others see religious figures and scenes from sacred writings. In some, the people talk together, in others they are silent. There are experiences that are only visual, or only musical or only tactile. The setting can be right there in their room or anywhere else. The people having the experience range from having a deeply developed life of faith to those who describe themselves as totally rational and "rooted in reality."

My experience has been that every pre-death dream and vision is unique to the person who experiences it and reflects their cultural situation (religion, ethnic background, family configuration, and so on). The pre-death dreams and visions incorporate the patient's own imagery, language and cultural mythology.

In view of all this variety, do pre-death spiritual experiences have anything in common? Yes. According to what has been reported to me, in nearly every case the experience has had a positive effect on the level of the patient's fear of death. The transformation of the dying person's worldview lessens anxiety. Some state unequivocally that their fear is gone. Others that it is greatly reduced. Some say that they are still afraid of the actual process of dying but no longer fear being dead.

Does the effect of the pre-death dreams and visions reach beyond just the patient experiencing it? Family members and friends say yes. Occasionally a person close to the patient will report a "companion" dream or vision where the imagery is related in substantive ways to the pre-death dreams and visions of the patient. For the most part, however, family reaction is centered on the patient's experience, and the reactions vary considerably. Some completely discount it saying, "It was only drug related." Or, "Uncle so and so always was a little crazy, this proves it."

In many cases, however, the patient's pre-death dreams and visions have a profound affect on his/her family. The story Michael told me is a good illustration.

Michael's wife Jane was dying of cancer. It was not his first acquaintance with the death of a loved one. His two sons had died before, one at the age of two of a disease and the other at fifteen in an automobile accident. Michael and Jane, both devout Roman Catholics, had stayed after Mass on Sunday to pray quietly. Jane's eyes were closed but Michael noticed that her lips were moving. He did not disturb her but waited until they were leaving the sanctuary to ask her about it. She told him the following:

"I became aware of Sammy and Teddy standing before me. They looked so natural and happy. I felt overcome by love and a desire to be with them. They laughed and said that in just a short while we would be together again and how wonderful that would be. I have a warm comfortable feeling all over just thinking of being with them."

In the days of pain and grief that lay ahead for both Michael and Jane, they both had Jane's spiritual experience to comfort them. Jane's view of death as a harsh interloper in the middle of life was softened considerably. Michael's sense of overwhelming grief at the impending loss of yet another beloved person in his life was now accompanied by feelings of hope. Jane would soon be united with their sons in God's loving presence and when Michael died he, too, would experience this wondrous reunion.

The effect of Jane's pre-death dream and vision continues as the story is told and retold. It causes others to wonder about their own deaths and what lies beyond. It opens the possibilities of new worlds and in the process can have a positive effect on our own sense of dread at the thought of death.

Is it possible to actually measure the fear-reducing effects of a pre-death dream and vision? Possibly, but only indirectly for the following two reasons. First, the person having the experience is in the process of dying. Communication is often limited at this time by physical impairments. I suspect, in fact, that the vast majority of pre-death dreams and visions are never made known or detected by others. So often a family member will say something like, "Right at the end Papa opened his eyes and reached his arms toward heaven. A look of rapture came over his face. Then he closed his eyes and died." We will never know what he saw. After death has in fact occurred, the person, of course, cannot tell us.

Second, I feel any attempt by a pastoral care giver or anyone else to impose on a patient a set of questions designed to measure fear would be inappropriate. A person's dying time is sacred to them and their loved ones. Interruptions, however well intended, could interfere with just the process of spiritual transformation we are seeking to understand. Death is a spiritual event and should be treated by all with reference and respect.

I do, however, have a wealth of information that has come from careful observation and first-hand conversations. I have been told the stories of innumerable pre-death dreams and visions. They reveal with few exceptions that the patient has become less fearful and less agitated. Most often the death is described as peaceful.

The following is the story of one woman's dying time that was profoundly affected by a pre-death spiritual experience.

Margaret, a counselor at Hospice, was concerned about one of our patients, Ruth, who had only a few weeks to live and who was extremely anxious and increasingly agitated. Her Christian faith, which had been a meaningful part of her life since childhood had, in her words, "just up and disappeared." She no longer believed in Jesus Christ, the Resurrection, or in any of the rest of that "stuff." Ruth was worried sick over what to say to her pastor of many years and she was angry that now, just now, when she really needed it, her religion had vanished. Margaret asked Ruth if she would be open to a visit from me. She was and we made an appointment for the following morning.

Ruth and her husband lived in a comfortable middle-class suburban home situated on one of the bay inlets. Sitting in the living room we could see their dock off the back deck and just beyond an inviting marine vista of white boats, colorful flags, and the sparkling blue waters of the lagoon. The room itself was comfortably filled with family pictures and mementos of the travels that had taken Ruth and John to the four corners of the world. Every table held bouquets of garden flowers brought by the many friends who dropped in to say hello. A large orange tabby cat lay peacefully sunning himself near the sliding glass doors. Every now and again his ear would flick, just enough to let us know that he was listening to the cadence of our voices.

Ruth and John had been married for thirty-seven years and had two grown children who were in their thirties. I was struck by Ruth's apparent lack of pain and level of energy. She told me that she had been sick for only two years. It was the kind of cancer characterized by little ongoing pain but a rapid decline in the end. Her doctor had recently told her that she was experiencing the onset of that decline now.

At the beginning of our conversation I told her that I was the person from the Hospice patient care team who was particularly interested in spiritual matters, that I was an interfaith minister bringing no particular message and that if she wanted to talk for a while, I was there to listen.

She laughed a little self-consciously and said, "Well, I don't know. You'll probably think what I'm going to tell you is just awful and want to leave."

I shook my head a little, smiled and replied, "Don't worry, I won't leave. What's going on?"

There was a long pause, then she heaved a great sigh and began to speak.

Ruth had been brought up in a family of committed Protestants and had learned her faith in an old-fashioned Sunday school from kindly teachers. She loved God and believed the stories in the Bible. Ruth's family had been poor, hard hit by the depression. However, they had managed somehow, and had been relatively happy in the process. Her parents placed a high value on education, and through hard work and sacrifice each child in the family eventually had been given the opportunity to go to college. Ruth majored in literature and all through the years continued to read good books and show an interest in new ideas.

She had continued also in her religious practices. She attended the local Methodist church on a fairly regular basis. When her children were young she taught Sunday school. Occasionally she took part in church-related projects. She knew the current pastor quite well and was planning to have him conduct her memorial service.

But, now, all of a sudden, her religious beliefs had evaporated and she was beside herself. How could she die without God? Was there no heaven after all? She wasn't even sure that she wanted a Christian funeral and that would upset everyone. "I'm scared to death," she said, and buried her face in her hands.

After a pause I asked her if she could remember what was happening at the time that she first noticed her faith changing. She said she had been reading some books on Eastern spirituality and one in particular by a "guru type" as she described him. "All of a sudden it didn't seem possible that God could be captured in any earthly frame of reference. All we can know is a Presence, that's it, a 'Creative Presence'." At that point she started to cry again, and then sobbed. "I've lost it all. What am I going to do? Now that I've told you I bet you don't want to talk to me anymore."

I took her hand in mine and waited a few moments. Then I said, "Ruth, I do want to talk with you. I know this has been very hard for you. Let's just take it slowly together. Maybe things aren't quite as bad as they seem. Because of the nature of faith development, a spiritual crisis often signals the beginning of significant spiritual growth."[2]

While listening to Ruth it occurred to me that she was probably in just such a time of faith transition and rather than losing her faith completely, as she feared, she was more likely to be undergoing a faith transformation. Because she was intelligent and open to new ideas, I asked if she would be interested in my thoughts about what was happening to her spiritually. She was eager to hear. As she listened to my explanation of faith development theories, I could see her body begin to relax.

"I guess I need to just let these new ideas about the Presence unfold within," she said. I agreed. We ended our time together then and made plans to meet again in three days.

When I arrived on Friday, Ruth opened the door as I was ringing the bell, and ushered me into the living room. Before I was fully seated, she said, "Something's happened! I've had a dream, in fact I've had the same dream three times in a row!"

"Tell me about it."

"It was the same dream every night just as I went to sleep. There were several huge deep blue boulders with eerie blue lights pulsating from them. They made a very loud wailing sound. All my attention was riveted right there. It was frightening, no, awesome, no, really frightening. Then I was awake again. The image of the boulders was gone, but all I had to do was close my eyes and it was back. And yet I didn't have a hard time going back to sleep. This happened three nights in a row."

I asked Ruth to tell me more about the noise.

"It was very loud and crashing, like whole mountains were moving. It didn't make me afraid I would be hurt. But it filled every possible space where noise could be and just engulfed me."

"Can you described the color and how it moved?"

"The blue was very deep, almost purple and had a metallic quality. Very deep and very blue, the most blue of blue. And it pulsated, sort of danced like the Northern Lights. It was alive and compelling. Those boulders were awesome. And that was it. It sounds so simple as I tell you but it was truly incredible to experience."

"What do you make of it? Does anything come to mind as you remember the dream?"

"It was like drums beating so loud that you think they are your heartbeat. It was the Presence, whatever that means. Not the boulders themselves or the noise itself. The Presence was all around. I was spellbound."

"The Presence?"

"Yes, it filled my heart and soul. I felt saturated, and then the whole thing faded. And there's something else. After the second night I called my daughter on the phone and told her about the boulders. She called me back the next morning to say that she had had a dream about boulders too. In her dream the boulders were stone gray and there wasn't any accompanying noise. Isn't that amazing? Imagine us sharing this dream! I feel like we're closer together."

"Really."

"We haven't always agreed on things but since I've been sick it has been different. Julie's really so wonderful and sensitive to what I'm feeling."

For the next week or so I continued to visit Ruth every few days. She became comfortable with her transformed understanding of God as spiritual Presence and reveled in the fact of God's great freedom in the vastness of space. "I don't need to know anything more than that," she said. "God is God, that's all that matters."

She even invited her pastor over and told him of her new spiritual insights. He was immensely supportive and together they planned her funeral. "It's full of surprises for the people I love," she told me later.

On the day before Ruth died I visited, knowing it was time to say goodbye. It was not easy because even in such a short time I had come to love her dearly. She was very weak and could hardly speak. She paused every moment or two to let me lightly brush her lips and teeth with cool water on a swab.

"Tish," she said quietly smiling, "I had the boulder dream again last night." I moved closer. "They had flattened into stepping stones and had moved to make sort of a path and were singing sweetly like the gentle wind. In the distance was a soft inviting clear golden light, it was the Presence calling me." Our eyes met. "It's calling me now and I want to go. The curtains no longer keep out the light. Nor the walls. He's here with us now. The light is right behind you." I wanted to turn and look but was afraid.

Ruth's sense of peace and rapture touched me deeply as I kissed her goodbye. Turning to leave her bedside I noticed that the nurse who had been in the room with us was crying softly. She too had been overcome by Ruth's words.

The next afternoon Ruth's husband called Hospice to tell us that she had died peacefully surrounded by her family.

I do not think that anyone can hear the story of Ruth's death without experiencing a myriad of personal feelings. For many people being part of another's death is like looking in the mirror. We see our own mortality staring back at us and are forced, at least momentarily, to consider it. We ask ourselves, what will death be like? How will it feel? What lies beyond? What is the meaning of life?

These are the big questions that have been asked throughout the ages. Unfortunately, these are also the questions that our society, for the most part, assiduously avoids. We shrink back in fear of the unknown. We cling to "the rational" as the only way of knowing and miss whole worlds of possibility. And we go to any length to perpetuate the "denial of death" our culture dictates. We lie to our children, place inordinate value on staying young, pay millions to authors to tell us that if we only have the right attitude we can cure a terminal illness. Our undertakers define their art by how natural and lifelike they can make a dead body look and we hide dying people out of sight in hospitals and so-called convalescent hospitals. Unlike other cultures where death is seen as a natural transition to another state of being, we go to any lengths to stave off death, spending billions on useless medical procedures and drugs in the last year of life.

I also do not think that anyone can hear the story of Ruth's death without being drawn into the wonder and mystery of it. We see reflected in her death the possibilities of significant spiritual insight and growing desire to venture into the unknown. Ruth's story shows us that death at home can occupy a valued place in the very midst of family life. No need to deny death here. She has the freedom to talk about her feelings as she reviews her life, almost complete in one sense, and yet in another stretching out far into the future through her children and grandchildren.

Her family can openly begin their work of grieving the physical separation to come. They can resolve old grievances and know the joy of forgiveness. They can express their love and hear those precious words in return. After Ruth's death these will be the treasured memories that comfort their grief and soften their tears.

Of course, all of death is not good. But it is not all bad either. My question is this. How can we make a dent, even a small dent in the excessive fear of death that grips our culture?

If the pre-death dreams and visions can be transformative for dying people and reduce their fear, why couldn't the same hold true for society? If people in general were to become familiar with pre-death dreams and visions perhaps their fear would lessen too.

Fear of death appears to stem from three main sources: the existential fear that at death we simply cease to exist, fear of facing the unknown alone and for some, religious-based fear of reprisal. The pre-death religious experience undermines all three fears. The dying person's world view is transformed into a new understanding. Life is experienced that transcends the grave, some of the unknown becomes known and fear of a vengeful God is for the most part dispelled.

My hope is that those who study dreams will draw attention to the important role pre-death dreams and visions play in our understanding and experience of death. The result would be a significant impact not only on our fear of death but also on the quality of our *life*. Few would disagree about the positive aspects of the pre-death dreams and visions for dying people and their loved ones. But the advantages need not stop there.

Imagine what would happen if the pervasive fear and denial of death in our society were to significantly decrease. The effects would be felt in everything from substance abuse, to family violence, to medical delivery systems, to religious concepts of the nature of God, just to name a few. Perhaps even the ultimate goal of death with dignity for every human being could become a reality. My challenge to those who work in the field of dreams is that this very real possibility for the betterment of society will be taken up in earnest.

𝒩otes

1. My use of transformative events as descriptive of pre-death dreams or visions is drawn from James Loder's excellent book *The Transforming Moment*. Loder explores the process which takes place resulting in a transformed perception of reality by carefully studying the "event" to determine its essential nature.

There are five steps in this process. First there is a felt sense of *conflict* which draws our attention. Next the unconscious conducts an underground search or *scanning* action which eventually results in a plausible solution or *insight* which transforms the previously held worldview. We then test the outcome to *verify* that the conflicting elements have indeed been transformed. Finally, the transformative event is *interpreted*. This process constitutes, according to Loder, "all the essential features of an event that transforms" (p. 36).

Let us now look at pre-death spiritual experience in terms of Loder's criteria for a transformative event. The conflict first appears in a situational context. Certain assumptions are taken as normative. Let us use the example of the Chinese gentleman who has the vision of his parents and grandparents. The assumption is that these people have been dead for several years. Then something happens, there is a "rupture in the inherent pattern of knowing" (p. 37). He has the vision.

Loder makes two interesting observations at this point in the process. He says that the more one cares about the conflict the more powerful will be the knowing event. And it is a knowing event of far greater personal significance if the initial conflict is not artificially generated from the outside but a conflict that the knower had had all along but not recognized. In our example, both observations have merit. This man cared deeply about his ancestors and he had for a long time been troubled by the conflict he felt between his religious value of ancestor worship and the pervasive American cultural denigration of the elderly.

Next in the process comes the interlude for scanning. The person is temporarily baffled, shifts through various possibilities, and searches for explanations. Our patient wonders how it can be that his dead parents are dead and yet right there in the doorway alive. Then comes "the constructive act of the imagination." At this point, an insight appears often with convincing force and a meaningful unity arises that resolves the conflict. Loder states, "This is the turning point of the knowing event" (p. 38). Our patient, through the vision, realizes that he has experienced while still in this world, a part of the world of his dead parents. He had always been told of the ongoing existence of ancestors. Now he has experienced it for himself. The construction of this insight is the transformation.

Next in Loder's process, there is a release of energy as the conflict is resolved and consciousness is expanded. A sense of liberation is felt and the person becomes open to further associations carrying the implications of the resolution even further. Our patient experiences a sense of peace in the context of his dying and begins to wonder about further possibilities of life in the next world.

In the fifth and final step the transformative event is completed. The event is interpreted and the knower's world is now reconfigured in a new way. In our example, the Chinese gentleman's vision of his relatives standing in the doorway holding orchids became the impetus for the transformation of his worldview. His interior spiritual life has been reclaimed from the shadows.

James Loder defines transformation by saying, "This key term does not refer merely to change in a positive direction, as common usage would suggest. Rather, transformation occurs whenever, within a given frame of reference or experience, hidden orders of coherence and meaning emerge to replace or alter the axioms of the given frame and reorder its elements accordingly" (p. 229). The pre-death spiritual experience activates a transformation. Spiritual reality for the patient is reconstructed.

2. It was here that I became thankful, as I have been many times in the past, for the work of James Fowler and the others who study and write about faith development. According to Fowler, faith development is a constructionist rather than developmental process. This means that between one stage and the next, the currently held faith stance is not simply added to, but breaks down during the transition and a new understanding of faith comes into being. In the process, religious beliefs that may have sustained a person for years can be shaken to the core. It is a time when knowledgeable ministers and spiritual companions need to be particularly supportive of those whose spiritual lives are in a process of transformation.

Chapter 9

Western Dreams about Eastern Dreams

Wendy Doniger

1. *What can we learn about dreams from the myths of other cultures?*

It is often argued that quantum physics confirms Zen Buddhism, that our own "modern" ideas were prefigured by "Oriental" mythologies. This may or may not be so, but I do not think it is a useful path to follow. Instead, I would argue that some of the insights of non-Western mythologies do indeed bear striking resemblances to some of the most abstract formulations of modern science, but only because the same basic human mind is searching for a limited set of metaphors with which to make sense of the same basic human experiences, be their expressions Eastern or Western, "factual" or imaginative. This is the bridge that justifies our attempts to gain insights about *our dreams* from the stories that other cultures tell about their dreams.

2. *What relevance does our understanding of lucid dreams, on the one hand, and orgasmic dreams, on the other, have for the interpretation of myths about sexual dreams?*

Stephen LaBerge has summarized the growing literature on what are called lucid dreams, which take place "when we 'awaken' within our dreams—without disturbing or ending the dream state—and learn to recognize that we are dreaming while the dream is still happening."[1] In addition to demonstrating that such dreams do occur, LaBerge goes on

169

to argue that they can be made to occur. He cites, first, a passage from Hervey de Saint-Denys:

> I dreamt that I was out riding in fine weather. I became aware of my true situation, and remembered the question of whether or not I could exercise free will in controlling my actions in a dream. "Well now," I said to myself, "This horse is only an illusion; this countryside that I am passing through is merely stage scenery. But even if I have not evoked these images by conscious volition, I certainly seem to have some control over them." I decide to gallop, I gallop; I decide to stop, I stop. Now here are two roads in front of me. The one on the right appears to plunge into a dense wood; the one on the left leads to some kind of ruined manor; I feel quite distinctly that I am free to turn either right or left, and so decide for myself whether I wish to produce images relating to the ruins or images relating to the wood.[2]

This is also a classical mythological image; the challenge of controlling a horse functions as a metaphor for free will and the harnessing of the senses in Plato, the Upanisads, and many other texts throughout the world. Here the image of controlling the horse seems to me to express for Saint-Denys his ability to control his own dreams.

For LaBerge, "This brings up two questions regarding control of lucid dreaming. The first is, how much is possible? . . . The second question regarding dream control involves what kind is desirable."[3] This is a problem on which the mythology of dream narratives, particularly orgasmic dream narratives, sheds some light.

On the one hand, orgasmic dreams seem to be significantly different, in physiological terms, from lucid erotic dreams:

> Wet dreams may result from genital stimulation and reflex ejaculation. . . . Wet dreams would be the result of actual erotic sensations accurately interpreted by the dreaming brain. In other words, first comes the ejaculation, then comes the wet dream. Apparently, the opposite normally holds for lucid dream orgasms. The erotic dream comes first, resulting in orgasm "in the brain." However, in this case, the resulting impulses descending from the brain to the genitals are evidently too inhibited to trigger the genital ejaculatory reflex. So, reflex dreams are only wet in the dream.[4]

In lucid erotic dreams, by contrast, there is some physiological change, but not as much as in a genuine, nonlucid wet dream. A woman named "Miranda" dreamt, in a lucid dream, that she was flying, found an attractive man, made love with him, and experienced an orgasm. "She said the dream orgasm had been neither long nor intense, but was quite definitely a real orgasm." In the laboratory experiments, measurements of vaginal blood flow and heart rate "provided the first objective evidence for the validity of Miranda's reports (and, by extension, those of others) of vividly realistic sex in lucid dreams."[5] And a man who had a lucid orgasmic dream reported, "Although I found I had not actually ejaculated, I still felt the tingling in my spine and I marveled at the reality that the mind could create."[6]

The mental intensity of nonejaculatory erotic dreams is still more complex than this evidence implies:

> Men whose spinal cords have been shattered through injury, so that there is no longer any nervous connection between their brains and their lower bodies, still have sexual dreams in which they experience all the feelings and sensations of orgasm. The basis of this experience is not in their isolated lower bodies. It is wholly within their brains.[7]

In other words, this man, incapable of a physiological orgasm, had a vivid lucid dream of orgasm.

Thus, as LaBerge points out, "In some respects, lucid dream sex has as powerful an impact on the dreamer's body as the real thing.[8] . . . What happens in the inner world of dreams—and lucid dreams, especially—can produce physical effects on the dreamer's brain no less real than those produced by corresponding events happening in the external world."[9] We are left, therefore, with a paradox: the lucid orgasmic dream produces erection, excitement (often said to be more mentally intense than in a real orgasm), but no significantly heightened heartbeat and no actual ejaculation. Is it, therefore, more or less real than a wet dream?

An orgasmic wet dream is physically real; a real orgasm has taken place, inside and outside the body of the dreamer, and it seems at first to have happened more or less as it would have taken place had the dream partner been physically present. In another sense, however, the orgasmic dream is emotionally unreal; one has had a fantasy of an experience that cannot be entirely real without a partner. The semen is a biological fact, but it is proof only of the fantasy. Unlike other "things" that the hero brings back from the dream world, the semen cannot prove the physical existence of the person who caused it to be present in the dream — the lover from the other world. Like the dream itself, semen is "emitted" by the dreamer in one of the basic processes of illusory creation.

Another way to approach this problem is to return to the question of control, for one cannot control an orgasmic dream as one can control a lucid dream. The element of control brings the lucid dream closer to the *mental* waking world but, there being less physiological response, farther from the *physical* waking world. Indian philosophical texts tell us a great deal about the control of lucid dreams, and Indian mythological texts tell us a great deal about the experience of orgasmic dreams. LaBerge attempts to apply the Oriental dream-control techniques of yogis and shamans to Western goals of improving one's life, or even, indeed, one's lifestyle. But this cannot be done.

The yogis' goals and assumptions differ from ours; their gods are not our gods. On the one hand, they are not trying to get ahead in the world of *samsara* (material life and rebirth); they are trying to leave it (as the texts that LaBerge cites show). They do not use dream techniques for the sorts of things that yuppies want to have; no Hindu would name a sexy perfume "Samsara," as Guerlain has done.[10]

Yet yogis are not control freaks; on the contrary, the key to all of their meditational techniques is the cultivation of a complete emptying out of oneself, a complete passivity, so that God, or the force of the universe, takes over. This approach is closer to the old Alcoholics Anonymous slogan—"Let go and let God"—than it is to any self-help creed. So, too, in the "Oriental" stories of shared dreams, the mutuality is always conceived of as passive, and the dreamer is at the mercy of the lover; these are myths of surrender, not myths of conquest. For both of these reasons, therefore, the control achieved in yogic dreams would never be applied to orgasmic dreams, since yogis would not want to have an orgasmic dream, and since orgasmic dreams are, in stories at least, passive.

But these are merely symptoms of the underlying, far more basic problem: that the healing techniques of India are designed to heal what Indians think of as the human person, more precisely to produce what Indians think of as a good (or normal, or healthy, or realized—choose your own ideal) person. And such a person is someone embedded in an Indian social system, someone whose expectations of relationships with parents, children, spouse, and everyone else are very different from our own. Ideas such as "individual" and "maturity' would have been utter nonsense to the authors of the textbooks on yogic techniques. It is therefore problematic—not impossible, perhaps, but certainly more problematic than is usually acknowledged—for a Westerner to achieve an Eastern enlightenment.[11]

3. *What can Hindu mythology tell us about the problems inherent in our attempts to study someone else's dreams?*

I have attempted elsewhere[12] to approach this problem through he use of a story that occurs in the great Sanskrit compendium of dream narratives, the *Yogavasistha*, a Sanskrit philosophical treatise composed in Kashmir sometime between the tenth and twelfth centuries C.E. The myth is the story of a hunter who meets a sage who has entered another man's body and lodged in his head:

> One day a hunter wandered in the woods until he came to the home of a sage, who became his teacher. The sage told him this story:
>
> In the old days, I became an ascetic sage and lived alone in a hermitage. I studied magic. I entered someone else's body and saw all his organs; I entered his head and then I saw a universe, with a sun and an ocean and mountains, and gods and demons and human beings. This universe was his dream, and I saw his dream. Inside his head, I saw his city and his wife and his servants and his son.
>
> When darkness fell, he went to bed and slept, and I slept too. Then his world was overwhelmed by a flood at doomsday; I, too, was swept away in the flood, and though I managed to obtain a foothold on a rock, a great wave knocked me into the water again. When I saw that world destroyed at doomsday, I wept. I still saw, in my own dream, a whole universe, for I had picked up his karmic memories along with his dream. I had become involved in that world and I forgot my former life; I thought, "This is my father, my mother, my village, my house, my family."
>
> Once again I saw doomsday. This time, however, even while I was being burnt up by the flames, I did not suffer, for I realized, "This is just a dream." Then I forgot my own experiences. Time passed. A sage came to my house, and slept and ate, and as we were talking after dinner he said, "Don't you know that all of this is a dream? I am a man in your dream, and you are a man in someone else's dream."

Then I awakened, and remembered my own nature; I remembered that I was an ascetic. And I said to him, "I will go to that body of mine (that was an ascetic)," for I wanted to see my own body as well as the body which I had set out to explore. But he smiled and said, "Where do you think those two bodies of yours are?" I could find no body, nor could I get out of the head of the person I had entered, and so I asked him, "Well, where *are* the two bodies?"

The sage replied, "While you were in the other person's body, a great fire arose, that destroyed your body as well as the body of the other person. Now you are a householder, not an ascetic." When the sage said this, I was amazed. He lay back on his bed in silence in the night, and I did not let him go away: he stayed with me until he died.

The hunter said, "If this is so, then you and I and all of us are people in one another's dreams." The sage continued to teach the hunter and told him what would happen to him in the future. But the hunter left him and went on to new rebirths. Finally, the hunter became an ascetic and found release. [13]

As we read the story of the hunter and the sage, we become confused and are tempted to draw charts to figure it all out. It is not clear, for instance, whether the sage has entered the waking world or the sleeping world of the man whose consciousness he penetrates, and whether that person is sleeping, waking, or, indeed, dead at the moment when we meet the sage. But as the tale progresses, we realize that our confusion is neither our own mistake nor the mistake of the author of the text; it is a device of the narrative, constructed to make us realize how impossible and, finally, how irrelevant it is to attempt to determine the precise level of consciousness at which we are existing. We cannot do it, and it does not matter. We can never know whether or not we have become trapped inside the minds of people whose consciousness we have come to share.

Inside the dream village, the new householder (*né* sage) meets another sage, who enlightens him and wakes him up. Yet, although he is explicitly said to awaken, he stays where he is inside the dream; the only difference is that now he knows he is inside the dream. Now he becomes a sage again, but a different sort of sage, a householder sage, inside the dreamer's dream. While he is in this state, he meets the hunter and attempts to instruct him. But the hunter misses the point of the sage's saga: "If this is so . . . ," he mutters, and he goes off to get a whole series of bodies before he finally figures it out. The hunter has to experience everything for himself, dying and being reborn;[14] he cannot learn merely by dreaming, as the sage does.[15]

This story can teach us many things. On the one hand, it may provide a wonderful example of a lucid dream, to encourage us in our attempts to find out more about our own lucid dreams. But, on the other hand, it may serve as a caveat, a warning of the possible dangers of attempting to get into other peoples' heads to understand their dreams. Since dreams are often the fulcrum of our whole unconscious personality, to apply *someone else's lever* at this point may uproot far more than we intended; it may tear out not only the roots of our own particular life but the deeper roots that our society has implanted in us, roots that are also, by this time, deeply imbedded in the unconscious. This may catapult us into an entirely different world—and, as the story of the hunter demonstrates, it is not always as easy to get out of such a world as it is to get in.

Notes

This essay is taken in large part from an invited address presented at the Seventh International Conference of the Association for the Study of Dreams, Chicago, 28 June 1990.

1. Stephen LaBerge, *Lucid Dreaming: The Power of Being Awake and Aware in Your Dreams* (New York: Ballantine Books, 1985).

2. Hervey de Saint Denys, *Dreams and How to Guide Them* (London: Duckworth, 1982). Cited in LaBerge, *Lucid Dreaming*, 116.

3. LaBerge, *Lucid Dreaming*, 117.

4. Ibid., 95.

5. Ibid., 91.

6. Ibid., 93.

7. Oswald, cited by Charles Rycroft, *The Innocence of Dreams* (New York: Pantheon, 1979), 111.

8. LaBerge, *Lucid Dreaming*, 93.

9. Ibid., 97.

10. See Wendy Doniger O'Flaherty, *Dreams Illusion and Other Realities* (Chicago: University of Chicago, 1984), passim.

11. For further discussion of the problems inherent in cross-cultural interpretations of symbols, see Wendy Doniger, "When a Lingam

is just a good cigar," in the Festschrift for Alan Dundes, ed. L. Bryce Boyer, forthcoming in a special issue of *The Analytic Quarterly.*

12. See Wendy Doniger O'Flaherty, *Other Peoples' Myths: The Cave of Echoes* (New York: Macmillan, 1988).

13. *Yogavasishtha-Maha-Ramayana* of Valmiki, ed. W. L. S. Pansikar, 2 vols. (Bombay, 1918), 6.2.136–57.

14. See the story of the hundred Rudras and the wild goose in chapter 5 of O'Flaherty, *Dreams.*

15. O'Flaherty, *Other Peoples' Myths*, 7-10.

IV.

Dreams
and
Critical
Reflections
on
"Our"
Culture

Political Dreaming

Dreams of the 1992 Presidential Election

Kelly Bulkeley

A couple of years ago I was working my way through the major works of Calvin Hall, as part of my doctoral dissertation research. As I read Hall's book *The Meaning of Dreams* (1966), I came across the following passage:

> Dreams contain few ideas of a political or economic nature. They have little or nothing to say about current events in the world of affairs. . . . Presidential elections, declarations of war, the diplomatic struggles of great powers, major athletic contests, all of the happenings that appear in newspapers and become the major topics of conversation among people are pretty largely ignored in dreams. (11)

For some reason this passage bothered me. Of course, I understood Hall's basic point, that we usually dream about personal matters like the health of our body and the relationships we have with family and friends. And I knew that other dream experts basically agreed with Hall; most psychologists, sleep laboratory researchers, and writers of popular books on dreams also regard dreams as speaking solely to the personal life concerns of the dreamer.

But still, I was bothered. Hall's claim seemed too strong, too sweeping. The more I thought about it, the more examples I found that challenged Hall. Jung's autobiography *Memories Dreams, Reflections*

(1965) presents a number of his dreams that spoke directly to the political situation of his world. Charlotte Beradt's moving book *The Third Reich of Dreams* (1966) contains dozens of dreams of people living in 1933–1939 Germany—dreams that directly addressed the rising political power of Nazism.[1] Carl Schorske (1987) wrote a fascinating article on the striking political references in Freud's "Count Thun" dream. Cross-cultural studies are filled with dreams that have direct relevance to the dreamer's social and political world.[2] And I myself have had many dreams in which politicians and political events play a prominent role.

As scattered as these references to politically relevant dreams were, I felt there were enough of them to refute Hall's claim, at least in its simplest form: politics do appear in people's dreams, and people do dream about the political affairs of their communities.

But now I had two new questions to ask. First, what do such dreams *mean*? Are these dreams *really* about politics, or are they just *using* political imagery to express other kinds of meaning? And, second, why are dream researchers like Hall so insistent that dreams are *not* relevant to political affairs, and relate *only* to personal, subjective realms of the dreamer's life?

As the 1992 U.S. presidential election approached, I realized I had a perfect opportunity to explore these questions in more detail. This election promised to be an exciting, passionately waged contest. Fear about the economy, anger at incumbents, disgust with "politics as usual," hopes for real change—no election campaign in years had stirred up such deep, powerful emotions in the American electorate. I decided that if people did *not* dream about politics during this presidential election, then Hall was right and I would just drop the subject. But I thought that if people *did* dream about the election, I might be able to get a better understanding of (1) what those dreams meant, and (2) why the field of dream studies has such difficulties in recognizing the political relevance of our dreams.

In the weeks leading up to the 1992 U.S. presidential election I conducted a small study on how people's dreams were responding to the campaign. I asked twelve people to keep detailed dream diaries from 25 October to 8 November, the two weeks straddling the election. These people did not know what my study was about. I also asked a second group of about forty people to tell me if they had any dreams relating to the presidential campaign. The members of these two groups were quite varied in terms of age, education, occupation, geographical residence, and political outlook.[3]

My basic finding was that many people dreamed about the presidential election. Not everyone in my study had dreams that referred to the candidates or the election campaign, but many people *did* have such dreams. Among my "blind" subjects, six of the twelve people (50%) had at least one dream relating to the election. Of the 113 total dreams reported by the twelve subjects, ten dreams related to the election, or about 9 percent of the total dreams. I want to emphasize that my study was not based on an absolutely random sample. If my findings have any value, it is not for what they prove, but rather for what they suggest about the relationship between dreams and politics.

The Debates

A number of dreams reacted to the four presidential and vice-presidential debates that were held prior to the election. The reactions were not favorable. Hank, a government employee in his late thirties, dreamed this right after the first presidential debate:

> I am watching something like a presidential debate on TV. . . . Bush is attacking Clinton because of a mistake that Clinton made in managing his financial accounts. Clinton apparently let one of his accounts get overdrawn, and has lost the account as a result. Bush is saying that this is bad. . . . A woman reporter comments that Clinton's position in the campaign was so strong that he is still a little bit ahead of the president, even after his mistake. She says to Bush that, if it weren't for this mistake, Clinton would have been able to "wipe your wild side for being so soft." Bush is enraged at this comment. He loses control of his emotions. He leaves his podium, goes over to the reporter, and physically attacks her. I can't believe this is happening. I tell my father that "George Bush just lost it." Some people are trying to subdue the president and get him back to his podium. The woman reporter is very shaken, and leaves the stage. Then there is a view of the room from straight overhead. As some people are leaving, some other people throw food at them. The whole situation degenerates into a fight, with people throwing things at each other and running around the room.

Hank proudly noted that this dream came *before* the rambunctious vice-presidential debate, which many pundits referred to as a "food fight." Maggie, an artist from Chicago in her early thirties, also dreamed of the political campaign as a kind of food fight:

> I am running down a spiral staircase. The staircase is in the middle of a duplex office where there is a food fight/political fight going on. I don't want any part of it.

This same distaste for the childish behavior of the candidates prompted Carla, a retired copywriter from Texas, to dream this the night after the vice-presidential debate:

> I was watching a two-year-old, blond baby boy. I latched the screen doors, but he hit the screen door and the hook slipped free and he ran out. I ran after him, calling, "Danny Quail, come back here. How did you get loose?" When I brought the child back I looked at the latch and saw the problem. The part that held the hook wasn't made right. It was too thick.

Carla says she knew in the dream that she was misspelling Vice-President Quayle's last name, and thinks it may be a reference to his infamous misspelling of "potato(e)."

Ross Perot

The candidate who appeared most often in people's dreams was Ross Perot. Perot's strong personality, controversial ideas, and roller-coaster candidacy made him the object of huge voter interest. Thus, it is not surprising that people would dream about him. What is surprising is that the people in my study tended to dream about him in very anxious, very skeptical terms. Julie, a community activist in her forties from California, reported that

> On October 22 I dreamt of Ross Perot all night! I was with him sometimes. I was nearby him at other times. And I watched his face on TV also during my dream. I woke up with a strong feeling of irritation.

Julie's dream seems to reflect her reaction to Perot's late reentry into the race, and to the heavy media blitz that accompanied it. For those last couple weeks of the campaign, Perot literally was everywhere.

Most of the Perot dreams referred to his prickly personality. Maggie had a long dream of hurrying around New York because she was late for a breakfast appointment. Toward the end she dreams

> I am in a big hurry but try to stop and buy olive oil and hot peppers. I stop in a very old country store/warehouse type place. They are very friendly and very, very slow. Ross Perot is the shopkeeper and I know if I try to rush him he'll get angry and won't serve me and all the time I have already waited for him will be wasted. I think I still leave without my goods because I cannot wait any longer.

Tim, a thirty-year-old writer in Los Angeles, also dreamed of being intimidated and somewhat frightened by Perot:

> Perot is in the living room of my parents' old house . . . talking to about thirty people. He's answering some question with a parable about a horse-like Australian rodent. He's describing the animal in detail. I grow impatient and interrupt him, "Fine, the thing is horse-like, Australian, and a rodent, so what? What does it do?" The crowd doesn't share my impatience and I'm embarrassed.

The following Perot dream was told to me by Jean, a young woman who works at the Marshall Fields department store in Chicago:

> For some reason I was going to work at a state mental hospital which was being closed down. People were carrying files out, wheeling patients away. It was a big, dingy building. I and some others were waiting for the new boss to come. Much to our surprise, Ross Perot arrived. He stated that he would be running the hospital and we would work for him. He was dressed casually in a tacky purple and white outfit. He looked ridiculous. The rest of the staff gathered, and instead of taking the elevator we all walked up the stairs to prove our dedication and endurance. The climb was longer than expected and we were all complaining and some people were sick. Ross didn't know how much farther we had to go, anymore than we did. One man had a fall and broke his neck. . . . Although there were nurses there, none would help him but me. Ross didn't know what to do.

Jean said she feels the dream is a commentary on the "lunacy" of the country, and the "double lunacy" of thinking a "crazy man could be the leader of a mental hospital."

George Bush

President Bush tried to present himself in the 1992 campaign as a champion of "family values" and of experienced leadership. The dreams I gathered suggest that he succeeded in this. Jean, who describes herself as a "die-hard Republican," had the following dream:

> Bush and Quayle are in town, to give a speech, and I'm asked to set things up and cook dinner for them. It's fine, I'm proud to do it all. I cook dinner for 12,000 people, set up the speaker's hall, and work everything out with the Secret Service agents. The dinner goes off, it's finished, and they say goodbye to me. I feel very good about it all.

In this dream Jean plays the traditional role of a hostess: taking care of her guests, cooking their dinner, helping them to be safe and comfortable. Although the work seems rather demanding (where do you find place settings for 12,000 people?), Jean gets great satisfaction out of it. Her dream suggests that traditional "family values" provide her with a sense of security and fulfillment.

Of the three candidates, President Bush appeared least often in the dreams of people in my study. This supports the conclusion of most political analysts that Bush lost the election because he was "out of touch" with the real-life concerns of voters.

Bill Clinton

Bill Clinton argued that he would be an agent of *change* as president. In people's dreams Clinton often did appear as a force for change—but also as a person who is somewhat unknown, and perhaps unaware of what true changes need to be made. Patty is a young woman working in a Chicago accounting firm. Although her job pays well, she is not happy with it; she has begun going to cooking school at night to become a chef. She dreamed the following:

> I am on the top of a high-rise building, looking across the way into an apartment's picture window. . . . I am with someone I feel comfortable with, although this person's identity is unknown to me. Through the apartment window I see a half dozen or more owls looking out. . . . I then look down to my right and see Bill Clinton seated beside me. My feeling is

one of slight surprise and friendliness toward him. I immediately say, "Oh, Hi Clinton . . . I'm sorry but I can't recall your first name. . . . You know, with the continual emphasis on the name Clinton by the media. . . ." He responds that his name is Bill, and we exchange conversational niceties of "glad to meet you's," while continuing to observe the owls.

Patty said that the dream addresses her hopes and fears about switching jobs: the dream image of Clinton embodies the concept of change. Interestingly, Patty does not really *know* Clinton that well in the dream—she doesn't recognize him at first, and when she finally does she can't remember his first name. It's as if the "change" that Clinton represents is, at the present moment, an unknown factor.

Jay, a writer from Wisconsin, also dreamed of Clinton as a figure of change. But like Patty's dream, Jay's dream indicates a concern that it's hard to grasp what exactly Clinton will *do*—what kind of change he will bring.

> Clinton is at the Shedd Aquarium in Chicago. . . . The aquarium is extremely dark. . . . Some sort of voting or polling is occurring which shows Bush beating him really badly. At this point a huge, portentous voice proclaims, "Clinton will have a huge answer!" I understand this to be a response from "God" as to what Clinton must do to win the election— what he must "sacrifice," offer. Then I am catapulted *into* the scene, into the aquarium which is now *crammed with people*, followers of Clinton. . . . I unfortunately, am attempting to make my way against the overwhelming human dream tide flowing against me . . . but no matter how hard I try I make no progress against such a flow of energy. . . . I have something, some message, some warning? It is terribly important to deliver. . . .

Jay felt that Clinton's call for a "New Covenant" at the Democratic convention was an inspiring vision of a changed, renewed nation. But Jay also felt that Clinton the *politician* might not understand, or be willing to make, the frightening sacrifices that will be required to achieve those changes.

Before the Election: Skepticism

In the days leading up to the election, people's dreams showed a strong feeling of skepticism towards politicians and the whole campaign process. Patty dreamed that

I am in a large public place watching political ads on a huge video screen. . . . The ad compares two candidates to two sandwiches—comparing and contrasting. I recall a vision of a huge "pastrami-like" sandwich. I begin to argue with people next to me, who prefer "sandwich A," while I prefer "sandwich B."

Patty's dream reflects the feeling of many voters that political ads are nothing more than slick efforts to "sell" a candidate, as if he or she were a sandwich. Sheri, a fifty-one-year-old administrative assistant, had a dream with a similar sense of skepticism, mixed with a degree of despair about the promises of politicians.

I'm talking to a woman I know. She's at my house. Her husband, DL, is running for office. I ask if she thinks he'll follow through and serve the full term if I vote for him. She says yes.

This is the final scene of a long dream in which Sheri deals with a troubling romantic relationship. In waking life she had been seeing a married man for many years, and while he told Sheri he was unhappy with his marriage he had in fact done nothing to end it. Sheri felt that her dream was illustrating her reluctance to believe the words of both husbands and politicians—they won't be "faithful" to what they've said. Sheri voted for Perot and was extremely unhappy with Clinton, which makes sense given the charges about his marital infidelities and his alleged tendency to "play loose" with the truth.

After the Election: Hopes and Disappointments

For those who voted for Clinton, his victory was cause for great celebration. Julie, the community activist from California, dreamed

I recall being a guest for a few days at an old friend's home and marvelling at the remodelling job she did. . . . She was very creative, I thought. She put in an art gallery, a meeting room, a business environment and clean, modern furnishings with ample room for growth. . . . I am surprised and pleased. This is more modern and forward thinking than I expected.

Julie said that her feelings in the dream "were exactly my feelings that resulted from the election the next day. I was surprised and pleased that we are becoming more flexible, modern, clean, and socially open."

The clearest example of a celebratory "victory dream" comes from Maggie, the Chicago artist:

> It is very dark out. Clinton and Gore have both given their acceptance speeches and are standing side by side. There is a spot light on them and everything but them is black. They have one of their arms around each other—shoulder to shoulder. Then (while keeping an arm around each other) they position themselves so that the tops of their heads touch and they are facing me—and the rest of the audience behind me. They sing "Amazing Grace." I am impressed that they sing, that they have the courage to do so alone because they have pretty bad voices—and they sing flat.

For a person like Maggie, who had never voted for the winner of a presidential election, Clinton's victory truly felt like an act of divine providence.

Some Clinton voters, however, felt a twinge of anxiety mixed in with their excitement. I had been a strong supporter of Clinton during the campaign, and I was thrilled when he won the election. However, the night after the election I had the following dream:

> I'm with my son, sitting outside a bank building. Clinton, Gore, and two others drive up in a car. I hope they'll stop and say hi, but they don't. They smile at us, but walk by into the bank.

When I reflected on the dream, I realized that I felt like a homeless person in it—sitting on a sidewalk with my child, asking some affluent people for a little token of recognition, only to be politely shunned. The dream made me look beyond my election-night optimism and ask a more sober, and sobering, question: is Clinton going to ignore the voters who had supported him and head "straight to the bank" to seize the spoils of his victory?

Those who voted for candidates who did not win were, naturally, saddened and disappointed. Rose, a retired engineer who lives outside Washington, D.C., had this somewhat mournful dream the night after the election:

> I am at the White House, I feel, a guest at a party or reception for the President Bush. . . . I am allowed to take a picture of the President before he goes downstairs. . . . In one of the upper rooms is a glass case, open at the top, into which are placed a large assortment of souvenirs of the President. Guests are allowed to take these and I'm enthralled and sur-

prised by the variety of things. . . . I cram my souvenirs into my evening purse which is small and suitable for an evening party like this.

Rose is an independent who voted for Bush because of his strong pro-life position. Her dream suggests that the Bush "party" is over—the time has come to celebrate his successes, gather whatever memories his supporters want to keep, and move on.

Concluding Reflections

So to return to the first of those two questions that initially motivated my study, what do these dreams mean? My strong impression is that the dreams express these people's feelings about their political world. One of the basic functions of dreaming is to help us make sense of things that are confusing, strange, or frightening.[4] In the fall of 1992, many people felt that the political state of the United States was confusing, strange, and frightening. It thus should not surprise us that people's dreams would express their concerns and hopes about the presidential election.

My other strong impression is that the dreams are not simply using political images to "symbolize" personal meanings. A Freudian interpreter might argue that a "manifest" dream about Bill Clinton is only masking a "latent" content having to do with the dreamer's relationship with his or her father. Similarly, a Jungian interpreter might claim that a nightmare of Ross Perot is only symbolically expressing the dreamer's unconscious fears of the "Ross Perot-like" parts of him or herself. I am emphatically opposed to such reductionistic, one-dimensional views. The dreams I gathered *certainly* related to the dreamer's personal lives, to their inner worlds—but they just as certainly related to the dreamer's *political* lives, to the *outer* world. A dream of Bill Clinton probably does say something about how one feels about one's father; but it probably also says something about how one feels about *Bill Clinton*. If there's anything we know about dreams, it's that they always have *many* dimensions of meaning. Dreams never mean just *one* thing.

But why, turning to my second question, have so many dream researchers ignored, downplayed, or entirely denied the possibility that some dreams have a political dimension of meaning? I imagine Calvin

Hall might defend himself by saying people don't dream about politics very much because politics aren't as *emotionally important* to them as are more personal subjects like relationships, health, and sex. Thus, he might argue, his claim that we do not dream about political affairs like Presidential elections is simply a description of the facts.[5]

It does seem that politics are not very important to people in American society.[6] Indeed, sociologists like Robert Bellah have argued that a serious problem in American society is the ever-worsening split between the public realm of political affairs and the private realm of personal affairs.[7] Our society's political system has become so complex and impersonal that many people feel alienated from it; more and more people see no point in actively participating in a system that is controlled by businessmen, lawyers, lobbyists, and bureaucrats. As a result, many people are simply giving up on the public world of politics, and seeking fulfillment in purely private, individual affairs like shopping and watching television. The problem, of course, is that the wider this public/private split becomes and the more alienated people feel from politics, the easier it is for the wealthy and powerful to keep their control of our political system.

So it is accurate to say that Americans do not dream much about politics because we do not care much about politics. But it is *not* accurate to say, as Hall does, that dreams *never* relate to politics and that dreams *cannot* relate to politics. On the contrary, the "facts" are that at certain times our dreams do relate, clearly and directly, to the political affairs of our community.[8] Indeed, if Bellah and other sociologists are right about the dangerous public/private division in American society, we in the dream studies field must be very, very careful not to make that division worse. By suggesting that dreams are only about the personal life concerns of the dreamer, and by quickly interpreting away political images in dreams as nothing more than "symbols" of those personal concerns, dream researchers may be *contributing* to the dangerous separation of public from private life in American society. Instead of merely "describing the facts," we may actually be *creating them*.

I will close by describing some of the constructive applications of a more careful and sophisticated study of dreams and politics. One clear implication is that dreams can be a powerful source of political self-awareness. Dreams provide insight into our deeper-lying feelings about politics and reveal to us the interplay of personal and political issues in our lives. Sheri's dream of the politician/husband who might or might not serve his whole term is a perfect example of this. The issue of *fidelity*, of keeping one's promises, is very important both in Sheri's personal life and in the broader political world; her dream brings this connection to Sheri's awareness, offering her an opportunity to reflect on the relationship between her feelings about *personal* fidelity and *political* fidelity. Patty's dream of watching the owls with Clinton is also an excellent example. For her, it is the issue of *change* that connects her personal life and the political world. Patty's dream brings forth the interplay of her uncertain feelings about changing jobs and about Bill Clinton's call for political change. The dream enables her to explore the relationship between her reactions toward change in the personal and the political realms.

Another implication is that dreams could help people defend themselves against the insidious effects of negative political advertisements. It's one of the most distressing features of contemporary American politics that voters are so deeply influenced by ads that unfairly and dishonestly slander opposing candidates. When pollsters ask voters what they think about such "attack ads," people generally claim these ads have no effect on them; but when election time comes, the winning candidate is all too frequently the one who has done the best job of persuading voters to fear and distrust the other candidate. The effectiveness of negative ads, then, seems to lie in their ability to manipulate *un*conscious fears: *consciously*, people ignore these ads; but *unconsciously*, the ads evidently succeed in stirring up people's fears, and influencing their votes. Perhaps voters could better resist the devious appeal of negative political ads if they devoted greater attention to their dreams. If we look to our dreams with an eye for their *political* relevance (in addition to their *psychological* relevance), we can develop a better understanding of the intimate relationship between the personal and the political realms of our lives. With that increased understanding to guide us, we may be better able to recognize how political advertisements often seek to stimulate our unconscious fears as a means of influencing our political beliefs, and our votes.

There has never been any rigorous, focused research on dreams and politics, and my study of the 1992 U.S. presidential election is nothing more than a preliminary exploration of the issues and questions that future research might consider in more detail.[9] But I feel strongly that we can learn a great deal from giving more attention to this subject. It promises to expand our understanding of dreams into new areas that many dream researchers have denied even exist. It also promises to give us insights into how Western society might overcome one of its more troubling problems—for dreams show us that the sharp division of our lives into public and private realms is nothing but an artificial separation of aspects of experience that are in fact deeply connected to each other.

Notes

1. See my essay, Dreaming in a totalitarian society: A Reading of Charlotte Beradt's *The Third Reich of Dreams* (1994b).

2. See Tedlock (1987) and Von Grunebaum and Callois (1966).

3. The names of the dreamers and some of the details of the dreams have been changed to insure the anonymity of the dreamers.

4. See Moffitt, Kramer, and Hoffmann (1993).

5. I'm always suspicious of simple "descriptions of the facts." They have a funny way of *masking* the facts rather than revealing them. Hall frequently characterizes his content analysis method of dream research as a purely "objective" means of describing dreams and dreaming. I have challenged Hall on this point in much more detail in section 3 of *The Wilderness of Dreams*.

6. Even in the exhaustingly long campaign of 1992, barely 50 percent of the country's total registered voters cast ballots—and huge numbers of eligible voters never even bothered to register.

7. Robert Bellah, Richard Madsen, William M. Sullivan, Ann Swidler, and Steven M. Tipton, *Habits of the Heart: Individualism and Commitment in American Life* (Berkeley: University of California Press, 1985). Bellah says, "The most distinctive aspect of twentieth-century American society is the division of life into a number of separate functional sectors: home and workplace, work and leisure, white collar and blue collar, public and private. . . . 'Public' and 'private' roles often contrast sharply, as symbolized by the daily commute from green suburban settings reminiscent of rural life to the industrial, technological ambience of the workplace. The split between public and private life correlates with a split between utilitarian individualism, appropriate in the

economic and occupational spheres, and expressive individualism, appropriate in private life. . . . Viewing one's primary task as 'finding oneself' in autonomous self-reliance, separating oneself not only from one's parents but also from those larger communities and traditions that constitute one's past, leads to the notion that it is in oneself, perhaps in relation to a few intimate others, that fulfillment is to be found. Individualism of this sort often implies a negative view of public life. The impersonal forces of the economic and political worlds are what the individual needs protection against. In this perspective, even occupation, which has been so central to the identity of Americans in the past, becomes instrumental—not a good in itself, but only a means to the attainment of a rich and satisfying private life" (43, 45, 163).

8. I discuss the question of how to interpret and understand the political relevance of dreams in more detail in section 3 of *The Wilderness of Dreams*.

9. Beginning with Bill Clinton's Inauguration in January of 1993, Bruce and Julia Miller began collecting "Dreams of Bill" from all over the country—asking people through newspaper ads, television and radio talk-shows, and so on, if they had experienced any dreams of President Clinton. The Millers have received a *huge* response, and are working on a book documenting their findings. Although theirs will not be a "scientific" study either, their work strongly supports my claim that *there is something here to study.*

References

Bellah, Robert, Richard Madsen, William M. Sullivan, Ann Swidler, and Steven M. Tipton. 1985. *Habits of the Heart: Individualism and Commitment in American Life*. Berkeley: University of California Press.

Beradt, Charlotte. 1966. *The Third Reich of Dreams*. Trans. Adriane Gottwald. Chicago: Quadrangle Books.

Bulkeley, Kelly. 1994. *The Wilderness of Dreams: Exploring the Religious Meanings of Dreams in Modern Western Culture*. Albany: State University of New York Press.

————. 1994b. Dreaming in a Totalitarian Society: A Reading of Charlotte Beradt's *The Third Reich of Dreams*. *Dreaming* (vol. 4, no. 2), pp. 115–126.

Hall, Calvin. 1966. *The Meaning of Dreams*. New York: McGraw-Hill.

Jung, Carl G. 1965. *Memories, Dreams, Reflections*. Trans. Richard and Clara Winston. New York: Vintage.

Moffitt, Alan, Milton Kramer, and Robert Hoffmann, eds. 1993. *The Functions of Dreaming*. Albany: State University of New York Press.

Schorske, Carl E. 1987. Politics and patricide in Freud's *Interpretation of Dreams*. In Harold Bloom (ed.), *Sigmund Freud's The Interpretation of Dreams: Modern Critical Interpretations*. New York: Chelsea House.

Tedlock, Barbara, ed. 1987. *Dreaming: Anthropological and Psychological Interpretations*. New York: Cambridge University Press.

Von Grunebaum, G. E., and Roger Callois, eds. 1966. *The Dream and Human Societies*. Berkeley: University of California Press.

ᎮᎭ*Healing Crimes*

Dreaming Up the Solution to the Criminal Justice Mess

Bette Ehlert

As America's confrontation with the external threat of communism has been winding down, her confrontation with a number of serious internal threats has been gearing up. One of the most vicious and strategic of these confrontations is happening now in the arena of crime and corrections.

Crime in America has become an intense issue in people's minds and lives. The fear of crime is widespread. A Gallup poll "records a feeling among people that crime is going up, up, and away. In 1990, 51 percent of respondents said there was 'more crime' in their area than 'a year ago'; only 17 percent said 'less.' No less than 84 percent thought there was 'more crime in the United States than there was a year ago.' Earlier polls showed similar opinions."[1]

The problem is not just in our minds. We do, in fact, have much to fear. It is as if "the period after the Second World War has been an age of crime; every category of serious crime has risen drastically from a base that was already high. In 1990, 2.3 million Americans were victims of "violent crime" according to figures compiled by the Bureau of Justice Statistics. These numbers came from surveys in which people were asked about their own experiences as victims. It did not include victims of the 23,000 homicides, whose mouths had been permanently and violently shut. The total number of crimes, including thefts, was something on the order of 34.8 million.[2]

Our situation is such that it is unlikely that the level of violent crime will ever again go low enough to abate the public's fear of assault or of criminals.[3]

In preparing for this confrontation with crime, America has been stockpiling armaments. *The New York Times* reported on 18 February 1993 "that sales of Mace in December, 1992, were ten times higher than one year before, that burglar alarm companies were flourishing, that self-defense seminars were springing up like weeds; and that thousands of people were buying car phones so they could dial 911 in case of sudden predation."[4]

America has also been building vast internal fortifications. She has attempted to strengthen her criminal justice system by enacting tougher laws, providing more and longer sentences, and building more and bigger prisons and jails. The purpose of these fortifications is what criminologists call "deterrence and incapacitation," although we euphemistically refer to what goes on within them as "corrections."

Constructing and maintaining our fortifications has become a mighty enterprise. We can begin to appreciate the size and impact of the endeavor with a look at the statistics on jail and prison populations. Statistics give both the gross numbers of incarcerants, and the per capita rate of incarcerations. The first figure correlates to the financial cost of corrections. The second figure correlates to the social impact.[5]

In 1925, there were nearly 92, 000 inmates in American prisons. Between 1925 and 1939, the population doubled. Between 1939 and 1981, it doubled again. Then, in the Reagan eighties, it doubled a third time, from 360,000 to over 700,000 inmates. At present, state and federal prisons hold over 800,000 inmates. At these rates of growth, American prisons will hold more than 1, 000, 0000 inmates by the mid-1990s and almost 2, 000, 000 by the year 2000. One not quite tongue-in-cheek commentator has projected that by the year 2053, one-half of all Americans will be in prison.[6]

The growth in our prisons has been paralleled by the growth in our jails. American jails held 158,000 inmates in 1978. This number grew to 225,000 inmates by 1983; to 340,000 by 1988; and to over 400,000 by 1990. Current estimates place the number of jail inmates at approximately 450,000. By the year 2000, America's standing jail population could approach 600,000.

However, we must note that jails are to corrections as McDonald's is to hamburgers. To understand the importance of an enterprise like McDonald's, we must consider not only the thousands of people that it "employs," but also the millions of people that it "serves." While jails held over 400,000 inmates on the 1990 census day, they processed over 10,000,000 people during the 1990 calendar year. While it is projected that jails will hold 600,000 inmates by the year 2000, it is also projected that they will process over 15,000,000 people in the same year. Jails therefore touch millions of American families every year.

Not only has the absolute number of American incarcerants grown, but the per capita rate of incarceration has also grown. In 1925, there were 155 people in prison for every 100,000 U.S. residents. Between 1925 and 1939, these rates increased to 273 people for every 100,000 U.S. residents, and remained fairly constant until 1980, when they again began to rise. Today, there are 630 people in prison for every 100,000 people in the general population.

Similarly, in 1978, there were 76 people in jail for every 100,000 U.S. residents. By 1988, this rate had doubled and there were 144 people in jail for every 100,000 U.S. residents.

Today, between our prisons and our jails, there are over 774 people incarcerated for every 100,000 U.S. residents. This means that nearly one percent of all U.S. residents is incarcerated. And even this is not the whole story. The 1992 *Corrections Yearbook*, published by the Criminal Justice Institute, tells us that on 1 January 1992, only 3 out of 10 people under correctional supervision were actually incarcerated. The remaining 7 out of 10 people under correctional supervision were on probation or parole. Using the ratio of 3 incarcerants to 7 probationers or parolees, we can say that if nearly one percent of all U.S. residents is actually incarcerated, then about three percent of all U.S. residents are somewhere within the correctional system.

If this 3 incarcerants to 7 probationers or parolees ratio holds through the year 2000, a projected incarcerated population of 2,600,000 prisoners would imply an additional 6,067,000 probationers or parolees—for a total correctional population of almost 9,000,000 Americans.

So, we may ask, how well are these vast internal fortifications working for us? How well do "deterrence and incapacitation" protect us from the predations of crime? What is the impact on America of putting so many people in prison and jail?

The financial impact of deterrence and incapacitation is staggering. In 1992, the total operating budget (not including capital improvements) of America's state and federal correctional agencies was 1.5 billion dollars. The total operating budget of our probation agencies was 1.9 billion dollars. The total operating budget of our juvenile correctional agencies was approximately 46 million dollars. In total, in 1992, America spent almost 3.5 billion dollars on corrections. We can only imagine what this number might become by the year 2000.

The human impact of deterrence and incapacitation is equally staggering. I invited a probation officer friend of mine to lunch. When I called to confirm the time before going by to pick him up, he told me "Be sure to tell my secretary that you're a friend, so that she doesn't treat you like a client." To be treated like a client of corrections is quite simply to be treated like a dirty and difficult child. The fact that a person has allowed himself to become a client of corrections is taken to indicate that he has no strong sense of self, that he has poor personal boundaries, that he lacks the ability to establish good priorities or make sound choices, and that he is therefore wholly incapable, mentally and emotionally, of holding his life together.

To develop his strong sense of self, corrections strips away family, job, social setting, personal effects, clothing, name, and identity. To teach him about choices, corrections relieves him of the need to make any. To help clarify his priorities, corrections puts him into an environment where simple survival is often the only priority. To instill good personal boundaries, corrections provides him the external barriers of an overcrowded, sometimes unclean, always poorly lit, deafeningly loud institution, where his every bowel movement is a public event, and where the only thing he must practice holding together is his temper and his mind.

If the financial and human impact of America's vast—and growing—prison and jail system is horrendous, what is its effect on the growing crime rate? Do "deterrence and incapacitation" have any effect? Unhappily, the answer from many experts seems to be that the impact is slight, and moreover, that "the criminal justice system cannot deliver a strong enough wallop of deterrence, beyond the way it is now, to justify a policy of toughening it up."[7]

Why on earth would this be? The following example may explain. In 1970, Hans Zeisel made a study of crime in New York City. He found that "of every 1,000 felonies committed, only 540 are reported to the police; these turn into 65 arrests and 36 convictions; exactly three of these felons are sentenced to prison for a year or more. If the system were three times as tough, it might put nine men in jail. If it were four times as tough, the number might be twelve. Even a tremendous increase in conviction rates, without something more, would hardly make a dent in the problem of crime.[8]

There is no doubt that deterrence does work. Most people are deterred from crime simply because they believe it is wrong. Still others are deterred by the prospect of punishment—which is real and severe. The problem is that: "The relationship between punishment and behavior is not a straight line but a curve; it flattens out as more and more people are, in fact, deterred. The few that are left become harder and harder to influence."[9]

What the public is asking for is more deterrence at the margins, deterrence where the curve flattens out, deterrence for the growing minority of people whose socialization and inner controls cannot contain the emotions that drive them to commit crimes. This minority might be deterred by the sort of draconian criminal justice system that Hitler ran, but it is not deterred by the sort of criminal justice system that is possible in a democracy. And this minority cannot really be incapacitated. If only 3 out of 1,000 felons are ever incarcerated, whatever would we do if we caught, convicted and had to incarcerate all the other 997? If it is not clear that America of the year 2000 will be able to afford the financial, social and moral costs of having 2,600,000 U.S. residents incarcerated and another 6,067,000 on probation or parole, how can we imagine that we could hope to handle even more?

What do we really know about this belligerent minority whose emotions cannot be contained and who cannot be successfully deterred from crime or incapacitated after it? The criminologists, sociologists, correctional educators, and psychologists who work with and study offenders have developed many theories about why people commit crimes. These theories have had direct effects on the administration of criminal justice—despite the fact that there is often little research to suggest the theorists are correct.[10]

One prominent theory of why people commit crimes is social bond theory. It suggests that delinquents have weakened bonds to their families, schools, and the law. It emphasizes that youths are naturally drawn toward delinquency, and that it is strong bonds to legitimate society that keeps them normal. Social bond theory is the theoretical basis for the intervention strategy represented by the Police Athletic League sports programs and the rhetoric of politicians arguing for a return to basic family values.

Another is "social learning theory." It suggests that all behavior, including crime and normal conduct, is learned in a process of reinforcement and punishment. Social learning theory drives programs like the many drug rehabilitation programs that involve the use of the therapeutic community.

Another is "anomie" theory. It suggests that there are direct ties between crime and the inability of individuals to deal with discrepancies between what they want and what they can achieve. Anomie theory undergirded the Great Society generally, and the Head Start Program in particular.

There is also "labeling theory." Labeling theory suggests that crime is behavior so labeled by society generally, and the agents of social control specifically. Labeling theory moved policymakers to implement the so-called 4-D's for juveniles: deinstitutionalization (or the removal of juveniles from correctional settings); diversion from the formal justice system; the extension of due process rights to juveniles; and decriminalization, whereby certain forms of criminal activity (so-called status offenses) were removed from the control of the law.

Some of these theories have been with us since the postwar period. None of them has helped significantly to stem the rising tide of crime. The bottom line is that, despite the theories, we do not know—really— why people commit crimes. In fact, our whole vast criminal justice system operates without benefit of knowing why people commit crimes. Lacking this knowledge, we have focused our efforts on the things that we do understand (armaments and fortifications) and we have more or less resigned ourselves to coping with crime by hiring more police and building more jails and prisons. As a result, our obvious problem is now that "the ability of any society to respond using such coping mechanisms has a limit. [And that] [p]erhaps we are at the edge of our limit."[11]

If we were to abandon coping, if we were to stop hiring police and building more correctional facilities, what else might we do? I think that we might take another—and a closer—look at our enemy, the offender. And I think, that based upon what we see, we might literally begin to dream up something new. I have seen astonishing things in my own dreams and in the dreams of the incarcerated offenders with whom I work. For me, looking into those dreams specifically for a solution to the problem of crime seems no more absurd—and certainly no more futile—than continuing the build-up of arms and fortifications.

In his book *Where People Fly and Water Runs Uphill*, Jeremy Taylor lists the basic assumptions that he makes when doing dreamwork. One of these assumptions is that dreams are "overdetermined," that all dreams have many levels of meaning. He states that some dreamers believe that all dreams have at least four levels of meaning: physical, psychological, social, and spiritual. He elaborates by saying that when something is found to be true internally or psychologically for a given individual, it will inevitably also be found to be true externally, for society, and vice versa. In other words, the personal is political.[12] My own dreams bear this out.

From 1978 to 1990, I pursued a confrontation-with-aggression theme in my dreams which seemed to parallel the confrontation going on between the American public and the American criminal. In 1976, at the age of twenty-eight I finished my formal education. I had an undergraduate degree in English and philosophy, two years as a TEFL teacher with the Peace Corps in Cameroon, a law degree, and a graduate law degree in taxation. Like lots of people from the sixties, I went to law school to "do good." But after I had been there a while, I found I was not comfortable with the competitive and combative emotional environment. So, I sought out a cerebral corner of the law (taxation) where I thought I could be far from the frontlines of battle and where I hoped I could "do (some) good" and also "be safe." In 1978, after two disillusioning years of (what felt like) combat experience, I read Patricia Garfield's book *Creative Dreaming*[13] and began recording and studying my dreams. My first recorded dream was the following:

I was supposed to fight some woman. It was something that had been arranged in another dream by other people who had thought it was the best way to resolve our differences. I agreed. I was walking around in the dark—probably early morning—looking for her—or wondering whether I should continue on to our appointed meeting place. I was wondering who would know or what would be lost if I did not go to meet her. I don't remember knowing her personally, so I had nothing to prove to her. I think that I am near a building on the University of New Mexico Campus—or it could also be the restrooms in a park. While it is dark and I am outside, the atmosphere is still and even stuffy, as if I am inside. I am anxious and uncomfortable about meeting this woman and I do not. I wake up.

"Unknown Foe," 1 January 1978)

In 1991, after thirteen more years of a love-hate battle with the practice of law, I had the following dream:

The setting is late at night on a military base. Artillery shells are exploding nearby. Missiles and tracer bullets streak through the sky. It looks like Baghdad during Desert Storm.

The action takes place in a small cinderblock building on the base. There is a glass and stainless steel front door to the building. Inside the door, and to the left as you are facing in, there is an untiled space of dirt in the floor which is a "planter," although there are no plants in it. The building does not seem to be either a prison or a hospital, but a woman is confined there. The building is small and it seems to lead to something underground.

A captain brings the base commander to confer with the woman in the building. The base commander has a bad situation. He is losing the battle. The captain thinks that this woman can help. She is apparently very wise and quite mad (meaning insane, but perhaps also angry). She emerges from below with a dueling pistol in her hand. It is an elegant old Southern plantation type dueling pistol. I can't tell, but it may be a toy/plastic gun rather than a real one. I think my brother had one like it when I was a child.

I observe the encounter from a place "in the air." I am above and to the right of the scene.

Each time the base commander poses a question, the woman lets rip with an answer. As she speaks, it may be that she fires the gun into the dirt of the planter which is to her right, but I do not hear the noise. She looks at the commander out of the corner of her eye, her tongue almost hanging out. She is slightly teasing and taunting. Her "delivery" is crazy. Each time she answers, I cringe. I keep waiting for her to make some completely nonsensical statement to this important, impatient (and officious?) man, and prove that she is as crazy as she seems. I am rooting for her to show herself to be sane.

Despite her lurching delivery, what she says about the use of guns and weapons, etc. is obscure, unusual, authentic and brilliant—and is punctuated by the use of her own gun.

Part of her agenda, and the captain's agenda for her, is to get her released from the house/building. The woman's closing remarks have something to do with going in or getting out and having to use the back door. The base commander goes off to use her information, but he is exploitative and uneasy and has not agreed to let the woman go.

"Guns of Work," 25 September 1991

Over the years from 1978 to 1991, I went from being an anxious student to being a generally disillusioned lawyer. The university/park became a military base under siege. The utility building/restroom became a bunker. The person looking for the fight had definitely found it. The still stuffy environment became a life-threatening asthmatic condition. The person hoping to avoid the fight had become a prisoner. The thing that might have been lost by not meeting with this woman prisoner was the battle, the war, and maybe the base itself. She was ridiculous but brilliant. She was armed, but apparently not intent on being deadly. She understood weapons. Her advice to the commander was not to lay down his arms. Her advice had to do with how best to use them.

During the same time, under the leadership of Ronald Reagan, I think that America was approaching her criminals in the same way that I approached the woman underground. America became big and belligerent and seemingly successful. She fortified her positions worldwide. She went on the offensive, cut loose with all the big guns, and planned to blow any opposition away. Then inexplicably, despite apparently sound strategy and considerable resources, she began losing the battle, and then the war. I cannot help but suspect that America will begin to discover a winning strategy in the war against crime in the same way that my base commander began to discover a winning strategy in his own personal war against the world. Both America and the commander have been needing to find out what the woman prisoner in the bunker knows.

In searching for the way out of my own embattled situation—a way to find out what the woman knew—I began trying to locate my other weapons. I tied to focus and hold onto my (right-brained) dreams, since my (left-brained) practice was exploding in my face. To formalize my focus on dreams, I decided to offer a community college course on dreamwork, where I hoped I would meet lots of good people to share my interest. To prepare for my course I began reading, and as I read, I discovered Gayle Delaney's book *Breakthrough Dreaming*. In this book, Delaney sets out her elegantly simple and beautifully effective "interview" method of dream interpretation.[14]

After much reading and some private sessions with Delaney and others, and armed with my years of client interview experience and a few basic dreamwork techniques, I started a private weekly dream group of friends and acquaintances, and began teaching "Practical Dreaming" through the University of New Mexico Community College.

Once I had got my feet wet in dream groups, one dream-related friend suggested, almost facetiously, that I should next contact Gordon Bernell, the education coordinator at our city/county jail. Envisioning nothing more noble than a lot of available dreamers to practice on, I called to volunteer. Gordon, who is also a lawyer, set aside his skepticism and allowed me to give it a try. He said, "We are open to new things here since, God knows, what we do doesn't work." He scheduled me a regular time and space to come offer dreamwork to women inmates.

I was not prepared for what I found. What I found was that jails are psychically filthy places—full of bloody dreams and gory feelings that are never mopped up. Pieces of them lie around in the corners and stick to your shoes. The odor of them clings to clothes and hair, and the feel of the place stays with you for hours after you leave. Dreamworking in a jail is like nursing in an E.R. People arrive in critical condition, present you their most horrific wounds for emergency treatment, and then leave again before you get to see anything heal.

What you do get to see is that people in jail live close to the bone. They have no cars, houses, jobs, families, clothes, jewelry, activities, or other props to announce who they are, or to hide behind. Their feelings of humiliation, frustration, indignation, and anger shine on the surface of their skin, a little like sweat. Just below the skin, and only slightly less visible, are the other feelings of guilt, pain, fear, self-doubt and loneliness.

You also get to see that people in jail live in a state of emotional starvation. They live with a near total deprivation of all the kinds of emotional nourishment that make it possible for the rest of us to survive from day to day. They are desperately hungry for the interest, attention, concern and affection of anyone with any emotional surplus to share.

My first dream groups (usually with four to eight women) met in a small conference cubicle designed to accommodate one lawyer and one client. The groups were interrupted by the incessant slamming of the glass and steel sliding doors that separate the women's "pods" from the hallway to the elevators. Groups were interrupted by the arrival of medications, methadone, commissary, caseworkers, lawyers, lunch, and recreation, as well as by the comings and goings of dreamers who got bored or "OD'd." We would start our meetings at about 10:00 am, when everyone was up and showered. Lunch could be served at any time from 10:30 am to 12:30 pm. Outdoor recreation (a walk on the roof) was at 1:00 pm. On most days, the corrections officers would allow me to stay for lunch, so that if some women decided to pass up recreation, the dream groups could last until 2:30 pm—which was lock down and head count.

To help us "clean up" after these groups, I was (after intercession from Gordon) allowed to carry in Tupperware containers of water and sand. We would all run our hands in the sand as we worked the dreams, and then at the end of the group, we would wash our hands, letting the water run off into the sand. After leaving the jail, I would drive down to one of the bridges over the Rio Grande, and dump the dirt into the river. In this way, I let the Great Mother dispose of the stuff that I couldn't carry.

Despite my lack of experience and the unbelievably lousy working conditions, the dream group, which met continuously for about nine months, was well received by the women inmates, and well worth the efforts. Three extraordinary gifts came to me as a result of it.

The first of these gifts was the support of Gordon Bernell, the education coordinator at the jail. Bernell was sufficiently impressed with the inmates' feedback to introduce me to other correctional educators and administrators. These introductions eventually led to the creation of other dream groups and the establishment of other invaluable contacts within the correctional system. The groups that grew out of the original Bernalillo County Detention Center women's group included the following: (1) a group for adult male offenders, offered as part of the "Comienzos" program, on the Men's Education Floor at the Bernalillo County Detention Center; (2) a group for male and female juvenile offenders offered to volunteers from the general population at the Bernalillo County Juvenile Detention Center; (3) a group for adult female offenders, offered as part of the "Pre-Release" program at the Corrections Corporation of America's New Mexico Women's Correctional Facility; and (4) a group in "Community Corrections" for adult male offenders with multiple DWI (driving while intoxicated) convictions.

The second extraordinary gift to come out of the original women's dream group was a personal discovery. In addition to Gayle Delaney's "interview" technique and Jeremy Taylor's "imaginative" or "If it were my dream, I would . . ." technique, I used the group to explore an adaptation of Anne Sayre Wiseman's "Mapping the Dream Problem on the Paper Stage" technique (described in her book entitled *Nightmare Help for Children from Children*.[15]) This technique seemed especially good for the days when I needed the dreamers to do more work than me. With this technique, the dreamer depicts or "maps" the important symbols of the dream using scissors, glue, and colored construction paper. When the map has been explained by the dreamer and commented on by the viewers, the dreamer is invited to consider how the shapes, colors, and arrangements are working and whether all elements are completely satisfactory, or if any aspect of the map "wants" something. If something is "wanted," the dreamer is encouraged to consider the options for change, the price of any change, and then whether and how to implement the change.

While the women were at work on their maps, I mapped my own dream from the preceding night. The dream was:

> Two hyenas are released into the wild, but in something like a game preserve. They are observed by two men seated before a radar screen. The radar tracks the animals through their body heat. They leave a "thermal signature" on the screen. The radar operators watch as two diagonal orange lines, representing the animals, intersect downward across the middle of the screen. One operator comments nervously to the other that the animals are moving more powerfully than had been expected.
>
> "Hyena in the Wild," circa November 1992

I mapped this dream by putting a small, round, explosive looking hyena on the left side of the page, and then a large square radar screen with an "X," and two male radar operators on the right side of the page. The next day, I introduced the mapping technique to my private group. I recalled no dreams from the night before, so while these women were working, I used the time to map my earliest remembered childhood dream. The dream was this:

> I am in the basement of the turn-of-the-century school building where I attended kindergarten. The room is small and rectangular, with a low ceiling of exposed pipes. It is filled with simple wooden benches. At the front of the room is one windowless wooden door which opens inward. The door, the walls, the pipes, and the benches are covered with many coats of pale 1950s green paint. I am there with my father. We are attending a parent-teacher's meeting. I am the only child. During the course of the meeting, a terrible and ferocious monster enters the back of the room. All the adults leap up and run out the front door, knocking over all the benches as they go. I run for the door, too, but because I am small, I have a hard time getting over the benches. I am the last to reach it and when I get there it is closed tight. Everyone else is outside, leaving me alone in the room with the monster. I am terrified. I pull on the knob with all my might. I manage to open it just far enough to look out. I see that many people are on the other side, pulling to keep the door closed. I see that my father is also right there. I cannot tell whether he is pushing against the crowd to let me out, or whether he is one of the people pulling the door closed to keep me in.
>
> "Monster in the Basement," circa 1954

I mapped this dream by putting an orange and black explosion on the left side of the paper, a bunch of criss-crossed lines to represent benches in the center of the paper, and a door with men's heads peeking in around it to the right of the paper.

As I put my "Monster" image away, I saw it side by side with my "Hyena" image. I realized that I was looking at two versions of the same dream, separated by forty years of experience.

The vague and terrifying monster from childhood had become a specific threat—one (or two) hyenas. The benches that had been the child's obstacles, had become the hyenas' paths. The closed door had become a "transparent" remote viewing device. The parent/teacher adults who had exerted themselves to keep the monster and the child shut in, were now focusing their whole attention on monitoring the hyenas' progress on the outside—in the wild—with the implication that not only were the creatures dangerous, but they were also precious and endangered.

Like all children, I needed to be safe from the monster. Ultimately, I, myself, became so good at containing the monster that I almost completely choked it off and could no longer hear its voice. Due to this harsh treatment, the monster developed asthma. Asthma for me was always a problem of the exhale—the expression. In cutting off the monster's voice, I had cut off the voice of my own inner wisdom that should have inspired and directed all of my positive, outgoing activities and expressions.

My personal struggle to find a way to contain but not crush the monster/mad woman within me has developed into a career activity. Inwardly, that activity has been to get to know both my wild and emotional inside and my containing and intellectual outside, and to attend to the doorway between the two, so that it works well and easily. For me, the dream is the doorway through which we can hear the underground voices most clearly, and through which all the monsters, children, hyenas, mad women, teachers, radar operators, captains, and base commanders must pass freely in order to conduct their essential business with one other.

Outwardly, that activity has been to seek out America's most powerfully symbolic doorways—the doorways to prisons and jails—and to get them to open and close for me as I go back and forth between the waking-life monsters, children, hyenas, and mad women on the one hand, and the teachers, radar operators, captains, and base commanders on the other. As more of us go back and forth through these doorways, the less opaque they will be, and the more like transparent remote viewing devices through which we can gather necessary intelligence about something natural, precious, and endangered that lives close to the source of the wisdom and energy that powers and guides all outer world activity.

In the course of conducting our war on crime and monsters, America has made herself into an armed camp. We are now staggering under the weight (and cost) of our own fortifications, and growing more and more hopelessly estranged from a growing number of "institutionalized" or chronically criminal citizens. While we need protection on the one hand, we also need these people on the other.

In corrections, there is—at least metaphorically—a peculiar equivalent to the remote viewing device that reads a thermal signature. It is the electronic bracelet. Because of the overcrowding of jails and prisons, and the horrendous expense of keeping people incarcerated, more and more jurisdictions are experimenting with "community corrections." In some instances "community corrections" means the offender is required to wear a bracelet and to check into a central computer from his home telephone at prearranged times throughout the day. It is a form of house arrest that accommodates a work schedule and does not uproot lives and families. If the offender does not answer the call for check-in so that the computer can "read" the bracelet, the computer will call every ten minutes for a certain number of hours, until finally an arrest warrant will issue. The average cost of a day's stay in jail is $50.00—and borne by the state. The average cost of a bracelet and phone is pennies a day— and is borne by the offender. We must focus on the offender and the doorway, not on the fortifications.

The electronic bracelet is an example of a "doorway" that provides security for the public, while it allows the monster its preserve, and permits the public and the monster to continuing observing and learning from one another. It is a promising solution from some right-brained innovator somewhere who no doubt dreamed it up.

The last and greatest gift to come to me out of the original women's dream group was my first opportunity to consciously stand in the doorway of the dream and hear the voice of the monster/child/hyena/mad woman. After hearing that voice (I have now heard it several times), I am prepared to make several outlandish assertions about crimes and criminals:

1. There is no such thing as *random* violence or crime. Victims become perpetrators, and perpetrators commit highly specific crimes. They commit crimes that are perfectly, metaphorically, linked to their prior experiences of victimization or abuse.
2. At the moment of the crime, the perpetrator experiences the precise form of mastery that was missing to him/her at the moment of victimization. Crimes are reparative attempts by victims.
3. Perpetrators are people who have poor boundaries. As victims, no perimeter stopped the world from impinging too far in. Now,

as perpetrators, no perimeter prevents them from spilling too far out.

4. Perpetrators are not deterred from crime by the prospect of punishment, or "rehabilitated" after crime by the experience of incarceration. Their crimes hold the promise of a ritual and symbolic benefit, the importance of which overshadows the concern for other consequences. For most offenders, this benefit is the healing of the childhood wound. The wound established the child as victim. Through crime, the child establishes himself as perpetrator. The wound and the crime are the two parameters within which adult self-boundaries will be established.

5. Dreamwork is the solution to much of what is wrong. Through dreaming, perpetrators confront the image of the wound and the image of the crime and recover the feelings attached to both. Through dreamwork, perpetrators "negotiate" the boundary between the two. As the skill of dream negotiation is perfected, it can be applied to future wounds, so that future crimes need only be committed in imagination, and future boundaries can be negotiated in accordance with preestablished rules of procedure.

The first dream in which I could hear the voice of the monster/child/hyena/madwoman was shared by a dreamer in one of the earliest women's dream groups at the Bernalillo County Detention Center. This person was a white female first offender in her early twenties. She had honey-blond hair, a kind and pretty face, and a soft Southern voice and was in every way the picture of the girl next door. I met her, and she had this dream, about one week after her arrest. She had never been arrested before.

Juliette and the Beast

I am in a room, sitting with my boyfriend, Richard. Maybe we're talking. The room is dark. The only thing I can see clearly is Richard. I feel sad and scared. Something is wrong. The room has doors. Richard leaves. I don't see what door he goes out. He just disappears. I walk around and can't find him. I feel abandoned and sad. Then the doors fly open. Except one door. It's a rubber door. Something is pushing it. I run to it and hold it closed. I can see fingers pushing through the rubber. The fingers have nails like a beast. There is no light. Nothing but darkness. I don't see anything. I'm screaming to Richard: "Come back! I want to go with you! I need help!" I don't want to let the door go and go after him. I need to hold the door. I am scared to even move.

Juliette cried bitterly throughout the retelling of the dream, and throughout the dreamwork, but the dream had kept her awake for many nights and she wanted to understand it. She gave powerful definitions of almost all of its elements, but I will relate only those most pertinent to this discussion:

Juliette described her boyfriend, Richard, as a wonderful man for whom she would do anything. He was totally accepting of her, and was "like her family." He was also a true multiple personality, who "had little voices", and did, in fact, slip out though different doors in his head. He was part intelligent, manipulative con-man, and part ruthless, violent thug. She attributed his violence to the fact that he had been sexually abused as a child. Like her own father, Richard was also notable for the fact that he had abandoned her into a life-threatening situation.

Juliette described the dark room where she felt sad and scared as being like the closet in her grandmother's house where, as a child, she used to hide from her uncle and grandmother. Juliette had repeatedly been abandoned by her teenaged mother into the care of her grandmother. During the periods she spent in her grandmother's home, she was sexually abused by her mother's younger brother. Her grandmother was aware of the abuse, did nothing to stop it, and sometimes punished Juliette for provoking it. Juliette also described the dark room with the many doors that opened and closed as being like the jail. Interestingly, she further defined "jail" as something like a father: "It keeps you safe, gives you food and shelter, and makes you do what you're supposed to do."

Juliette described the hands with pointy, long nails coming through the door as belonging to a beast or a creature, or to something that she did not want to see. She identified the hands with her mother who had also had long clawlike fingernails, and who had used them to scratch and threaten her. Juliette said that mother would drink and beat her and then lock her in her room.

Juliette described her crime as follows: She was hitchhiking with Richard. A man gave them a ride. Richard assaulted the man. As the victim was struggling, Richard told Juliette to go through the man's pockets and possessions to find his wallet and valuables. At the end of the terrible drama, Juliette was in a car, groping for a wallet through the clothes of a beaten and terrified man, just the way that her uncle had so often been in the closet, groping through the clothes for her. After the crime, Richard vanished. Juliette was apprehended and charged with "strong-armed robbery."

Juliette went from being the good, innocent, defenseless little victim in the closet, to being the evil, premeditated, and powerful perpetrator in the car. She went from being strong-armed herself, to strong-arming another.

At the end of the dream interview, Juliette could see herself as both the victim/child, and the perpetrator/beast. The victim/child and the perpetrator/beast, however, could not see each other. We encouraged Juliette to find a way to make the dream come out better. We suggested that she find out what the beast wanted and then try to negotiate. We offered her the following "If it were my dream, I would . . ." suggestions for revision: Get the beast to chill out, and then go around and close the doors until you feel more comfortable. Or, get the beast to chill out and then, since there are a lot of doors open to you, go out and look around for your boyfriend. Or, since Richard and the beast are both outside, ask the beast to go look for Richard. Or, just ask the beast what it knows about Richard.

Juliette listened to our suggestions and came back a week later with one final dream before transferring out of the institution. In this second dream, she was running through the woods, pursued by a gang of men. As she jumped over a stream, a huge alligator rose up, grabbed her pants and began pulling her down.

This second dream was less frightening than the first. The perpetrator was no longer a mythical beast, but only an alligator. Juliette was no longer trapped in a closet, but on the move in the woods. While Juliette's self-as-victim and self-as-aggressor images were by no means reconciled and integrated, they could at least see each other. Juliette and the beast were almost touching.

This second dream also seemed to have richer possibilities for negotiation and revision. We made several suggestions. Maybe the alligator only wanted the pants. Maybe Juliette could trade the pants to the alligator in exchange for protection from the gang in pursuit. Maybe Juliette could tame the alligator by rubbing its stomach. Maybe the gang in pursuit was not really after Juliette, but only wanted the alligator. Maybe she could trade the alligator to the alligator hunters in exchange for help in getting out of the woods. Maybe with help from the gang, Juliette could transform the alligator into a purse—something with a prized but tough exterior that could hold her I.D.

Juliette's first dream was typical of many first dreams that offenders bring to dreamwork. It presented, in one tableau, an overview of all the interlocking conflicts at many levels of Juliette's life. It presented, on its face, a dream victim and a dream perpetrator, in conflict, at opposite ends of a spectrum, and connected by a metaphor. That is, it presented the good and defenseless child who was strong-armed, fighting the evil and powerful beast who had the strong arm. At another level, the dream implied a present day, waking-life perpetrator (Juliette the strong-armed robber), and a present day, waking-life victim (either the man in the car, or Juliette in the jail). At yet another level, the dream implied the historical, waking-life perpetrator (the uncle), and the historical, waking-life victim (Juliette as a little girl).

Juliette's second dream was also typical of many subsequent dreams that offenders bring to dreamwork. It showed the confrontation continuing, but improving. It also showed possibilities for further negotiation and improvement emerging more clearly. As the image of Juliette in the dream is reconciled with the dream image of the beast, I believe that healing is happening at all the levels, and that a good *and* well-defended young woman is beginning to emerge.

The following dream came to a man named Daniel whom I worked with on the Men's Education Floor at the Bernalillo County Detention Center. Daniel was a very handsome, very fair-skinned African-American in his late twenties. He had a quietly commanding presence. He was big, soft-spoken, intelligent, and aware of everything going on around him. There was something very genteel and heart-felt about him. He should have been well on his way up the corporate ladder. He was, in actuality, a successful crack dealer who lived in a house full of beautiful women junkies who brought him money. He had this dream a few days after being sentenced to an unusually long jail term, given his record. At the time of the dream, he had already served almost two years jail awaiting disposition on the same charges. Daniel's dream was also a recurring dream, although earlier versions had had different details.

Daniel and the Dark Entity

I don't remember how this started. I am asleep. All of a sudden, this entity is in my bed, holding me down. He is dark. I can't tell if it's his clothes or his skin that is dark. He exudes darkness. He has a thick mane of bushy hair. He is holding me down hard, as if to say, you can't get up—I won't let you. He's on my back, but somehow I can see him. I feel highly frustrated. I can't believe I can't get up. This thing tricked me. He deceived me. He had to get my permission to get this close. I didn't have to allow this to happen. I am really going. I finally get up and run away. He either let me go, or I broke away. While it is happening, it isn't too scary—but it is more scary afterwards.

In fact, Daniel had been so disturbed by this dream that he had persuaded the corrections officer to let him out of his cell, so that he could spend an hour or so in the day room until he found the courage to go back to sleep.

Daniel mapped this dream, depicting himself in a bed, pressed beneath a large, dark entity. To help the small dream ego in the bed—to get it some "perspective"—he eventually moved it to a floating position in the upper right corner of the paper. There, it was safely disassociated from the frightening activity below.

During the dream interview, Daniel gave a wordless acknowledgement that he had been abused sexually as a child. He associated the large dark entity to his childhood assailant, to the judge in black robes who had sentenced him, and interestingly, to a "dope fiend" customer of his whom he often befriended with free "product," and who wore a similarly strange hairdo.

During the dream interview, Daniel conceded that he himself had been a "large dark entity" on a lot of people's backs and that about eighty users had needed desperately to "get out from under" him. His crime was "pushing."

Like Juliette's dream, Daniel's dream showed interlocking conflicts at many levels. On its face, Daniel's dream gave the child-victim and the Dark Entity–perpetrator, in conflict, at opposite ends of a spectrum, and connected by a metaphor. The connecting metaphor was that the good and defenseless little kid who "got fucked," grew up to be a real "Evil Fucker." The little kid who got pushed down on the bed grew up to be the pusher. (The metaphor continued to explain the "trick" in the dream. The trick was that when you deal with the "Dark Entity"—in this case, the devil, the drug business, or the child molester—you get "fucked in the end." Sensing this, he had developed "eyes in the back of his head.") At another level, Daniel's dream implied the first historical victim (the innocent little boy), and the first historical perpetrator (the original evil fucker). At still another level, it implied the present-day victims (all the people with someone "on their backs"—meaning both Daniel himself and his customers), and the present-day perpetrators. In this case there seemed to be two: the judge who gave the stiff sentence, and the junkie. I believe that the junkie appeared because he was the one who "ratted Daniel out," although I didn't discuss this part with Daniel.

The Dark Entity's unusual hair proved to be a clue for how the little boy who "gets fucked" and the "Evil Fucker" might eventually be integrated. When Daniel mapped the entity, he depicted its hair as being bound into two large bunches. When asked what this hair might look like if it were untied, he replied that it might look like a lion's mane.

From here, Daniel connected to the expression "King of Beasts." Daniel himself had roughly the skin color of a lion. As a wealthy drug dealer, he had, in fact, been a sort of King of Beasts. He had also allowed his females to hunt for him and bring him food. However, in the image of the lion, the potential for "beastliness" co-exists with the potential for kingly, magnanimous, and noble behavior—which I think is the direction in which Daniel is headed. We also talked about the story of Androcles and the Lion, in which the slave first frees the beast, and then the beast frees the slave.

We encouraged Daniel to think about ways to make this dream come out better. Within about a week, he reported that he had had the dream again, but that this time, instead of getting so scared, he had been able to simply stand up and walk away. My feeling was that Androcles' lion had come into his own.

The following dream gives an example of victim-perpetrator negotiations which conclude successfully in rapprochement. This dream came to an eighteen-year-old Hispanic man named Arthur, whom I worked with at the Juvenile Detention Center. He was there on his second or third offense and would remain in custody until his twenty-first birthday. Like Juliette and Daniel, Arthur was an unusually attractive, intelligent person who was also an extremely gifted artist. It would have seemed more natural to be meeting him in some studio in the art department of the university than to be seeing him in jail. His dream was this:

Arthur and the Knife

I am watching a knife falling. It's falling I slowly and turning end over end. It lands and sticks in this square piece of wood. Dark blood begins to ooze out of the wood. It spreads until it gets my feet wet. I wake up real scared.

The message of this dream was so powerful that when Arthur did awake, he found himself standing in his stocking feet, in his driveway, in the rain. He had sleepwalked out of his house and down to his car.

Arthur gave an action/feeling summary of his dream as follows: (1) "I am curious about a falling knife." (2) "I watch the knife stick and the board begin to bleed. I am still curious, but feeling like I should get out of there." (3) "When my feet get wet, I am real scared, like I should get out of there." He connected this action/feeling summary of the dream with the events leading up to his arrest. Even after he had got his feet wet, he failed to get the message that it was time to get out.

Arthur described the knife in his dream as follows: The blade of the knife was the blade of a hunting knife. It was black steel with big, serrated teeth. He had seen his stepfather use a hunting knife to "field dress" game. He defined "field dressing" as the process whereby the hunter cuts the guts (the stomach and intestines) out of the deer, so he can haul home only those parts of the carcass that are valuable to him.

The handle of the knife was the handle of a kitchen knife. It was pearlized white plastic. Arthur had seen his mother use such a kitchen knife to chop meat and vegetables for dinner.

We asked Arthur if there were some way in his life that he was involved in stripping, chopping, or "field dressing" big game. He said yes, that he was a car thief, and that all his many convictions were related to auto theft. Car thieves, he said, may strip, chop or gut the vehicle, so that they can dispose of the desirable parts in the most effective way.

We asked Arthur if there was also some way that he, himself, was being "field dressed." He eventually said yes, and explained that there was a lot of "bad blood" in his family because his mother and stepfather were afraid he had become a "chip off the old block." Arthur's biological father was an offender and was incarcerated at the time of the dream.

Arthur conceded that, in a way, his mother and stepfather were "ripping his guts out," as they did not want to take with them any of his deep feelings, or any other parts of himself that might be connected to his father.

Like Juliette's and Daniel's dreams, Arthur's dream implied a present day, waking-life perpetrator (Arthur the car thief), and a present-day, waking-life victim (the auto owners who got "stuck" and Arthur who went to jail). It also implied an historical, waking-life perpetrator (his stepfather and mother), and an historical, waking-life victim (Arthur as a young child). But, Arthur's dream is also very different from either Juliette's or Daniel's. While it *implied* both a deer and a hunter, it *featured* a knife.

There was surely a time in Arthur's life when he was a deer. There was also clearly a time in his life when he was a hunter. The deer was innocent, natural, and without adequate defenses. It got killed and field-dressed. With respect to the hunter, it was only prey. The hunter was deliberate, premeditated, well-armed, and destructive. With respect to the deer, he was only a predator. The knife, however, knew both the deer and the hunter, and yet, a full understanding of "knife" could not be reached just through understanding "deer" and "hunter." The knife was an unusual composite with enormous possibilities of its own.

As the dreamwork progressed, some of the knife's possibilities proved to be that it was "sharp," was "hard but subtle," "had a point," could "cut through the bullshit," could "cut to the heart of the matter," and could "chop things down to size."

Arthur's knife was an image of authentic self. It was also the basis of a new self-image. It united Arthur's self-as-victim with his self-as-perpetrator. It joined the innocent naturalness of the deer to the protective power of the hunter. The image of "knife" seemed to spring from a level of self that is beneath the level of wounds and crimes, and it seemed to contain the energy needed to sustain the behaviors that it suggested. Upon Arthur's transfer from jail to prison, the knife self-image was already doing its work. He seemed to leave with a serenely optimistic state of mind—something for which he had not been noted during his other incarcerations.

Juliette, Daniel, and Arthur all found in crime an experience of mastery that precisely, metaphorically, offset an earlier experience of abuse and victimization. However, in the time we had available, only Arthur was able to get beyond the wound and the crime to secure an *image* of integrated authentic self. In mythological terms, all these heroes got the "call to adventure." All these heroes entered the "Heart of Darkness" and confronted the dragon. But after the confrontation, only one hero actually "seized the treasure."

This third step—achieving the integrated image of self, or "seizing the treasure"—is indispensable. It is also the step that all repeat offenders fail to take. Seizing the treasure is, after all, the real point of the whole journey. Heroes who leave the underworld without integrating the decency of the victim with the power of the perpetrator—without seizing the treasure—those who leave without the handbag or the lion or the knife, are obliged to return again for them later.

The three steps: (1) the wound, (2) the crime, and (3) the integrated image of authentic self; or (1) the call to adventure, (2) the confrontation in the heart of darkness, and (3) the seizing of the treasure, are the three acts of one play, variously titled "integration," "individuation," or initiation."

The drama begins at birth, when we inherit a life situation. For some, the inherited situation includes a list of high-risk factors like poverty, unloving caregivers, addiction, neglect, and various kinds of physical or emotional abuse. Some one of these adverse inherited circumstances becomes the central childhood "wound."

As we mature emotionally, we learn ways to tend the wound. These include: exploring it, nursing it, protecting it, hiding it, denying it, and overcompensating for it. The sum of the treatments we learn to give ourselves becomes our repertoire of coping skills.

Nature however seeks healing and wholeness. It wants to be free of both the wound and all the treatments. It favors a direct approach that either kills or cures—definitively. When a person reaches the end of childhood, nature craves a test. It craves something so difficult as to exceed the power of all the puny skills acquired through tending the childhood wound. Those who don't die of the test, succeed in drawing out of the depths of themselves some heretofore unknown quality. This new quality is unique with each individual. Seen in dreams, it is the image of the authentic, adult self. With the emergence of this quality/image, the individual becomes more than just the sum of the problems—and solutions—given in childhood. He or she becomes healed of them and "initiated" into adulthood and the authentic self.

Traditional societies supplied ritual challenges through which young people could test their way into their authentic adulthood. Contemporary society supplies similar challenges. The acceptable ones include military service, college, graduate school, professional training school, trade school, marriage, and responsible parenthood.

Unfortunately, too many of us arrive at the end of childhood too battered and too uneducated to undertake these acceptable challenges. Where no acceptable challenge is available, nature reverts to the default. The default initiation is, like the straight line, the shortest distance between two points. It makes use of the ancient eye-for-an-eye, tooth-for-a-tooth principal. The default initiation is simply stepping through the childhood wound, and turning it inside out. In this way, the initiate becomes his/her own worst nightmare. The child in the closet becomes the beast at the door. The little kid who gets fucked grows up to be the Evil Fucker. The deer becomes the hunter.

The default initiation can entrain terrible complications. These complications often obscure the benefits to be derived. For example, where the original childhood wound is horrific, the offsetting reparative act is horrific. It takes place under dangerous, volatile (and probably illegal) circumstances, and it involves a high risk of police intervention and consequent criminal penalties. Under such circumstances, there is little likelihood that the restaged reparative drama can be made to come out better than the disastrous original. There is every likelihood that it will result in new wounds to the offender, the other participants, and maybe the bystanders, too. Then, even the benefit of the sought after symbolic triumph is lost in the confusion.

The last and best gift of my original women's dreamwork group at the Bernalillo County Detention Center was my understanding that dreams will get us to the solution for what is wrong with our criminal justice system. When we approach the fortifications that are our prisons and jails, we can look through the doorway of the dream to see the answer to the question, "Why do people commit crimes?"

The answer is that crimes are nature's default initiation into healing and adulthood. They are designed to provide the victim with precisely the form of mastery that was missing to him or her at the moment of the victimization. After the crime, the offender is poised between the two parameters within which his or her adult self-boundaries will be drawn. The offender is poised between the decent self-as-victim, and the powerful self-as-perpetrator. After the crime, the offender is finally in a position to grow up—to fabricate the handbag, become the real King of Beasts, or seize the knife. Knowing how to do dreamwork, and knowing why people commit crimes, we should be able to see to it that no one ever commits more than one.

By looking through the doorway of dreams, we should also eventually be able to fix it so that crimes won't be necessary at all for healing. We should be able to reorganize our fortifications so that, in the future, they will protect the public, but without imprisoning the children, the monsters, the hyenas, or the mad women. We need to learn how to turn our fortifications into a preserve and an obstacle course for the benefit of our wild and belligerent minority whose emotions are likely to explode out into crime. We need to offer them something besides the conventional initiations (school, military service, apprenticeship, marriage, etc.) for which they do not qualify, so that we can prevent them from seeking the default initiations (crimes and incarcerations) which unnecessarily endanger, impoverish and disrupt the rest of us.

Finally, by looking through the doorway of dreams, we can help the children and monsters already trapped in the fortifications. Through dreams and dreamwork, offenders can begin to develop many of the cognitive skills in which they are so notoriously deficient. These include problem-solving skills like "critical reasoning" (issue-spotting, fact-finding, identifying causal connections, estimating and anticipating developments) and "social perspective taking" (developing empathy, awareness, and sensitivity, leading to better interpersonal problem-solving).

When a unified image of authentic self emerges from two opposing images of self-as-victim and self-as-aggressor, I imagine that what has gone on behind the scenes is a sort of process of negotiation. All negotiation is founded on the premise that each party has something of value to the other. In a negotiation, the details of both parties' needs and resources are explored for ways that things can be combined or exchanged to everyone's advantage. The objective of negotiation is to arrive at a win-win result. Unless the win-win result can be reached, it effectively becomes a lose-lose situation.

Dreaming and dreamwork are about possibilities for negotiation. They bring things to consciousness. They bring disparate characters to the table together. They permit the dreamer to familiarize him/herself with everyone's fears and desires, strengths and weaknesses, motives and goals. They help the dreamer to understand who seeks what changes, and what the costs and benefits of each change might be. They also permit the dreamer to explore the implementation of change. Then, as the dreamer explores, understands, and appreciates the position of each dream character, he/she somehow also incorporates, integrates, and absorbs them.

It is interesting to me that in the default initiation, the offender generally does not attempt to bring about the better outcome by *revising* the traumatic scene. Instead, he/she tends to seek the better outcome by simply *recasting* him/herself in the aggressor's more powerful and more desirable role. The offender thereby changes an I-lose-you-win situation into an I-win-you lose situation. This is like switching places with the opposition in a negotiation. It does not efficiently advance the parties toward a win-win outcome. It suggests, among other things, a lack of skill at negotiating.

Good dreamwork demands the same cognitive skills as good negotiation. Dreamwork, like negotiation, trains the dreamer to explore the opponent's position. This exploration leads to the discovery of increased possibilities for action and outcome. Dreams are nothing if not expositions of possibilities. As a reliable method for exploring the possibilities is learned, the inevitable connection between trauma and crime as the default healing response, is broken.

At present, despite all the lip-service that we give to "criminal justice" and "corrections," we want not just "deterrence and incapacitation," but also punishment and revenge. We send people off to prison the way we might send them off to the woodshed to deal with a stern father. Like stern fathers, prisons have to do with structure, containment, organization, rules, and discipline. The guidance they offer usually takes the form of reprimand. We expect prison barriers to *instill* boundaries in people. We expect offenders to *imbibe* good boundaries from the experience of being in prison. It is almost as if we expect people to "set up" in prison the way Jell-O sets up in a mold. We cannot make Jell-O without a mold, and we cannot make Jell-O if we do not allow enough time, but all the molds and all the time in the world won't help us get the dessert if we fail to add the magic power. Given the right mold, the right time, and enough Jell-O, the dessert takes shape. Offenders are the same. With enough dreams, everyone takes shape. Up until now, we have been forgetting the real magic powder.

Notes

1. Lawrence M. Friedman, *Crime and Punishment in American History* (1993), 450, New York: Vantage.

2. Ibid., 451.

3. Ibid., 452.

4. Ibid., 452.

5. L. Thomas Winfree, Jr., Professional excellence and correctional education in the 1990s: A criminologist's perspective, *Journal of Correctional Education* 44:3 (September 1993), 116–21. Unless otherwise specified, the statistics cited herein on jail and prison populations were gathered and digested by L. Thomas Winfree, Jr., an academic criminologist. My discussion adapts and paraphrases Mr. Winfree's observations and conclusions.

6. Luis J. Rodriguez, author of *Always Running*. The statistic quoted was taken from Mr. Rodriguez' presentation to the 48th International Conference of the Correctional Education Association, Chicago, 11–14 July 1993.

7. Friedman, *Crime and Punishment*, 457.

8. Ibid., 457–58.

9. Ibid., 458–59.

10. Thomas Winfree, Jr., Professional excellence and correctional education in the 1990s, 116–21. This discussion on theories of criminal behaviour is adapted and paraphrased from Mr. Winfree's article.

11. Ibid., 458–59.

12. Jeremy Taylor, *Where People Fly and Water Runs Uphill: Using Dreams to Tap the Wisdom of the Unconscious* (1992) New York: Warner.

13. Patricia Garfield, *Creative Dreaming* (1974) New York: Ballantine.

14. Gayle Delaney, *Breakthrough Dreaming: How to Tap the Power of Your 24-Hour Mind* (1991). In this book, Delaney develops what she calls the "interview" method of dream interpretation. It is an approach

well suited to people who love literature, and who have some experience at interviewing. In other words, it is something almost all of us can use. The method approaches the dream like a story. Each dream will have some or all of the elements that any story has: plot, setting, action, characters, animals, objects, mood and feeling. Each such element is also a symbol for all of the things that the dreamer knows about it or associates to it. The interview method is dedicated to calling up that knowledge and retrieving those associations. The steps of the interview are: (1) Have the dreamer tell the dream. (2) Have the dreamer fully define and describe each element of the dream. (3) Read each definition and description back to the dreamer, and ask the dreamer to "bridge" the definition or description to someone or something in waking life, or to some part of him or herself. (4) Wait for the "bridge." (5) Read the entire dream back to the dreamer, deleting all "elements" and inserting instead their full definition or description, as well as any "bridges." (6) Ask the dreamer to bridge the "expanded dream" to someone or something in waking life, or to some part of him or herself. (7) Wait for the "bridges." (8) Go back over and "unpack the bridges" to verify the waking-life connections and develop the interpretation.

In conjunction with defining and bridging the elements, Delaney suggests that you also ask the dreamer for a summary of the dramatic structure of the dream. Simply put, this means, ask the dreamer: (1) What is the beginning of the dream and what is the feeling at that point? (2) What is the middle of the dream, and what is the feeling at that point? and (3) What is the end of the dream, and what is the feeling at that point? This summary reveals the "punch line" of the dream. It shows you the emotional direction of the action: whether, for example, something big and scary is becoming small and wonderful, or the other way around.

As a back-up to Delaney's method, when ideas come but technique fails, I make use of Jeremy Taylor's "imaginative" or "If it were my dream, I would think . . ." method. This method allows all dream group members to participate effectively, regardless of perceived levels of interview skill.

15. Anne Sayre Wiseman, *Nightmare Help for Children from Children: A Guide for Parents and Teachers* (1986). Berkeley: Ten Speed Press.

Let's Stand Up, Regain Our Balance, and Look Around at the World

Johanna King

The myth of Narcissus, as recorded by the brilliant Roman poet Ovid, tells the story of a beautiful young boy who fell in love with his reflection in a pool of water, could not tear himself away, and eventually died by melting in his own tears of anguish—this despite the fact that he eventually developed insight into his dilemma (Knoespel, 1985). I want to make the argument that we (modern dreamworkers) may self-destruct like Narcissus if we continue to be so enamored with our own reflection—focusing excessively on intrapsychic dream meanings. We must realign our perspective to give more weight to the dreamer's waking experience. We must bring the dream back into the world, and learn how to identify, understand, honor, and make use of the complicated network of threads and webs (and sometimes broad roadways) that weave together our dreams and our everyday waking life. We live, we exist, we are in the world, and we also *dream* in and of the world.

I base my argument on a critique of a perspective about dreams, one that is in my view unbalanced at best, and hurtful and damaging at worst. This perspective states that the dream is always a deep spiritual experience that has something profound, momentous, and new to say about the dreamer's inner self, and that it has as its major function the raising of repressed or unacknowledged psychic material from the unconscious to the conscious. This perspective has certain assumptive bases: (1) an intrapsychic emphasis is more important and valuable than an interpersonal or extrapersonal one; (2) it is more difficult and more important to focus inward, to "work on one's own stuff," than it is to focus on issues out in the world; (3) nightmares are best understood as reflections of internal struggle, imbalance, repression, or personal shadow; (4) spiritual, mythical, archetypal, and lucid dreams are "better"; and (5) personal growth is the most important life goal. A near-religious sense of fervor often accompanies explications of this perspective, and nonbelievers are sometimes viewed as unenlightened or "psychologically delayed."

I do not argue for the elimination of this perspective, which in many cases is a useful and appropriate one. Rather, I want to see it balanced with a perspective that gives substantially more weight and emphasis to the view that generally dreams are understood in terms of the *dreamer's waking-life experience, and the dreamer's relationship, psychological and physical, to that waking experience.* I do not see these positions as mutually exclusive. Harry Hunt, for example, presents evidence of the complex interplay between "big," "archetypal," and other culture-pattern dreams and the collective social and cultural reality of the dreamer (Hunt 1989). And of course many dreams are probably best understood by taking into account *both* positions. So it is not, in my mind, a matter of choice but one of balance.

This overemphasis on intrapsychic dream meaning has developed for many reasons. Most obviously, it satisfies the narcissistic urge that exists within all of us. After all, Ovid did not invent the story of Narcissus from scratch, any more than great writers ever invent their best stories from scratch. Rather, he based it on his understanding of certain fundamental and irrefutable elements of human nature. We all share this natural, and generally healthy, tendency to be at times introspective meditative self-oriented, and focused on inner processes of thought and feeling. This natural tendency becomes unhealthy only when it comes to dominate experience, and interfere with judgment and perception.

Secondly, as E. Fuller Torrey so convincingly argues (1992), our entire culture, from child-rearing patterns to ideas about behavioral genetics, has been profoundly influenced by Freud and his emphasis on the examination of intrapsychic processes. Torrey claims that this is

Freud's most negative legacy: "the main ingredient in the alphabet soup of American psychotherapies is 'Me.' . . . There have always been narcissistic individuals, but 20th-century America may be the first culture in which the quest for self and happiness has been equated with the greater good" (p. 248).

Finally, contrary to popular opinion, I believe it is easier to focus inward than outward. Even the thought of trying to effect changes in the external world can make one tired. Issues of world poverty, political repression, degradation of the environment, and war are so overwhelming that it is generally very difficult to visualize a personal role in their amelioration.

Whatever the reasons, attention to the intrapsychic is a growth industry in the United States today. Torrey (1992) estimates that there are about 200,000 mainstream therapists in the country—a twenty-two-fold increase over the number in 1945, when the population was about half its present size. In addition, we have untold numbers of numerologists, iridologists, rebirthing experts, massage therapists, aura readers, and so on. Perhaps ironically, I myself am a therapist, and I personally value the presence of therapists of all stripes in our culture.

But I am concerned that a major consequence of overemphasis on the intrapsychic, in addition to a failure to give the worldly elements of our dreams their due, is the sapping of attention and assets from the arena of social action and reform. The energy, resourcefulness, creativity, and commitment that might be available to deal with critically important *social* issues are being lost in the rush to focus on *personal* issues. Torrey calls this a tragic misallocation of national resources.

James Hillman (Hillman and Ventura 1992) states the case in a very strong voice. "We've had a hundred years of analysis, and people are getting more and more sensitive, and the world is getting worse and worse. . . . We're working on our relationships constantly, and our feelings and reflections, but look what's left out of that. . . . What's left out is a deteriorating world" (p. 3). He worries that righteous anger about conditions in the world are converted in therapy into intrapsychic fear and anxiety, thus depriving the world of the energy needed to effect changes. He is especially critical of "inner child" work. He says, "the child archetype is by nature apolitical and disempowered. . . . This is a disaster for our political world, for our democracy. Democracy depends on intensely active citizens, not children . . . [w]e're disempowering ourselves through therapy" (p. 6). He envisions a redefinition of the self as an *interiorization of community*, and says in a metaphor worthy of dreamworkers that "therapy is going to have to go out the door with the client, maybe even make home visits, or at least walk down the street" (p. 81).

It must be said that this point of view has its critics, in turn. Charles Simpkinson (1992) argues that intrapsychic therapy does *not* cause people to lessen their community or political involvement. Jane White-Lewis (1994) makes much the same point, adding that the very intrapsychic-extraphyschic distinction may be an artificial one. I would like to be convinced by these optimists, but I worry.

It is easy, in my view, to find examples of dreams that are best understood in terms of the dreamer's waking-life experience, and the dreamer's psychological and physical relationship to that waking experience, rather than in terms of personal growth or deep inner meaning. I offer here a few examples.

A Dream about Sexual Abuse

In the course of our therapy with survivors of childhood sexual abuse, and in reading and hearing about the work of others, my colleague Jacqueline Sheehan and I have examined a great many dreams about that early damning experience, and have tried to understand how it has influenced the lives of the dreamers (King and Sheehan 1996). We find that to work with these dreams without explicit and early reference to the abuse experience is countertherapeutic and can be actively destructive.

Consider the following dream:

> I am standing with a man. We are face to face. I am small—about waist high to him. We are playing a game that is horrible. It is called "ants in your pants." He has tricked me into the game. He is very pleased with the game and he knows that I am not. Part of the game is to touch each other's genitals.

The imagery presents a faithful, if not literal, rerun of the dreamer's early abuse experience. She *was* small at the time; she *was* confused and did not understand how a "game" could be so negative for her; she *was* sexually and psychologically victimized by an adult man; and she did *not* avoid the "game," despite her distress. Any constructive work with this dream must focus first on the in-the-world experience of the victimization itself. Premature or exclusive focus on the more intrapsychic issues of coping with feelings of victimization, difficulties "standing up" to men, or patterns of doing things she does not really want to do would promote an atmosphere of blaming the victim, and indeed create a new process of victimization.

Germans' Dreams in the Early Days of Hitler's Regime

The fascinating book by Charlotte Beradt called *The Third Reich of Dreams* (1968) is filled with dream accounts which the author calls "parable(s) par excellence on how submissive subjects of totalitarian rule were produced" in Germany (p. 7). These dreams clearly and dramatically chronicle the dreamers' physical and psychological relationship to the fast-moving sociopolitical events going on around them. The dreams also reveal an uncanny, sharp-witted awareness that might not have been evident in waking life.

The following dream is from the book:

> I was sitting in a box at the opera, dressed in a new gown, and with my hair beautifully done. It was a huge opera house with many, many tiers, and I was enjoying considerable attention. They were presenting my favorite opera, *The Magic Flute*. When it came to the line, "that is the devil certainly," a squad of policemen came stomping in and marched directly up to me. A machine had registered the fact that I had thought of Hitler on hearing the word "devil." I imploringly searched the festive crowd for some sign of help, but they all just sat there staring straight ahead, silent and expressionless, not one showing even pity. The old gentleman in an adjoining box looked kind and distinguished, but when I tried to catch his eye he spat at me. (p. 25)

The dream occurred early in the Hitler era, 1933, and is a chilling prognostication of things to come. The dreamer already sees clearly that wealth and beauty will not serve as protection from the tyranny, and she is already aware of the incredible cost of calling attention to herself and of having even private thoughts of resistance. She envisions a range of positions that members of the society, and perhaps she herself, might take in an attempt to cope: the expressionless passivity of the crowd; the hostile rejecting stance of the old gentleman; the active identification of the policemen with the military-political machine. She does not explore in the dream the possibilities for active resistance, as do some of Beradt's other dreamers. The feelings and options for action (and failure to act) so coherently reviewed in the dream only make sense in terms of the dreamer's physical and psychological imbeddedness in-the-world of the socio-political context of her time, not as intrapsychic elements to be "worked on." To focus in an unbalanced way on the intrapsychic would produce, I fear, a sense of paralysis and capitulation on the part of the dreamer, and allow little room for the social action so desperately needed in those years.

A Dream of a Young Sandanista Soldier

At the time of this dream, the young soldier was stationed "deep in the countryside," and his unit was not seeing much action. He was the only person in the unit with any university education, and in the evenings, in his off-duty time, he walked about two miles to a nearby town to teach physics and math to the locals. He wore his uniform and carried his rifle, because at one spot the path dipped between hills, and there was the possibility of ambush. He felt a little afraid at times, but was never attacked on these walks. This was, paradoxically, a very peaceful time in his life.

The dream:

> A nightmare (written down a few days after it occurred). It is about suffering women in a cobalt radioactive chamber driven by computers. Still today I hear her cries and see terminal screens calling the roll listed in white-blue lines on the terminals. Heavy-water. Tanks, like huge water tanks. Buildings with strong pillars, squared.

Eight years before the dream, when he was fourteen, the dreamer's mother died of cancer. During her last days, he carried her in her arms to get her radiation treatments in a facility called in Nicaragua a "bomb." She died in great pain. The dreamer immediately had to assume the support of his four younger sisters and a year-old brother born retarded and with a pulmonary deficiency; the little boy died from pneumonia within the year. The dreamer felt a certain relief at both of these deaths, but never had the time, opportunity, or support to grieve properly. At last, in the relative peace of his Army days, he let himself explore the still frightening event that had exploded into his young adolescence. An understanding of this barren and lonely dream, filled with suffering, danger, tanks, computers, lines, and angles, must refer to his painful early life, in which he was required by fate and history to suffer terrible loss and to prematurely be a "strong pillar" for his siblings. A failure to deal with these worldly events, or any minimization of them in favor of current intrapsychic desolation, would be a grave disservice to the dreamer.

A Dream after Sexual Assault

This nightmare occurred about a week after the young dreamer was awakened by her boyfriend when he returned to her room after taking a friend home. They were both astonished to see that another man was in her bed, and in their confusion, they allowed him to escape out the window by which he had apparently entered. The man had sexually assaulted her, though not raped her, while she slept. The dream:

> I went to sleep in my roommate's room, then found myself sleeping on the sidewalk outside the house. Someone was sneaking along with a flashlight, and I was afraid he would see me. My dog and another one were running around the house, and then came up to me. Then the guy knew where I was, and flashed his light on me. I tried to get back into the house before he got to me, and I woke up.

The dreamer's sense of security was shattered by the event, and she felt exposed and defenseless. Neither her dog (who had slept through the whole thing) nor her boyfriend had been able to protect her, and she felt for the first time in her life that terrible things could happen to her. Any discussion of this adolescentlike sense of invulnerability, this expectation that others would care for her, and the feeling of betrayal she felt when they did not, would be premature and even destructive outside the context of a full exploration of the event which prompted the dream.

Torture and Dreams

Surprisingly, the literature on the psychological effects of torture, the treatment of torture victims, and treatment countertransference issues pays little attention to dreams. Of twenty-one recent articles which I reviewed, fifteen mention nightmares, most simply as part of a list of sequelae of the torture experience. Four mention reduction in nightmares as a marker of successful therapy. Perhaps this is because the authors erroneously view dreams as exclusively intrapsychic experiences, while they realize that torture itself must be understood as a sociopolitical, extrapersonal event.

Becker and co-workers (1990) report the recurrent dream of a torture victim:

> In the dream, democracy has arrived and now (the dreamer) will be the torturer. (The dreamer) is waiting to begin the torture of his own torturers, but while he is waiting he begins to feel unwell, vomits, and awakens. (p. 145)

The dreamer, a bright and active community leader who had grown up in poverty, was tortured by agents of the Pinochet regime in Chile, primarily via the application of electrical shock to his head, his most valuable asset. In therapy, the dreamer realized that despite the tremendous rage he felt toward his torturers, he could not and would not allow himself to become one of them or to behave like them. The dream is impossible to understand without reference to his experience, his social and political alliances and orientation, his in-the-world relationships, loves, hates, and fears. The dreamer undertook the painful healing process of testimony, which involves the careful, thorough sharing and recording of the torture experience as a way of increasing understanding, reestablishing trust in others (via trust in the therapist or witness), and putting a balancing in-the-world perspective on what is a profoundly lonely experience. Eventually his symptoms of depression, nightmares, and skin disease faded.

Dreams of the Jonestown Tragedy

Lawrence Wright (1993) wrote a poignant and gripping *New Yorker* article about the tragic self-annihilation of over 900 members of the Peoples Temple in Guyana in 1978, after the Temple relocated there from Redwood Valley and Oakland, California. He based the article on interviews with three of the sons of the infamous Temple leader, Jim Jones. These sons survived because they happened to be away from the compound that fateful day. They have been tormented since not only by their incredible loss, but also by fantasies and doubts about what they would and could have done had they been there.

Two of the sons, Jim and Stephan, told Wright a series of their dreams, remarkable for their similarity as well as for their touching poignancy. The dreams document the slow process of their coming to terms with the terrible personal and social tragedy that they and so many others endured in Jonestown.

Jim had recurrent dreams about his first wife, one of the Jonestown victims, in which he would catch glimpses of her and run after her, but be unable to catch up with her. Finally he had a dream in which he caught up with her sitting on a bench in Japantown in San Francisco, where they used to go together before the Temple moved to Guyana. She looked up at him and said "Goodbye, Jimmy," and he replied "Goodbye, honey." This was his last dream about her.

Stephan had similar dreams in which he would catch a glimpse of someone who had died in Jonestown, and run after them, only to have them disappear. In later dreams he would hear of them being alive. In still later dreams, he would catch up with them, and experience feelings of warmth, forgiveness, and good will. This dream pattern repeated itself with many friends and relatives.

His dreams about his father followed a similar progressive pattern. As Jim Jones began to deteriorate, Stephan, then a teenager, felt increasing contempt and hatred for him. He thought constantly about killing him, but passed up several opportunities, saying, "if anything kept me in check, it was the love for the father that I had already lost" (p. 78). Stephan had grown up in the People's Temple, and was imbued with many prosocial values: a commitment to social activism; ethnic and racial equality; a communal orientation that emphasized shared goals, resources, and energy. He held on to the values, the relationships in memory with people that he had lost there (he was especially close to his mother), and his sense that, had it not been for his father, the Temple's ideals might have been realized. In the first of his dreams about his father, Jim Jones was always an evil, adversarial figure. In later dreams, he became the "bumbler, the inept, the ridiculous bad guy, and (then) almost a neutral figure . . . with no influence" (p. 89). He had the following dream, the last about his father, thirteen years after the tragedy:

> I was in this beautiful wooded area. It was in a time well into the future, but it was of the past. It was unspoiled, very lush, and I'm standing on top of an elevation, the highest elevation in this wooded area. I'm looking down this path that works its way down the hill. I can see a group of people walking toward me, and there's this figure in this white—all-white—robe, long white hair, and a walking stick. It's clear that this is good. These are good people. I'm drawn to these people, but I wait for them. The leader is this man in white. The people love him and he loves them, and he's of them. He's one of them. They're all around him. They make their way up the path and when they finally get upon me I see my father as an old man. He's a man that can be trusted. He's wise and loving. (I felt) love and security from the time that I saw that group, and his eyes met mine, and I woke up. (p. 89)

In this dream, set in a beautiful Guyana-like location, Stephen visualizes his father as perhaps he would have been late in life had not his paranoia, drug abuse, and unbridled persecutory misuse of power destroyed him and so many others. His charisma and personal potency, as well as his capacity to create community, are evident in the image. Stephan had been tormented by the question of why people surrender their authority to people like Jim Jones, and why, once things change, they persist in their loyalty. And the dream helps him answer this social, interpersonal, in-the-world question. The figure in white *is* Jim Jones, as Stephan saw him at the time of the dream, not some inner wisdom figure. To reexperience the security and love that the Temple had once provided him, he had to take into account the positive qualities his father had once radiated, and realize how very powerful they were. He had to perceive the good in order to understand the evil; he had to know why peopled flocked to his father to understand why they followed him into annihilation.

All of these dreams, and many other less dramatic ones, make *primary* reference to the waking-life circumstances of the dreamers and illustrate, I hope, how unbalanced or premature focus on the intrapsychic can sadly miss the dream message. In striving to understand and work with these dreams, we must be willing to look at and engage the ugly, disturbing, dark parts of the *world*, without mislabeling them as projected shadow, repression, or any other intrapsychic construct. If we fail to do this, we lose the opportunity each dream provides to (1) see the waking experience more clearly, frequently from a new perspective, (2) better understand the complex network of connections between the dream and waking experience, and (3) enable the dreamer to envision being in the situation, and in the world, in a different, new, enhanced, or more constructive way. Only when we explore these opportunities can we begin to really access the remarkably perceptive and creative ability of the dream state to envision both problems and solutions in the world. These problems and solutions can never clearly be visualized from a purely intrapsychic perspective, which too often emphasizes *internal* changes and adjustments, not changes in the world. Insight, self-awareness, and positive affective states do not by themselves produce contextual change.

And so, I fear, if we cannot reduce our societal preoccupation with our intrapsychic reflection, we, like Narcissus, will allow our world to fall down around us, despite whatever insight we might develop along the way.

Note

This chapter is based on a paper presented at the June 1992 Conference of the Association for the Study of Dreams in Santa Cruz, California, and printed in the Winter 1993 *ASD Newsletter* 10(1): 13–15, 17.

References

Becker, David, Elizabeth Lira, Maria Isabel Castillo, Elena Gomez, and Juana Kovalskys. 1990. Therapy with victims of political repression in Chile: The challenge of social reparation. *Journal of Social Issues.* 46(3): 133–49.

Beradt, Charlotte. 1968. *The Third Reich of Dreams.* Chicago: Quadrangle Books.

Hillman, James, and Michael Ventura. 1992. *We've Had a Hundred Years of Psychotherapy and the World's Getting Worse*. San Francisco: HarperSanFrancisco.

Hunt, Harry. 1989. *The Multiplicity of Dreams*. New Haven: Yale University Press.

King, Johanna, and Jacqueline Sheehan. 1996. The use of dreams with incest survivors. In Deirdre Barrett (ed.). *Trauma and Dreams*. Cambridge, MA: Harvard University Press.

Knoespel, Kenneth J. 1985. *Narcissus and the Invention of Personal History*. New York: Garland Publishing.

Simpkinson, Charles. 1992. Soul work: A matter of timing. *Common Boundary* 10(6): 9.

Torrey, E. Fuller. 1992. *Freudian Fraud: The Malignant Effect of Freud's Theory on American Thought and Culture*. New York: HarperCollins.

White-Lewis, Jane. 1994. Dream maker as feminist. Paper presented at the July 1994 Conference of the Association for the Study of Dreams. Leiden, the Netherlands.

Wright, Lawrence. 1993. Orphans of Jonestown. *New Yorker* 69 (39) (22 November 1993): 66–89.

Chapter 13

Conclusion

Kelly Bulkeley

The field of dream studies has emerged in the second half of the twenti-eth-century as an outgrowth of research in various academic disciplines—psychology, neurophysiology, anthropology, religious studies, and literary criticism, among many others. Its emergence has not, however, been due to the work of academic researchers alone. The development of dream studies has also been nourished by the tremendous and increasingly widespread interest in dreams among the general public. Of course, people have been "studying" dreams since the beginnings of human history. But it is only quite recently that people have begun studying dreams *in this particular way*: focusing specifically on dreaming as a distinct type of experience, applying a wide variety of research methods to examine dreaming, and seeking in dreams answers to a broad range of theoretical and practical questions.[1]

The multiple roots of the field of dream studies reflect the complex nature of dreaming itself. For better or worse, dreams are very hard to study. Consider the following characteristics of dreams:

- Dreaming is both rational and irrational; dreams portray perfectly reasonable, "lifelike" situations and utterly bizarre, illogical, otherworldly happenings.[2]
- Dreaming involves both the mind *and* the body; it is rooted in psychological and physiological processes, in the mental world of thoughts and beliefs and in the physical world of instincts, urges, and bodily processes.[3]

- Dreaming relates to both individual experience and to social reality; it draws upon the personal life concerns of the dreamer and upon the language, customs, and common beliefs that characterize the social world in which the dreamer lives.
- Dreaming points back to the past and points forward towards the future; it brings forth memories of long-forgotten childhood experiences and presents visions of new possibilities lying ahead of us.   Tribal views
- Dreaming shows both the good and the evil within us; in dreams we find our noblest, most virtuous ideals and our most violent, destructive urges.
- Dreaming reveals both the finitude and the infinitude of human existence; it shows our rootedness in the trivial, inescapable details of our everyday lives and it discloses our freedom to imagine, to create, to transcend ourselves and our waking world.

To many people, these paradoxical features of dreaming make it seem baffling, disturbing, and nearly impossible to understand. To other people, however, these same features make dreaming appear fascinating, exhilarating, and capable of leading us into those realms that lie beyond the boundaries created by the conceptual structures that govern our waking lives. Dream studies has emerged as a distinct field because no single academic discipline has been able to do justice to the complexity, richness, and diversity of the phenomenon of dreaming. No single discipline has been able to make sense of the inexhaustably mysterious world of our dreams.

Dream studies has begun assuming the institutional forms that conventionally define a research field in modern Western academics. There are journals, book series, associations, and conferences, all devoted to the multidisciplinary study of dreams. So now that we can speak of dream studies as a distinct field, it is well to reflect on what the field's potentials might be, on what its future might hold.

The essays collected in *Among All These Dreamers* have presented the ideas of people from a wide variety of backgrounds and disciplines, all offering visions of the possible future of dream studies.[4] As diverse as the twelve essays are, they share a common premise: that it is crucial to recognize the *social and historical context* in which the field of dream studies has emerged. The modern study of dreams has been directly and

profoundly influenced by the distinctive characteristics of late twentieth-century Western society. We must have a clear understanding of
that society if we are to understand what the field of dream studies *is*
and what it may *become* in the future.

This concluding essay is an effort to describe the social and historical context of modern dream studies—it is an effort to *historicize* the
dream studies field.[5] The essay offers an analysis, based on both classic
and contemporary social theories, of the distinctive characteristics of
modern Western society.[6] The goal of this analysis is to help us better
understand the historical roots, the present nature, and the future
potentials of the field of dream studies.

Dream studies, as a distinct field of inquiry, has emerged in a particular time and place: the late twentieth-century world of the United
States, Canada, and Western Europe. The societies in which this field
has emerged are, in political terms, constitutional democracies; in economic terms, they are governed by the structures, principles, and mores
of advanced industrial capitalism; and in religious and cultural terms,
they have their roots in both the Judeo-Christian and the Graeco-
Roman traditions. This social and historical milieu is generally known
as "modern Western society" or "the modern West," and the field of
dream studies was born squarely within that milieu.

Naturally, there has long been a rich debate about when exactly
modern Western society "began." But for many scholars, the pivotal
moment in the rise of the modern West was a winter day in November
of 1619 when René Descartes sat alone in his "warm room," and pon-
dered the ultimate nature of his knowledge.[7] After very careful reflection, Descartes decided that he could trust nothing *absolutely* but his
own individual reason. Sense perceptions, emotions, religious teachings, cultural traditions, none of these could provide Descartes with the
pure, complete certainty that his reason could give him. Descartes
emerged from the solitude of his warm room to write *Discourse on
Method, The Meditations Concerning First Philosophy*, and other works
which laid the new philosophical foundations of what would become
modern Western society.

These new foundations rested upon a basic division between the
rational individual and the rest of existence.[8] Descartes' first principle
was the now famous assertion that "I think, therefore I am."[9] Descartes
claimed to know the truth of this assertion with a certainty that sur-

passed all other knowledge. He could easily imagine, he said, that "nothing whatsoever existed in the world, that there was no sky, no earth, no minds, and no bodies";[10] but he could not imagine that *he* did not exist, for in the very act of conceiving the question of his existence he proved that he did in fact exist. From these reflections Descartes concluded that his *essence* was his reason; "Thought is an attribute that belongs to me; it alone is inseparable from my nature. . . . I am therefore, to speak precisely, only a thinking being, that is, a mind, an understanding, or a reasoning being."[11]

The revolutionary philosophy of Descartes promised to bring the clarity, the rigor, and the absolute certainty of mathematical reasoning to bear on all the important questions of human life and society. Thanks to the efforts of other Enlightenment-era thinkers like Thomas Hobbes, David Hume, John Locke, and Immanuel Kant, Descartes' philosophy soon became the dominant worldview of Western society. His ideas shaped the research methods that scientists used to study the natural world; his mode of skeptical analysis was used to make far-reaching reforms in education, politics, and religion; and his declaration of the sovereignty of individual reason gave people the philosophical resources to resist the oppression of governments, churches, and all other authorities whose actions could not be rationally justified.

From that basic philosophical split between the rational individual and the rest of existence derived other fundamental splits, other basic conceptual divisions that have become defining features of modern Western society. One of the most important of these splits was the division of humans from *nature*, from the natural environment. Descartes' philosophy helped to destroy traditional beliefs that humans are integrally *connected* to nature, that we *participate* in nature, that nature is itself a *subject*.[12] The philosophical freedom that Descartes offered was, with regards to nature, taken as the freedom to manipulate, exploit, and plunder. Nature was increasingly seen as nothing more than inert matter, a source of raw material to serve human purposes and satisfy human desires.

A classic statement of this view of nature comes in Locke's *Second Treatise on Government* (1689), a work that served as a philosophical touchstone for the American revolution. Locke, writing of the rational foundations of civil society, asserted that nature has no value until it is

touched by human labor: "I ask, whether in the wild woods and unculti-
vated waste of America, left to nature, without any improvement,
tillage or husbandry, a thousand acres yield the needy and wretched
inhabitants as many conveniences of life, as ten acres of equally fertile
land do in Devonshire, where they are well cultivated?"[13] Nature, in
Locke's view, has value only insofar as it can be "improved" to provide
"conveniences" for humans. Gone is any sense that humans stand in a
living relationship with the natural world, a relationship that might set
limits on efforts to "improve" the environment.

Along another Cartesian fracture line, humans became split from
ourselves, that is, from everything that was not rational within us: emotions, wishes, fantasies, urges, intuitions, and passions. Descartes
argued that only reason can be trusted to give us certain, objective truth;
as a result, it became necessary to purify our minds of anything that
might "cloud" its reasoning. Descartes claimed, "I know manifestly that
nothing of all that I can understand by means of the imagination is pertinent to the knowledge which I have of myself. . . . I must remember
this and prevent my mind from thinking in this fashion, in order that it
may clearly perceive its own nature."[14]

And to the extent that the irrational could not be eliminated
entirely, it could at least be *controlled*; Western society could strive to
domesticate the irrational, to tame it and make it serve the master of reason. As one contemporary philosopher says, "At its core, the ethos of
the modern world, from Descartes to Freud, [is] rooted in expectations
of *self-command*."[15] Indeed, the philosophical connection between
Descartes and Freud is very strong on this point. The primary goal of
psychoanalysis, as Freud saw it, was to increase rational control over the
irrational.[16] At the conclusion of lecture 31 of the *New Introductory
Lectures on Psychoanalysis* (1933), Freud describes this goal with a telling
analogy: The "intention" of psychoanalysis is "to strengthen the ego, to
make it more independent of the super-ego, to widen its field of perception and enlarge its organization, so that it can appropriate fresh por-
tions of the id. Where id was, there ego shall be. It is a work of
culture—not unlike the draining of the Zuider Zee [a lake in
Switzerland.]"[17]

But almost 400 years after Descartes, and 60 years after Freud,
Western society seems far from eliminating or even modestly controlling the irrational elements of human life. Despite all the fabulous pow-

ers of scientific reason, we seem to be doing no less murdering, tortur-
ing, raping, stealing, abusing, oppressing, hating, and warring than we
ever have. Indeed, our failure raises the unsettling possibility that the
very effort to control the irrational forces of the human psyche has actually made those forces stronger and more violent. The more forcefully
we assert that we are "thinking beings" and try to increase the power of
our rational egos, the more viciously rebellious the powers of irrationality seem to become.

Along yet another fracture line, the philosophical revolution of
Descartes created a profound split *between* humans: humans became
objects *to each other*. In the Cartesian view of the world, people are not
integrally, essentially connected to any other humans, to any group or
community. Rather, we are first and foremost *individuals*, autonomous
thinkers, dependent on no one, related to no one, answering to no one
but our own private reason. And what Descartes described in philosophical terms, the political economist Adam Smith enshrined in
Western society's economic system. Smith's *The Wealth of Nations*
(1776), the Ur-text of capitalist economics, asserted that this split of
humans from each other is *the* basic fact of economic life: "It is not from
the benevolence of the butcher, the brewer, or the baker that we expect
our dinner, but from their regard to their own interest."[18] Smith argued
that the exclusive and vigorous pursuit of individual self-interest was
not only "natural," that is, a primary, universal human instinct, but was
in fact the best means to the well-being of society as a whole. When an
individual works to maximize his own self-interest, Smith claimed,

> he is in this, as in many other cases, led by an invisible hand to promote an
> end which was no part of his intention. Nor is it always the worse for the
> society that it was no part of it. By pursuing his own interest he frequently
> promotes that of society more effectually than when he really intends to
> promote it. I have never known much good done by those who affected to
> trade for the public good.[19]

Capitalism's encouragement of individual self-interest has indeed
increased the "wealth of nations," or at least of some nations. But what
it has done to human relationships is another matter. Countless social
critics have charged that the highly competitive, individualistic, greed-
driven ethos of the modern West, while producing great quantities of
material riches, has terribly impoverished the quality of human rela-

tionships. In *The Economic and Philosophic Manuscripts of 1844*, Karl Marx put it this way:

> [N]o eunuch flatters his despot more basely or uses more despicable means to stimulate his dulled capacity for pleasure in order to sneak a favour for himself than does the industrial eunuch—the producer—in order to sneak for himself a few pennies—in order to charm the golden birds out of the pockets of his Christianly beloved neighbors. He puts himself at the service of the other's most depraved fancies, plays the pimp between him and his need, excites in him morbid appetites, lies in wait for each of his weaknesses—all so that he can then demand the cash for this service of love.[20]

Marx argued that in a capitalist society human relationships are ground down into merely instrumental exchanges: each individual strives to use other people, to *seduce* them, to *exploit* their vulnerabilities in order to satisfy his or her own individual desires. Marx claimed that this makes it impossible for a society to maintain any traditional standards of personal morality or to preserve humane economic and political systems.[21]

The mistreatment of others was not invented by modern Western society. But the modern West has not eliminated such mistreatment, either, and in fact seems to have provided distinctly "rational" justifications for it. After Descartes the inferior social status of women, for example, could be justified on philosophical grounds. Women appeared to be less "logical" than men (although, as Simone de Beuvoir notes in *The Second Sex*, "A syllogism is of no help in making a successful mayonnaise, nor in quieting a child in tears; masculine reasoning is quite inadequate to the reality with which [a woman] deals"[22]). Women are less capable of assuming the position of a Cartesian "thinking thing," and thus undeserving of any greater social or political power. It therefore appeared *rational* to restrict women to serving only sexual and reproductive functions in society. Similarly, the mistreatment of non-Western cultures were now legitimated by the respectable philosophical argument that the indigenous people of Africa, India, the Americas, and so forth were pre-rational savages who should have been grateful that Western settlers and colonists had arrived to take control of their lands.[23]

With all of these harmful splits, divisions, and fractures pervading their experiences of the world, many modern Westerners have come to suffer from a sense of *spiritual meaninglessness*. Many modern Westerners have great difficulties believing that their lives have any ultimate cohesiveness, meaning, or purpose. Despite our society's scientific achievements and material gains, there is a widespread anxiety that these do not suffice for a truly *good*, truly *human* life.[24]

In other times and places, this kind of spiritual meaning was provided by religions, cultural traditions, and family and social networks. Emile Durkheim was one of the first social scientists to recognize the vital necessity of such "moral communities" in giving people a trustworthy sense of existential purpose and moral guidance—in short, a *faith* in the ultimate meaningfulness of life. Durkheim, writing in the early decades of this century, argued that only in healthy, stable communities could individuals find the security, support, and nurturance that such a faith requires. But modern Western society has produced an incredibly rapid series of changes in people's lives—sweeping changes in technology, in economics, in politics, in culture. Durkheim feared that all these changes were threatening the viability of our moral communities. He said,

> [W]e are going through a stage of transition and moral mediocrity. The great things of the past which filled our fathers with enthusiasm do not excite the same ardour in us . . . ; but as yet there is nothing to replace them. . . . In a word, the old gods are growing old or already dead, and others are not yet born.[25]

As we have seen, Descartes believed that each person could find meaning, purpose, and moral guidance in his or her own individual reason. But Durkheim argued passionately that it is both naive and dangerous to ignore the vital role our moral communities play in providing us with spiritual meaning, with the "warmth, life, [and] enthusiasm"[26] that make human existence truly fulfilling.

There is no doubt that modern Western society has made many noble achievements. We have developed a highly sophisticated knowledge of the natural world. We have accomplished incredible technological feats. We have defeated many deadly diseases and found ways to increase food production dramatically. And, we have championed the political ideals of freedom and democracy. Nevertheless, these achievements have been made at a heavy cost. I find Max Weber's account of this cost to be most persuasive. In his essay "Science as a Vocation" he says, "The fate of our times is characterized by rationalization and intellectualization and, above all, by the *'disenchantment of the world.'* Precisely the ultimate and most sublime values have retreated from public life."[27] Weber's notion of the "disenchantment of the world" conveys in a phrase the primary theme of my analysis: the "progress" of modern Western society has robbed us of our sense of *enchantment*, our sense that the world is alive, our sense that life is sublime and mysterious, our sense that human existence has meaning and purpose and value. At the conclusion to *The Protestant Ethic and the Spirit of Capitalism*, Weber compares our lives in the economic and social order of modern West to being imprisoned in "an iron cage."[28] He says,

> No one knows who will live in this cage in the future, or whether at the end of this tremendous development entirely new prophets will arise, or there will be a great rebirth of old ideas and ideals, or, if neither, mechanized petrification, embellished with a sort of convulsive self-importance. For of the last stage of this cultural development, it might well be truly said: "Specialists without spirit, sensualists without heart; this nullity imagines that it has attained a level of civilization never before achieved."[29]

Creating new meanings for a disenchanted world—that is the great challenge facing Western society as we step, or stumble, into the new millennium.

If the foregoing analysis of the modern West is valid, ours is a society rent by deep philosophical conflicts, plagued by an anxious sense of spiritual meaninglessness, and bereft of secure, stable communities. My belief, the belief that motivated me to gather these essays together, is that dream studies can play a small but valuable role in the process of creating new meanings, new "enchantments," that can help us address the individual and communal problems afflicting modern Western society. This is not to suggest, however, that the study of dreams is the one great solution to the world's problems. The unsettling reality of the late twentieth century is that there are no single solutions to our troubles. Not the free market, not the Bible, not technology—the yearning for a single magical answer must yield to creative new efforts to devise, integrate, and practically apply *multiple* responses to our problems. The essays collected here illustrate a number of particular roles that dream studies can play in promoting these efforts. The roles may be limited to quite specific contexts and locations, but they are no less valuable and effective for those limitations.

Notes

1. In all of these ways the contemporary field of dream studies is significantly different from the various other ways in which people have studied dreams through history. Dreams are usually not distinguished sharply from other ecstatic phenomena like visions, trances, and possession; they are usually studied from one perspective, like theology or medicine; usually the goal is a relatively limited one like healing, or prophecy, or divine communication. I do not want to push the uniqueness of the modern dream studies field too far, because there are obvious and important ties with other traditions of exploring dreams; nevertheless, I think it is very important to recognize what is genuinely distinctive and unique about the way *we*, in our particular social and historical context, go about studying dreams.

2. See Harry Hunt, *The Multiplicity of Dreams* (1989), and Kelly Bulkeley, *The Wilderness of Dreams* (1994), for more on the interplay between rationality and irrationality in dreams.

3. Paul Ricoeur speaks of the "mixed discourse" that psychoanalysis must use to make sense of phenomena like dreams. At the outset of *Freud and Philosophy* (1970) he says, "by turns we will see psychoanalysis as an explanation of psychical phenomena through conflicts of forces, hence as an energetics; and as an exegesis of apparent meaning through a latent meaning, hence as a hermeneutics. . . . I hope to show that there are good grounds for this apparent ambiguity, that this mixed discourse is the raison d'être of psychoanalysis" (62, 65).

4. These essays are not, however, meant to offer anything like an exhaustive survey of the dream studies field.

5. In this I am following up on the work done by Lucy Bregman (1982), G. William Domhoff (1985), Deborah Jay Hillman (1987), Montague Ullman (1987), and Mary-Therese Dombeck (1992) in trying to understand the social and historical context of dream studies. The perspective I am developing in this conclusion departs from those works in two important ways. First, I am trying to clarify the context of dream studies *as a whole*; previous research has tended to focus on par-

ticular aspects of the dream studies rather than on the field as a whole. Second, I am not working to clarify this context just to analyze the *present* status of dream studies (which is the major concern of the works mentioned above) but rather to help us consider the *future* possibilities of the field.

6. I expect that readers will find some, and perhaps many, points on which they disagree with the following analysis. My hope, however, is that the general purpose of this analysis will not be ignored in the midst of any particular failings: the general purpose being to provide a clear and detailed analysis of the social and historical context of modern dream studies. Whether or not I succeed in adequately analyzing this context, I hope that I have succeeded in demonstrating the need for an analysis of the social and historical context of the dream studies field. This is essentially the same claim I make in *The Wilderness of Dreams* (1994), where I argue that dream studies needs explicit, well-grounded statements of a theory of interpretation, a theory of religious meaning, and a theory of secularization in order to develop as a field. I offer my own proposals, which may or may not be adequate; but my broader project, in that book and in this one, is to begin developing the core philosophical principles that will be needed to orient the future development of the dream studies field.

7. *Discourse on Method*, trans. Laurence J. Lafleur (Indianapolis: Bobbs-Merrill, 1960), 10.

8. The irony is that Descartes' philosophy appears to have been generated in some measure by his experience of a series of three dreams, as argued in John R. Cole's book *The Olympian Dreams and Youthful Rebellion of René Descartes* (1992).

9. Descartes, *Discourse on Method*, p. 24.

10. Ibid., p. 82.

11. Ibid., p. 84.

12. See, for example, Carolyn Merchant's *The Death of Nature* (1980) and *Ecological Revolutions* (1989), Bill Mckibben's *The End of Nature* (1989), Roderick Nash's *Wilderness and the American Mind* (1967) and *The Rights of Nature* (1989).

13. Locke, *Second Treatise on Government*, 24.

14. Descartes, *Discourse on Method*, 85. See also pp. 95 and 127.

15. Stephen Toulmin, *Cosmopolis: The Hidden Agenda of Modernity* (1990), 163, emphasis added.

16. For some interesting reflections on the relationship between Descartes and Freud, see François Meltzer, Descartes' dreams and Freud's failure, or the politics of originality (1987).

17. Freud, *New Introductory Lectures on Psychoanalysis*, 71.

18. Smith, *The Wealth of Nations*, 18.

19. Ibid., 477–78.

20. Marx, *The Economic and Philosophic Manuscripts of 1844*, 94.

21. Jürgen Habermas, in *Knowledge and Human Interests* (1971), provides a detailed analysis of the negative effects of capitalist social structures on human communications.

22. De Beauvoir, *The Second Sex*, 564.

23. It is true that modern Western society has provided such groups with the economic means to overcome their mistreatment. This is capitalism's chief claim to moral virtue. But in my line of argument, such tools at best enable these groups only to overcome one problem while embracing another (i.e., the sharp and harmful split of humans from each other). Thus, a newly "modernized" group of people may well use capitalism to overcome problems associated with sexism and colonialism—and thereby become dehumanized, alienated, and spiritually disoriented like everyone else. And that is assuming that they can even succeed in making *that* much "progress", which in many cases has yet to happen.

24. See, for example, Paul Tillich, *Systematic Theology* (1951–1963), Reinhold Niebuhr, *The Nature and Destiny of Man* (1964), and Mircea Eliade, *The Sacred and the Profane* (1957).

25. Durkheim, *The Elementary Forms of the Religious Life*, 475.

26. Ibid., 473.

27. Weber, Science as a Vocation, 155, emphasis added.

28. This is from the translation of Talcott Parsons. Other translators render Weber's German original as "Iron Cloak."

29. Weber, *The Protestant Ethic and the Spirit of Capitalism*, 182.

References

Bellah, Robert, Richard Madsen, William M. Sullivan, Ann Swidler, and Steven M. Tipton. 1985. *Habits of the Heart: Individualism and Commitment in American Life.* Berkeley: University of California Press.

Bregman, Lucy. 1982. *The Rediscovery of Inner Experience.* Chicago: Nelson-Hall.

Browning, Don. 1987. *Religious Thought and the Modern Psychologies: A Critical Conversation in the Theology of Culture.* Philadelphia: Fortress Press.

Bulkeley, Kelly. 1994. *The Wilderness of Dreams: Exploring the Religious Meanings of Dreams in Modern Western Culture.* Albany: State University of New York Press.

Cole, John R. 1992. *The Olympian Dreams and Youthful Rebellion of René Descartes.* Urbana: University of Illinois Press.

De Beauvoir, Simone. 1970. *The Second Sex.* Translated by H. M. Parshley. New York: Bantam Books.

Descartes, René. 1960. *Discourse on Method.* Translated by Laurence J. Lafleur. Indianapolis: Bobbs-Merrill.

Dombeck, Mary-Therese. 1991. *Dreams and Professional Personhood.* Albany: State University of New York Press.

Domhoff, G. William. 1985. *The Mystique of Dreams: A Search for Utopia through Senoi Dream Theory.* Berkeley: University of California Press.

Durkheim, Emile. 1965. *The Elementary Forms of the Religious Life.* Translated by Joseph Swain. New York: Free Press.

Eliade, Mircea. 1957. *The Sacred and the Profane: The Nature of Religion.* Translated by Willard R. Trask. Princeton: Princeton University Press.

Freud, Sigmund. 1965. *New Introductory Lectures on Psychoanalysis.* Translated by James Strachey. New York: W. W. Norton.

Habermas, Jürgen. 1971. *Knowledge and Human Interests.* Translated by Jeremy J. Shapiro. Boston: Beacon Press.

Hillman, Deborah Jay. 1987. Dream work and field work: Linking cultural anthropology and the current dream work movement. In *The Variety of Dream Experience.* Montague Ullman and Claire Limner (eds.), New York: Continuum.

Homans, Peter. 1979. *Jung in Context: Modernity and the Making of a Psychology*. Chicago: University of Chicago Press.

———. 1989. *The Ability to Mourn: Disillusionment and the Social Origins of Psychoanalysis*. Chicago: University of Chicago Press.

Hunt, Harry. 1989. *The Multiplicity of Dreams: Memory, Imagination, and Consciousness*. New Haven: Yale University Press.

Locke, John. 1980. *Second Treatise of Government*. Indianapolis: Hackett Publishing Company.

Marx, Karl. 1978. The Economic and Philosophic Manuscripts of 1844. Translated by Martin Milligan. In Robert C. Tucker (ed.), *The Marx-Engels Reader*. Second Edition. New York: W. W. Norton.

McKibben, Bill. 1989. *The End of Nature*. New York: Anchor Books.

Meltzer, Françoise. 1987. Descartes' dreams and Freud's failure, or the politics of originality. In Françoise Meltzer (ed.), *The Trial(s) of Psychoanalysis*. Chicago: University of Chicago Press.

Merchant, Carolyn. 1980. *The Death of Nature: Women. Ecology, and the Scientific Revolution*. New York: Harper & Row.

———. 1989. *Ecological Revolutions: Nature, Gender, and Science in New England*. Chapel Hill: University of North Carolina Press.

Nash, Roderick. 1973. *Wilderness and the American Mind*. New Haven: Yale University Press.

———. 1989. *The Rights of Nature*. Madison: University of Wisconsin Press.

Niebuhr, Reinhold. 1964. *The Nature and Destiny of Man*. 2 volumes. New York: Scribners.

Ricoeur, Paul. 1970. *Freud and Philosophy: An Essay on Interpretation*. Translated by Denis Savage. New Haven: Yale University Press.

Rieff, Philip. 1966. *The Triumph of the Therapeutic: Uses of Faith after Freud*. New York: Harper & Row.

Smith, Adam. 1976. *An Inquiry into the Nature and Causes of the Wealth of Nations.* Edited by Edwin Cannan. Chicago: University of Chicago Press.

Tillich, Paul. 1951–63. *Systematic Theology.* 3 volumes. New Haven: Yale University Press.

Toulmin, Stephen. 1990. *Cosmopolis: The Hidden Agenda of Modernity.* Chicago: University of Chicago Press.

Ullman, Montague. 1987. Dreams and society. In Montague Ullman and Claire Limner (eds.), *The Varieties of Dream Experience.* New York: Continuum.

Weber, Max. 1946. Science as a vocation. In *From Max Weber: Essays in Sociology.* Translated by H. H. Gerth and C. Wright Mills. New York: Oxford University Press.

———. 1976. *The Protestant Ethic and the Spirit of Capitalism.* Translated by Talcot Parsons. London: Unwin Paperbacks.

List of Contributors

Kathryn E. Belicki is Associate Professor of Psychology at Brock University, St. Catherines, Ontario, Canada, where she both teaches and conducts research. Research into sexual abuse, dreams, and nightmares are her primary interests. She also maintains a private practice in partnership with Dr. Denis Belicki.

Kelly Bulkeley is a dream researcher living in Kensington, California. He has authored two books, *The Wilderness of Dreams: Exploring the Religious Meanings of Dreams in Modern Western Culture* and *Spiritual Dreaming: A Cross-Cultural and Historical Journey*, as well as numerous articles on the relationship of dreams to psychology, religion, and culture. He teaches at the Graduate Theological Union, at the University of California, Berkeley, and is the chair of the board of directors of the Association for the Study of Dreams.

Patricia Bulkley is a Presbyterian minister from Kentfield, California. She is chaplain at Hospice of Marin, and teaches pastoral counseling and Christian spirituality at the San Francisco Theological Seminary. She is currently completing a Doctor of Ministry degree at Princeton Theological Seminary.

Marion A. Cuddy is a clinical psychologist in Ontario, Canada. She divides her time between providing psychological services to geriatric clients in a psychiatric hospital and a general private practice. She continues to collaborate on research with Dr. Belicki in the areas of sexual abuse and nightmares.

Wendy Doniger is Professor of the History of Religions at the University of Chicago Divinity School. Among her many books are *Dreams, Illusion, and Other Realities*, *Other People's Myths*, and *Women, Androgynes. and Other Mythical Beasts*. She is just finishing a work on the theme of sexual doubles in mythology.

Bette Ehlert is an attorney in private practice in Albuquerque, New Mexico. She operates a dream consultation service there, and leads dream workshops in various New Mexico correctional facilities.

Jayne Gackenbach is a psychologist who has written and edited many books and articles on dreams, including *Sleep and Dreams: A Source Book*, *Control Your Dreams*, and *Conscious Mind, Sleeping Brain*. She is a former president of the Association for the Study of Dreams and is one of the pioneers in research on lucid dreaming. Ms. Gackenbach currently teaches in Edmonton, Alberta, and is doing research on the culture of Canada's aboriginal peoples.

Johanna King has recently retired after more than thirty years of working as a clinical psychologist at the student health facilities of California State University, Chico. She has long been involved with the Association for the Study of Dreams, and is currently the organization's president-elect.

Carol Schreier Rupprecht is Professor of Comparative Literature at Hamilton College, New York. She has edited two books, *Feminist Archetypal Theory: Interdisciplinary Revisions of Jungian Thought* and *The Dream and the Text: Essays on Language and Literature*, as well as authoring numerous articles on Renaissance views of dreams and dreaming. Ms. Rupprecht is a former president of the Association for the Study of Dreams.

Herbert W. Schroeder is a research social scientist with the USDA Forest Service, North Central Forest Experiment Station in Chicago, Illinois. He received his doctorate in environmental psychology from the University of Arizona in 1980. Since then he has been conducting research on people's perceptions of and preferences for trees, forests, and other natural environments. His current research interests focus on the symbolic, experiential, and spiritual values of natural environments.

Anthony Shafton is a writer and community dreamworker in Chicago. He has written *Dream Reader: Contemporary Approaches to the Understanding of Dreams*, and he is continuing his research on how African-Americans experience, interpret, and use their dream experiences.

Jeremy Taylor is a Unitarian-Universalist from San Rafael, California, and he is the former president of the Association for the Study of Dreams. He has written *Dream Work* and *Where People Fly and Water Runs Uphill*, and numerous articles on dreams and dreaming. He teaches classes on dreams at many Bay Area schools, and travels extensively to give workshops, lectures, and seminars on practical techniques of dreamwork.

Jane White-Lewis is a Jungian analyst practicing in Guilford, Connecticut and New York City. In addition to her private practice, Ms. White-Lewis has been active in the Association for the Study of Dreams for many years and has published work on nightmares and on Virginia Woolf. Her current interest in the political and social importance of dreams has grown out of her teaching a course on dreams in an inner-city high school.

Author Index